Korean Studies of the
Henry M. Jackson School
of International Studies

James B. Palais, Editor

Korean Studies of the Henry M. Jackson School
of International Studies

*Over the Mountains Are Mountains: Korean Peasant Households
and Their Adaptations to Rapid Industrialization*
by Clark W. Sorensen

Cultural Nationalism in Colonial Korea, 1920-1925
by Michael Edson Robinson

*Offspring of Empire:
The Koch'ang Kims and the Colonial Origins
of Korean Capitalism, 1876-1945*
by Carter J. Eckert

*Confucian Statecraft and Korean Institutions:
Yu Hyŏngwŏn and the Late Chosŏn Dynasty*
by James B. Palais

*Peasant Protest and Social Change
in Colonial Korea*
by Gi-Wook Shin

Peasant Protest
& Social Change
in Colonial Korea

Gi-Wook Shin

University of Washington Press

Seattle and London

*For my mother
and in memory of my father,
who taught me the importance
of knowledge and praxis*

© 1996 by the University of Washington Press
First paperback edition © 2014 by the University of Washington Press
Printed and bound in the United States of America
18 17 16 15 14   5 4 3 2 1

All rights reserved. No part of this publication may be reproduced or transmitted in any form or by any means, electronic or mechanical, including photocopy, recording, or any information storage or retrieval system, without permission in writing from the publisher.

University of Washington Press
www.washington.edu/uwpress

Library of Congress Cataloging-in-Publication Data
Shin, Gi-Wook.
  Peasant protest & social change in colonial Korea / Gi-Wook Shin.
    p. cm. — (Korean studies of the Henry M. Jackson School of International Studies)
  Includes bibliographical references and index.
  ISBN 978-0-295-99380-5 (pbk. : alk. paper)
  1. Peasant uprisings—Korea—History. 2. Land tenue—Korea—History. 3. Korea—History—Japanese occupation, 1910–1945. 4. Korea—History—1864–1910. 5. Social movements—Korea—History. I. Title II. Series
DS916.55.S55   1996   96-31636
951.9'03'08624—DC20   CIP

The paper used in this publication is acid-free and meets the minimum requirements of American National Standard for Information Sciences—Permanence of Paper for Printed Library Materials. ANSI Z39.48–1984. ∞

Contents

Preface vii

Chronology xi

Note on Romanization xiii

Introduction 3

1/ Explaining Peasant Protest:
An Integrated View 9

2/ Social Change and Land Tenure
in Traditional Korea 22

3/ Colonialism and Korean Agriculture:
Growth without Development 39

4/ Tenant-Landlord Conflict, 1920-32:
Ideology or Interest? 54

5/ The Red Peasant Union Movement,
1930-39, Part I: An Overview and Critique 75

6/ The Red Peasant Union Movement,
1930-39, Part II: History from Below 92

7/ Tenant-Landlord Conflict, 1933–39:
Class and Nation   114

8/ Japanese Militarism and
Everyday Forms of Resistance, 1940–44   133

9/ Historical Origins of Peasant
Radicalism in Liberated Korea   144

Conclusion:
Toward Reform and Revolution   174

Appendix 1
Main Activities of Red Peasant Unions   181

Appendix 2
Peasant Radicalism Index in Relation
to Number of Red Peasant Unions and Socioeconomic,
Demographic, and Religious Variables   185

Appendix 3
Leadership Characteristics
in Selected Red Peasant Unions   188

Appendix 4
List of Counties Analyzed   191

Notes   193

Bibliography   209

Index   231

Preface

This book concerns the role ordinary people play in shaping history. In particular it explores the origins, forms, and legacy of peasant activism in Korea during its most turbulent years, 1876-1946. This period saw Korea open its market to foreign powers and undergo Japanese colonialism, agricultural commercialization, industrialization, and postcolonial revolutionary movements. Throughout, Korean peasants were not passive; their activities crucially affected these transforming events.

The role of the Korean peasant in social and political change has been neglected because of the current trend in Korean historiography to interpret peasant activities as simply part of a nationalist or communist movement. Some see nationalism and communism as incompatible and others do not, but neither side takes peasants seriously as independent actors. For them, the 1920s, 1930s, and early 1940s featured a nationalist peasant movement or communist peasant movement, but not a peasants' peasant movement. To correct this overemphasis on the role of a nationalist/communist elite or a politics of revolution or nationalism, I assume the peasants' perspective.

I do not present a general history of Korean peasant activism, but try to explain its various forms and nature. Korean peasants engaged in several forms of protest: tenancy disputes from 1920 to 1939, the red peasant union movement from 1930 to 1939, "everyday forms of resistance" from 1940 to 1945, and finally the rebellions of 1946 (see Chapters 4-9). Furthermore, the intensity and nature of protest varied over time and

---

An earlier version of Chapter 4 was published in the *Journal of Korean Studies* 7 (1990) and part of Chapter 9 in the *American Journal of Sociology* 99 (1994). I thank the publishers for permission to reprint them here.

across regions. Such variation offers a unique opportunity to examine contending approaches to peasant protest (see Chapter 1). Accordingly, this study is theoretical and comparative as much as empirical and historical.

A sociohistorical approach is required because variation in Korean peasant activism cannot be properly explained by mere reference to the devastating impact of imperialism on the peasant economy, success or failure of leadership, or the repressive power of the state—factors past scholarship has stressed. The complex nature of protest is best understood by looking at the peasants' changing socioeconomic situations from a historical perspective (see Chapters 2 and 3). This does not suggest structural determinism. The effect of imperialism was mediated through the rural class structure, whose differentiation resulted in protest of diverse forms and nature.

The concluding chapter discusses the impact of peasant activism on later socioeconomic and political changes. Korean peasant activism in the first half of the twentieth century provided a social basis for subsequent social revolution in the north and social (land) reform in the south. This is consistent with the revisionist view of postwar Korean society and politics, but traces its origins back even to the colonial period. Also, I challenge the popular view of Korea's political economy which overemphasizes the roles of the world system and the state. A comprehensive understanding of development and change in contemporary Korea cannot be achieved without an account of the historical role of the peasant class.

This study began with work on my Ph.D. dissertation at the University of Washington and was extensively revised adding new chapters during my stay at the University of Iowa and University of California, Los Angeles. I am very grateful to Daniel Chirot for his support for my earlier as well as postgraduate work. It was he who introduced me to a sociological understanding of peasant protest action, and he never failed to offer warm encouragement of my examination of Korean peasant activism. Thanks also to Herbert Costner, Paul Burstein, and Edgar Borgatta for reading parts of this work in various stages. Bruce Cumings, Michael Robinson, Carter Eckert, Clark Sorensen, Elizabeth Perry, Stephen Vlastos, Jae-On Kim, Scott Eliason, Stephen Wieting, Charles Mueller, Kimura Mitsuhiko, and Chang Yun-Shik provided valuable comments on several chapters. In particular, I appreciate Bruce Cumings's detailed comments on my critique of his work in Chapter 9. Two anonymous readers from the University of Washington Press shared many valuable comments and suggestions for revision.

The Faculty Development Fund of the College of Liberal Arts and Sciences, the Professional Development Fund of the Center for Asian and Pacific Studies, and the Central Investment Fund for Research Enhancement, all at the University of Iowa, provided institutional support for my trips to Korea during the summers of 1992 and 1993 to collect additional data, including interviews. Also, a leave of absence from teaching in the fall of 1994 at UCLA allowed me to finish revision. I appreciate all their generous support.

Various chapters were presented at professional meetings, seminars, and colloquiums: Chapter 1 at a colloquium sponsored by the sociology department of Seoul National University in Seoul (June 1992) and at a workshop on "Culture and Social Movements" in San Diego (June 1992); Chapter 7 at a monthly seminar of Yonsei University's Institute of Korean Studies in Seoul (June 1992) and at the annual meetings of the Association for Asian Studies in Los Angeles (March 1993); Chapter 9 at a colloquium sponsored by Yonsei University's sociology department in Seoul (June 1992), at the annual meetings of the American Sociological Association in Pittsburgh (August 1992), at a colloquium sponsored by Harvard University's Korea Institute (April 1993), at a seminar convened by the University of Washington's Center for Korean Studies (May 1993), and at the annual meetings of the Korean Sociological Association in Ch'unchŏn (June 1993). I deeply appreciate the forums to present my work and the sharpening of my arguments which those host institutions afforded.

Further thanks to James Palais for his interest in my work and his encouragement to turn my Ph.D. dissertation into this book. I owe him a great intellectual debt, because his efforts made me rethink Korean history carefully and thoroughly. Also, I am grateful to my former teachers at Yonsei University in Korea, Professors An Kyech'un, Cho Hyechŏng, Chŏn Pyŏngje, Chŏng Chaesik, Pak Yŏngsin, and Song Pok, who not only taught me "sociological thinking" but encouraged me to pursue graduate work in the United States. They continued to show interest and support even after I had completed my Ph.D., offering me various intellectual forums to discuss and refine my arguments. Choe Yoonwhan of the East Asian Library of the University of Washington helped me locate materials during my graduate and postgraduate work. Ko Jongwook assisted in data collection and analysis. Michele Shade greatly contributed to polishing my English. Julidta C. Tarver and Leila Charbonneau of the University of Washington Press helped improve the quality of this publication. In particular, I am very grateful to Leila for her careful copy editing.

Family support was crucial in completing this work. I cannot express enough gratitude to my wife, Mee-Sun, for her warm and patient support. She has especially provided a comfortable and encouraging environment at home so that I can concentrate on my work. Kelley and Ashley, my lovely daughters, perhaps gave me the best kind of psychological support with their charming smiles.

Finally, and not least, I thank my parents, who taught me the importance of knowledge and praxis. Certainly, childhood experiences influenced many of the arguments made in this book. My father was a landowner in North Korea before he went south during the Korean War. To be sure, in escaping the communist regime he nonetheless lost all he had, including land. Already a church elder in the North, during his escape he decided to become a minister, specifically in a rural area. In late 1952 he started his ministry in a village a few miles west of Seoul. Influenced by An Ch'angho, a prominent nationalist during the colonial period, he believed that education could best enlighten and improve peasants' lives, so he started a Christian night school. This marked the beginning of the peasant movement he initiated in the 1950s.

He insisted that critical to the movement's success was understanding the peasants' way of life and also living like them. By no means was his movement revolutionary; it was reformist, improving peasants' living standards, educating their children, eradicating superstition—programs reminiscent of the cultural nationalist movement of the 1930s. I saw some intellectuals come to my village to help the movement, but most refused to live as the peasants did. They could not conceive that peasants who lacked formal education could do well in business and have a rationality different from their own. My father, who sadly passed away in January 1995, had never failed to remind me of this intellectual fallacy. Thus I owe a great intellectual debt to my parents. They taught me about peasant rationality not through theory but through experience. It is my great pleasure to dedicate this book to them.

Chronology

1876	Korea opens its market to Japan.
1894	Tonghak peasant wars start in North Chŏlla province. Sino-Japanese War breaks out.
1904	Russo-Japanese War breaks out.
1905	Korea becomes a Japanese protectorate.
1910	Korea becomes a Japanese colony.
1914	The colonial government promulgates the land tax ordinance.
1918	The cadastral land survey is completed.
1919	The March First nationalist movement begins in Seoul and P'yŏngyang.
1920	The colonial government launches the Program to Increase Rice Production. The Korean Workers Mutual Aid Association is established.
1924	The Korean Worker-Peasant League is established.
1925	The Korean Communist Party is established. The Peace Preservation Law is promulgated.
1926	The colonial government organizes the agricultural associations in rural society.
1927	Sin'ganhoe is established.
1928	The Sixth Comintern Congress in Moscow delivers the December Theses to the Korean Communist Party.
1932	The Tenant Arbitration Ordinance is promulgated.
1934	The Agricultural Lands Ordinance is promulgated.
1937	The Japanese invade China.
1938	The Japanese Diet passes the National General Mobilization Law.

1939	The colonial government issues the Rent Control Order.
1941	The Pacific War breaks out.
1943	The colonial government issues the Staple Food Management Law.
1945	Japan surrenders to the Allied forces.
	The Committee for the Preparation of Korean Independence is organized.
	The American and Soviet Occupation forces come to South and North Korea, respectively.
1946	The North Korean Provisional People's Committee carries out land reform.
	The uprisings begin in Taegu on 1 October.
1948	The Republic of Korea is formed in the south.
	The Democratic People's Republic of Korea is formed in the north.
1948–50	South Korea carries out land reform.
1950	Civil war breaks out.

Note on Romanization

Korean and Japanese words and names are romanized by the McCune-Reischauer and Hepburn systems, respectively. Korean names cited in the text are the given full names in Korean order (surname first, no comma). Korean and Japanese names in the bibliography are also listed in that order (surname first, no comma). Some authors who have published in Korean and English are cited in two forms (e.g., Yongha Shin [Sin Yongha]), but all such cases are cross-referenced in the bibliography.

Peasant Protest
& Social Change
in Colonial Korea

Korea

Introduction

What this book attempts to do is understand socioeconomic and political changes of twentieth-century Korea by looking at the role of rural conflict. In particular it focuses on those historical processes and politics of peasant activism in the first half of the century that crucially affected social and political changes in the second. This approach significantly departs from the currently dominant political economy approach that stresses the importance of a particular world system and the state in the successful Korean transformation from a poor, agrarian country to a viable industrial society (Amsden 1989; Cole and Lyman 1971; Jacobs 1985; Lim 1985; Mason et al. 1980; Song 1990; Woo 1991). Like other works of historical sociology, this book views agrarian conflict as a way to understand diverse paths to modernity (Moore 1966; Brenner 1976, 1977). It also agrees that "Korea's path to modernity and industrialization has not been a smooth evolutionary process but rather a discontinuous, uneven, and conflict-ridden one determined not by some immutable logic of modernization but by historical contingencies and a dialectical process of social change" (Koo 1993, p. 231). Accordingly this book examines the historical origins and legacy of peasant activism in colonial and post-World War II Korea that have shaped subsequent social and political changes.

No one doubts that South Korea represents a success story of the interplay of the state and world system in capitalist transformation. It recorded an annual gross domestic product (GDP) growth of 9.7% from 1965 to 1988, reached $6,300 GNP per capita in 1991, and has become a major trading partner of the United States and Japan. Such economic prowess is especially dramatic because the civil war of 1950–53 almost destroyed Korea. As Vogel recently pointed out, "No nation has tried harder and come so far so quickly, from handicrafts to heavy industry, from poverty to prosperity, from inexperienced leaders to modern planners, managers, and engineers" (1991, p. 65). It is well recognized that effective state involvement and foreign capital, technology, and market played key roles in this successful capitalist transformation, and Korea is now expected to become Asia's "next giant" after Japan (Amsden 1989).

In addition to fast, successful economic growth, relative income and land equality also characterize the Korean development pattern. In 1985 the wealthiest 10% of Korean households garnered 27.5% of the national income, while the figures for Brazil and Mexico were 50.6% and 40.6%, respectively. Gini coefficients of land inequality also show that South Korea had much more equitable land distribution (coefficient of 37.2 in 1970) than Brazil (83.3), Mexico (77.0), or even Japan (47.5) (Taylor and Jodice 1983).[1] This relative equality in Korean development contrasts with Latin America's "dependent development," which produced high social and economic inequality (see Evans 1979).

But despite widespread recognition of Korea's developmental success, most research studies tend to overlook *historical* conditions that made possible an effective state role and relative equality in the Korean transformation. Some scholars concentrate on the colonial legacy of a strong and efficient state bureaucracy: bureaucrats who had served the colonial state came to play an important role in the state apparatus during the industrialization of the 1960s and 1970s (Cumings 1984a). Other scholars go further, arguing for "colonial origins of Korean capitalism" by showing that the postwar interplay of the state and the world system in Korean development can be traced back to the colonial period (Eckert 1991; McNamara 1990). No less significant but little noticed in understanding the active role of the Korean state is the historical process that witnessed the destruction of the old regressive landlord class and the restoration of rural political stability. When an old ruling class controls the state or when society is subject to constant turmoil, strong and efficient state action is severely hindered (Huntington 1968). The Taewŏn'gun's failure to strengthen state power at the expense of the landed aristocracy in late nineteenth-century Korea attests to the importance of such conditions (Palais 1975). As Rueschemeyer and Evans point out, state autonomy from dominant class interests is a prerequisite to effective state action, and increased state autonomy obtains where "subordinate classes acquire sufficient power to undo monolithic political control by the dominant classes" (1985, p. 64).

It was land reform, started in 1948 and completed during the civil war, that toppled the once powerful landlord class and established political stability in Korea, clearing the way for an active state role (Amsden 1989). It also created the relatively equitable income and land distribution. When Korea was decolonized from Japan in 1945, big landlords, 3% of the rural population, owned 60% of the land; a remaining 80% of the rural population were landless tenants or semi-tenants with little land. But by 1957, after land reform, 88% of the rural population were full owner-cultivators. The smallholder structure of Korean agriculture not only created far more equitable land distribution but also fomented a large-scale rural exodus, which provided the labor force needed for rapid industrialization in the 1960s and 1970s (Koo 1990).[2]

While the economic and political consequences as well as the processes of land reform have received fairly extensive study, the historical origins and politics remain to be explained. Some scholars see land reform mainly as an American military government policy to prevent the rise of communism or the Korean politicians who sought support from the populace (Cho 1964; Mason et al. 1980). But this approach is *ahistorical* and downplays the role of the peasant class that fought for land reform (Kang 1988). Still others trace land reform to widespread postwar rural unrest. Landlords could not collect rents from their tenants and the state still lacked power to enforce collection (Chang Sanghwan 1985). The widespread peasant radicalism in liberated Korea, however, did not flare up overnight simply with the removal of Japanese rule. Nor was it the "anomic" and "pathological" expression of the "rootless" mass, as Henderson (1968) argues; nor merely a result of "social mobilization," of agitation by those who had been forced to leave their home villages for Japan and Manchuria during the colonial period and returned home after liberation with new radical ideas such as socialism (Cumings 1981b).

Rural unrest had much deeper historical origins. As this study will show, postwar peasant radicalism built on the "class," "political," and "national" consciousness of the peasant class developed through their experience in protest and resistance during the colonial period. In the North, peasant radicalism provided a crucial basis for social revolution with sweeping land reform. In the South, strong reactionary forces under the auspices of the American military government rendered social revolution "incomplete" (Cumings 1981b; Song 1989). But in both cases the peasants' pressing demand for land reform was crucial. In the words of Powelson and Stock (1987), land reform in both South and North

Korea was achieved "by leverage" instead of "by grace"; that is, peasants obtained land reform by their "economic and political strength" rather than by "gracious government" or "intellectual compassion."

This book attempts to explain the historical process and politics of peasant activism in the first half of twentieth-century Korea that greatly affected social and political changes in the second. This historical attention to peasant activism corrects the overemphasis, in previous studies, on the interplay of the world system and the state to the neglect of "societal pressures."

In investigating the historical roots and legacy of peasant activism in the first half of twentieth-century Korea, this book focuses on four major forms of peasant protest and rebellion: tenancy disputes (1920–39), the red peasant union movement (1930–39), "everyday forms of resistance" (1940–45), and the peasant rebellions of 1946. These movements had different roots, characters, regional variations, and historical legacies. For instance, tenancy disputes were centered in southern commercialized regions, and revealed the class conflict between tenants and landlords over rent reduction and secure tenancy contracts. The more radical and violent protests led by red peasant unions, on the other hand, were centered in the northeastern regions with a high ratio of owner-cultivators, who demonstrated against local government tax policy and police interference in village affairs. This movement was more a "state-society" conflict than a class conflict.

During the war years, direct and overt protest became difficult because of the highly repressive and fascist colonial regime. Yet peasants found "passive" ways of resisting colonial power, such as hiding crops from government officials and changing crops from rice to barley and wheat in order to avoid uncompensated rice collections. These methods can best be conceptualized as "everyday forms of resistance" (Scott 1985). This book will also examine the ways class, nation, and the state combined to produce such diversity and complexity in rural conflict and protest. It will be further shown how such protests influenced the course of postwar peasant radicalism, culminated in the 1946 uprisings.

In explaining such diverse forms of colonial and postcolonial peasant activism, the approach adopted here rejects the currently popular thesis of "colonialism-pauperization-revolution" (Asada 1973; Cho Tonggŏl 1979; Hŏ Changman 1963). That thesis simplistically contends that Japanese colonialism created structural conditions conducive to peasant revolution: impoverishment or pauperization of the peasant class and subsequent polarization of rural class structure. Factional leadership or colonial/state repressive power then supposedly hindered the revolutionary potential of peasant activism. Clearly colonialism should be considered, and poverty and exploitation existed in rural Korea, but to attribute peasant activism to them requires substantiation. Also, such simplification of rural economy and class structure blurs the diverse forms, roots, and nature of peasant activism. This book closely attends to how the effects of structural changes, such as colonialism and commercialization, on rural economy and society were mediated by a differentiated rural class structure, resulting in diverse forms and motives of peasant protest and resistance.

Also rejected is the view, still popular in studies of Korean peasant activism in colonial and liberated Korea, which focuses on the revolutionary elite and their ideology (Henderson 1968; Lee 1978; Scalapino and Lee 1972). That approach traces peasant protest and resistance to the influence of nationalist or communist intellectuals. While these intellectuals could provide organizational skills and articulate peasant interests, in nationalist or communist terms, this view ignores the role that common people played in making their own history. Purportedly, "peasants followed the leaders blindly" (Lee 1978, p. 37) or "were too scattered to have more than atomized . . . cohesion," leading to "social incohesiveness and incapacity for common action" (Henderson 1968, p. 50); they needed only correct ideas and leaders to become radical or revolutionary. From this perspective, what happened from the 1920s to the 1940s was the Korean *nationalist* or *communist* peasant movement, not the *peasants'* peasant movement.

A sociohistorical perspective, looking at rural social structure and process, should eclipse an ideological perspective focused on the revolutionary elite.[3] Attention to social structure, however, should not be taken as structural determinism. Some scholars argue that "revolutions are not made, they come" (Skocpol 1979, p. 17); certain forms of agrarian class structure lead inexorably to certain forms of rural conflict (Paige 1975; Stinchcombe 1961). But history is too rich and complex to be so neatly packaged. Revolutions do not simply come in response to structural conditions; they require human action. A perspective is necessary that relates peasant political action to rural socioeconomic structure and to how peasants understood their interests in historically specific situations. Organizational efforts of nationalist or communist leaders, or exploitation and impoverishment of the peasantry, may have a bearing on peasant political collective action, but this must be explained from the peasants' perspective. Imperialism or colonialism may have figured in peasant activism, but this effect was mediated through peasant action. The dynamic relations between socioeconomic structure and peasant action must be considered. This book serves as a theoretical guide to the roots, forms, rationalities, and nature of peasant activism in the first half of twentieth-century Korea from a sociohistorical perspective.

CHAPTER I

Explaining Peasant Protest

An Integrated View

In *The 18th Brumaire of Louis Bonaparte,* Karl Marx identified the social basis of the monarch's dictatorship of nineteenth-century France as "smallholder peasants." He did not regard peasants as historical agents of social change, but as a conservative mass, like "potatoes in a sack." Marx wrote that peasants "cannot represent themselves, they must be represented" ([1852] 1981, p. 124). As capitalism developed, they would disappear as a class. Workers must and would lead the social revolution.

Contrary to Marx's prediction, major revolutions in the twentieth century did not occur in advanced countries, led by the working class, but in backward countries such as Russia, China, and Vietnam, where the majority of the population were "peasants" (Wolf 1969). In Skocpol's words, "revolutions have occurred in agrarian countries caught behind foreign competitors, not in the most advanced capitalist industrial nations" (1979, p. 292). Lenin was the first Marxist to see the importance of the peasantry in social change. As early as 1903, in "To the Rural Poor," he recognized the revolutionary potential of the peasant class and urged contemporary Marxists to mobilize them for revolution (Kingstone-Mann 1985). (His position was dubious, however, in holding that peasants were petty bourgeoisie in outlook and thus ready to ally themselves with the proletariat, but would never become the leading class.) Bukharin, another important Russian Marxist, agreed that revolution could succeed only through a combination of "a *peasant* war against the landlord and a *proletarian* revolution" (Cohen 1980, p. 166).

Mao Zedong (1967) went one step further, arguing that in an agrarian society such as China the peasantry was not simply an ally in a proletarian revolution, but *the* revolutionary force. His analysis of classes in prerevolutionary China asserted that the semiproletariat of poor peasants should be the carrier of revolution. Frantz Fanon, an influential Algerian revolutionary leader, agreed that "in colonial countries the peasants alone are revolutionary" (1963, p. 48). Such claims that the peasantry is the revolutionary force in the Third World seemed supported by the North Korean, Vietnamese, Mexican, as well as Chinese revolutions (Wolf 1969).

Social scientists have also recognized the importance of the peasantry in social change. Early anthropological studies of peasant society describe conservative and backward-looking attitudes and behavior. Robert Redfield's "little tradition" and George Foster's "image of the limited good" provide typical examples of this view that peasants would or could not change their situation because they lacked a sense of progress (Redfield 1960), or because of mutual distrust or competition with each other (Foster 1965). These arguments accord with modernization theory, which characterizes Third World countries as backward because they are tradition-bound and thus reluctant to change their environment.

Critics of modernization theory, however, question the conservative nature of the peasantry and emphasize their importance in social change. Barrington Moore, Jr. (1966) convincingly shows how important the agrarian class structure is in understanding modern societies. According to Moore, the various routes to the modern world (i.e., democratic capitalism, fascism, and communism) result from differences in rural class structure. Also, Eric Wolf (1969) describes social revolutions in the Third World, as well as the Russian and Chinese revolutions, as peasant revolutions.

Scholarly concern with the peasantry as a main agent of social change accelerated with U.S. involvement in Vietnam in the 1960s. Whether they were intrigued or perplexed by the strong resistance of Vietnamese peasants, the anthropologists, political scientists, and historians, as well as sociologists, tried to explain the nature of peasant society and the source of power in peasant protest. The moral economy versus political economy debate, as represented in the work of James Scott (1976) and Samuel Popkin (1979), highlights the significance of the peasantry in social and historical change. Along with other scholars, Scott and Popkin ask whether poor landless tenants or middle peasants are more prone to revolution and why; whether it is moral outrage, class consciousness, or pursuit of individual interests that foments peasant revolution; and how capitalist imperialism relates to peasant protest. Korean scholars, in their efforts to explain Korean peasant activism during the colonial period, also discuss these issues.

The following section explores three major dichotomies, two theoretical and one methodological, concerning peasant protest: (1) landless tenants versus middle peasants; (2) moral peasants versus rational peasants; and (3) structural forces versus individual action. An integrated view emerges to guide this book's subsequent analysis of Korean peasant activism in the first half of the twentieth century.

THEORETICAL AND METHODOLOGICAL ISSUES

Landless Tenants or Middle Peasants?

One issue confronting revolutionary leaders has been which rural class stratum to mobilize for revolution. Both Mao and Fanon sensed the revolutionary potential of poor, landless peasants or tenants, whose weak ties to the land leave "nothing to lose and everything to gain." For Fanon, "the starving peasant, outside the class system, is the first among the exploited to discover that only violence pays. For them there is no compromise, no possible coming to terms" (1963, p. 48). This pauperization-revolution thesis is also the dominant approach to the study of Korean peasant protest during Japanese colonialism. Cho Tonggŏl (1979), who represents South Korean nationalist scholarship, attributes the rise of tenancy disputes in the 1920s to the exploitation and impoverishment of starving peasants; and Hŏ Changman (1963), a North Korean scholar, and Asada Kyoji (1973), who is Japanese, similarly interpret Korean peasant movements during the colonial period. All three characterize tenant protests of the twenties and thirties as a major form of nationalist or national-liberation movement by poverty-ridden Korean peasants.

Stinchcombe (1961) and Paige (1975) rigorously theorize concerning the revolutionary potential of landless tenants and the conduciveness of the tenancy system to revolution. Envisioning rural conflict in terms of class relations, Stinchcombe identifies five modes of organizing commercial agriculture that engender corresponding interclass responses: the hacienda system, family-sized tenancy, family smallholding, plantation agriculture, and the ranch (capitalist agriculture with wage labor). Among them, he argues, family-sized tenancy is most likely to produce intense rural conflict: tenant-landlord friction over how the crop is shared, the immense social distance separating the two groups, peasant technical knowledge, and the leadership of wealthier tenants combine to foster political and class conflict.

A more sophisticated explanation of class conflict, in Paige's *Agrarian*

Revolution, also posits diverse forms of peasant protest as primarily functions of different rural class relations. However, "income source" is the fundamental variable that differentiates forms of class relations in commercialized enclaves of developing countries. The rural elite depend on either land or capital return for their income. Cultivators receive either land rights or wages. Combining these two dichotomies yields four types of relations between elite and cultivators, each with a characteristic political outcome. Typically a landed upper class combines with wage laborers or sharecroppers to engender class conflict that fuels a revolutionary movement, while a commercialized elite seldom provokes such radical behavior (see Paige 1975, p. 11, fig. 1.1). According to Paige, in terms of class conflict the sharecropper possesses characteristics similar to those of the working class: weak ties to the land, occupational homogeneity, and work-group interdependence (1975, p. 60). Thus, Paige echoes Stinchcombe: a tenancy or sharecropping system is more likely to provoke radical or revolutionary peasant protest than are relations with a commercializing elite.

Zagoria's (1974) study of peasant radicalism in India, Indonesia, and the Philippines supports such arguments for the revolutionary potential of the tenancy system. Tenancy was in fact widespread in many parts of Asia, including Korea, Japan, and China; and some evidence implicates that system in rural conflict (Cho Tonggŏl 1979; Smethurst 1986; Waswo 1977; Wiens 1980; see also Chapters 4 and 7), though whether such conflict was revolutionary or reformist remains debatable.

In contrast, others view middle, rather than landless, peasants as revolutionary. Hamza Alavi's (1965) discussion of the Russian, Chinese, and Indian revolutions depicts such a role. Speaking of Russia, he writes (pp. 246–47):

[I]n the case of the poor peasant, the sharecropper, his livelihood depended on his being able to get the land, from the landlord, for cultivation. Although he was exploited he was too dependent on the landlord to be able to oppose him as the middle peasant could. . . . When the great upheaval began in 1905 it was the middle peasant who provided its main force [and] . . . inaugurated the revolution of 1905.

Eric Wolf (1969) agrees with Alavi regarding six "peasant wars" of the twentieth century (pp. 290–91):

The poor peasant or the landless laborer who depends on a landlord for the largest part of his livelihood, or the totality of it, has no tactical power: he is completely within the power domain of his employer, without sufficient resources of his own to serve him as resources in the power struggle. . . . [He is] unlikely to pursue the course of rebellion. . . . The only component of the peasantry which does have some internal leverage is either landowning "middle peasantry" or a peasantry located in a peripheral area outside the domains of landlord control.

For Wolf, the key to revolution is not found in mere exploitation or poverty but in the realm of social power structures and human ecology. Barrington Moore, Jr., also usefully separates "conservative solidarity," in which rich peasants or landlords control village resources and organizations and dominate smallholders, tenants, and laborers, from "radical solidarity," in which the peasants themselves share in resources and run a village organization that can oppose landlords or the state (1966, pp. 475–76). Middle peasants then are those likely to develop the "radical solidarity" needed for political action.

Some historical evidence supports this middle peasant thesis. Roy Hofheinz (1977) finds an inverse correlation between rates of tenancy and communist strength in the 1920s and 1930s in South China. This is, he explains, because a powerful gentry usually accompanied high tenancy rates. Mitchell (1968) writing about Vietnam and Cumings (1981b) about liberated (post-1945) Korea also detect a negative correlation between tenancy rates and peasant radicalism. Also, as Chapters 5 and 6 portray, most radical peasant movements (i.e., red peasant union movements) in colonial Korea occurred in areas with low tenancy and a high owner-cultivator (middle peasant) ratio.

Why these seemingly contradictory findings on the relation between land tenure systems and peasant radicalism? Do they suggest incompatible models or can additional factors integrate them? This issue similarly dogs two general theories of peasant protest motives—moral versus rational.[1]

Moral or Rational Peasants?

James Scott's *The Moral Economy of the Peasant* (1976) enhances the development of theory in the study of peasant protest movements.[2] Drawing largely on A. V. Chayanov's theory of subsistence economy, Karl Polanyi's (1944) idea of the devastating effect of the market on society, and E. P. Thompson's (1971) concept of the moral economy that guided the actions of English crowds in eighteenth-century food riots, Scott develops a general theory of peasant economy and peasant protest: at the center of peasant politics is the peasant's overriding concern with obtaining a secure subsistence for his family. This concern stems from his precarious position, the product of a shortage of land, capital, and outside employment opportunities. Constrained by "the vagaries of weather and the claims of outsiders" (Scott 1976, p. 4), the peasant is conscious that he lives near the margin of hunger and that a bad harvest can mean starvation. Fear of such a subsistence crisis produces a highly risk-averse peasantry; what dominates is a safety-first strategy, to minimize the probability of disaster, rather than a maximum average return approach. A "subsistence ethic" involving "reciprocity" between "patron and client" of the same moral community reinforces this strategy. Colonial domination and penetration by market forces directly erode not only already precarious peasant security and welfare, but the buffering moral economy. A peasant protest movement, then, is basically defensive and restorative against threats to subsistence and intrusions by the colonial state and impersonal capitalist market forces.

Scott's characterization of peasant protest as antimarket and defensive receives some empirical support. Ann Waswo's analysis of Japanese tenancy disputes (particularly of the depression years of the late 1920s and early 1930s) attributes their increase to landlords' abandoning their traditional benevolent role, becoming "distant figures, unfamiliar with local customs or with the personal ties of the people who farmed their land" (1977, p. 92). Stephen Vlastos's study of peasant protests and uprisings during the Tokugawa period of Japanese history (1600–1867) maintains that peasants protested "in the name of the right to subsistence," although he disagrees with Scott in that such protest did "not necessarily imply a desire to return to earlier modes of production" (1986, p. 157). The dominant line of Korean scholarship interprets Korean peasant protest during the colonial period similarly: the Japanese destroyed traditional tenant rights (e.g., *tojigwŏn*) through the land survey, aggravating rural poverty (Cho Tonggŏl 1979; Sin Yongha 1979). This in turn fueled the rise of tenancy disputes in the 1920s and 1930s (see Chapters 3 and 4).

Samuel Popkin, in *The Rational Peasant* (1979), directly challenges this moral economist view of peasant protest. For Popkin, contrary to Scott, a peasant economy is not always subsistence oriented, but often produces for the market. Rather than avoiding risk, peasants are willing to invest and gamble whenever possible to further their own interests. Popkin criticizes as utopian the moral economist's description of precapitalist peasant villages, arguing that traditional villages did not provide insurance or welfare for poor peasants and that frequent conflicts and substantial stratification occurred. He contends that the modern central state and capitalism did not introduce new subsistence crises, but rather new political openings that might allow peasants to turn the terms of trade in their favor through collective action. Peasant protests, far from being backward-looking and defensive, are forward-looking endeavors to exploit the new opportunities transformation creates.

This rational peasant view is also empirically supported. Richard Smethurst's (1986) analysis of tenancy disputes in Japan of the 1920s and 1930s criticizes Waswo's interpretation. According to Smethurst, early twentieth-century Japanese tenants were no longer subsistence peasants but entrepreneur-farmers, actively engaged in the market. In addition, the relative scarcity of labor increased the bargaining power of tenants and better education raised their consciousness, all of which helped them pursue their interests through collective action such as disputes. James White's (1988) study of popular protest in Tokugawa Japan similarly views peasant protest as progressive and rational. However, no study of peasant protest in colonial Korea adopts this perspective, a fact challenged in Chapters 4 and 7.

As with the landless versus middle peasant debate, the moral versus rational peasant question remains inconclusive, again posing the quandary whether inconclusive and often conflicting findings are irreconcilable or can be integrated. But first, a final, methodological issue must be discussed.

Structural Forces or Individual Action?

Of methodological concern to scholars of peasant studies is the relative importance of structural forces versus individual peasant action in accounting for collective peasant protest.[3] Skocpol (1979) and Paige (1975) offer structuralist views of peasant protest, whereas Scott and Popkin represent voluntarist explanation. Structuralists trace peasant protest to forces such as class relations or state power, while voluntarists stress motivational aspects of protest participation given such structural conditions.

In *States and Social Revolutions* (1979), Skocpol rejects any voluntarist or individualist explanation of peasant collective action, and attributes structural outcomes such as revolutions strictly to structural causes. For her the social revolutions of 1789 in France, 1917 in Russia, and 1911 and especially 1949 in China are to be explained in terms of the relations of each of these states to other states as well as to its own social classes. Similarly, the origins of revolutionary movements in Third World countries after World War II should be sought in the destruction or weakening of colonial power. For Skocpol, neither individual behavior, nor attitudes, nor interests can explain revolutions, because "revolutions are not made; they come" (1979, p. 17).

Paige's analysis of peasant rebellions and revolutions, as discussed above, is another important structuralist work. Linking rural class structure to political outcomes—rebellions and revolutions—he introduces intervening variables such as the economic power of the elite, the socioeconomic characteristics of the labor supply, structural features of reward systems, and the social structure of the cultivating class. However, he incorporates no individual motivational or behavioral variables and little variation in patterns of political behavior of a certain class (e.g., the tenant class). The political behavior of the peasant class is seen as a direct function of local economic structural characteristics.

Most Korean scholarship on peasant protest during the colonial period seems to follow this structuralist perspective, though no study offers a clear methodological articulation. The apparent assumption is that while colonialism and capitalism brought subsistence crises to rural Korea and polarized its class structure, creating the potential for revolution, strong colonial state repressive power prevented it from occurring. No logic of protest other than Marx's renowned "nothing to lose but chains" seems to explain peasant protest. Similarly, the Japanese defeat in World War II created a revolutionary situation in Korea, but again the repressive power of the American military government and reactionary forces hindered mobilization.

Popkin adopts a radically different methodological position. Following Mancur Olson's (1965) well-known "logic of collective action," he argues that the existence of shared interests among members of the same class does not automatically lead to collective action. For example, the improving or declining economic situation does not suffice to explain the absence or presence of protest; also relevant is whether the individual peasant expects participation in collective action to be of ultimate personal benefit. Structural forces do not directly lead to structural outcomes; individual actions mediate, and thus individual peasant rationality or motivation must be considered, although within a given set of circumstances, such as agricultural commercialization and repressive state power. White's (1988) work on popular protest in Tokugawa Japan and James Tong's (1988) analysis of collective violence, rebellions, and banditry in Ming China adopt the same methodological position as Popkin.

Scott's moral economist argument is in accord with the voluntarist perspective, though he doesn't directly deal with this methodological issue. Yet his meaning of rationality differs from Popkin's. Popkin's peasant is rational in that he evaluates the possible outcomes associated with choices compatible with his preferences and values, in order to maximize his interests. By contrast, Scott's peasant is risk-averse, and therefore his rationality or motivation for protest can be understood only within the context of a subsistence ethic.

This macro-micro issue again poses the question raised by the theoretical debates: Are the apparently divergent models of peasant protest incompatible, or can an integrated view accommodate their various findings?

AN INTEGRATED VIEW OF PEASANT PROTEST

The approaches discussed above thus reveal three different faces of the peasantry. First, a peasant to some degree produces directly for his household's consumption; production decisions are accordingly shaped in part by household needs. This is the image of a peasant that moral economists present. Second, a peasant is also something of an entrepreneur, for most peasants produce in part for the market, and must consider prices, supply and demand, and costs and returns. This is, of course, Popkin's rational peasant. Finally, Paige and Wolf emphasize the peasant as a member of a stratified society under a state system, whose surplus production supports the needs of noncultivating classes.

Scott, Popkin, Paige, and Wolf variously enhance understanding of a particular dimension. Yet this purposeful focus fosters a narrow vision of theory and research. The result is irresolvable debate such as that between the moral economy and political economy viewpoints; and this situation continues as long as each approach insists on one of these characteristics to the exclusion of the others. Breaking this stalemate, Philip Huang's integrated view of the peasant as "an entity that fused the characteristics of entrepreneur, subsistence producer-consumer, and exploited cultivator into a single, inseparable unit" (1985, p. 6) recognizes each of the three faces as one aspect of a multidimensional being.

At the same time, however, the mix of these characteristics varies with the peasant's social stratum. An upwardly mobile, rich peasant-farmer or tenant using hired labor and producing a substantial surplus is much closer to Popkin's rational peasant than is an exploited cultivator, such as Paige's sharecropper, whose surplus supports a ruling (noncultivating) class. An owner-cultivator producing mainly for family consumption, on the other hand, suggests Scott's subsistence peasant. What Popkin, Paige, and Scott all overlook is the differentiated nature of the peasant class (see Huang 1985).

To illustrate this differentiated view of peasants, consider the cultivation and commercialization of rice in colonial Korea. Korean scholars attribute the increasing cultivation and commercialization of rice in the 1920s and 1930s to the forced policy of the colonial government. They argue that to meet rice demands in Japan, the colonial government forced peasants to cultivate rice at the expense of other subsistence crops (Cho Tonggŏl 1979; Pak Kyŏngsik 1986). But closer examination reveals a complex of motivations that varied by peasant stratum and the different class relations of each. Larger, well-to-do peasants were unmistakably motivated to a great extent by profit when they increased the proportion of rice in their crops. Yet even the largest and most commercialized peasants still devoted a substantial proportion of their cultivated area to subsistence crops for household consumption. They also paid part of their surplus in tax to the state. In the case of poorer peasants, survival was often more important than profit in their decision to switch to rice. Their land, whether owned or leased, was too meager to sustain their households; they simply hoped that the returns for that year would meet their subsistence needs. Poorer peasants who were landless tenants often had no choice: once rental terms on land that could grow rice were set according to that crop's market potential, few tenants could afford to grow other cereals. Yet when market conditions changed, poorer households could and did adjust their cropping "portfolios" accordingly, in ways not unlike the more well-to-do peasants. Thus, all three approaches figured in peasant response to rice cultivation, with entrepreneurial calculations looming much larger for the rich owner-cultivators or upper tenants, and subsistence considerations (albeit through cash crops rather than cereals grown directly for household consumption) and class relations much more important for the poorer peasants and tenants. (See Chapters 2 and 3 for detailed discussions of the peasant economy in traditional and colonial Korea.)

Also, peasant attitudes vary according to changing socioeconomic situations as well as different rural strata. Walthall (1986) and Vlastos (1986) in their studies of Japanese peasants show that as the economy changed from a subsistence to a profit-oriented market economy, values of peasants changed. In a subsistence economy it was rational to accept the lord's benevolence—periodic tax adjustments in tight times—but once it became possible to generate a surplus, producers redefined the "rational" and the "just" in favor of whatever rules, customs, and authoritative bodies helped the process of capital accumulation (see Bowen 1988). Similarly, a period of economic boom encourages peasants to maximize their own interests, like Popkin's rational peasant, disregarding the safety-first rule of Scott's subsistence peasant. Depression years, on the other hand, dissuade them from risks that threaten survival. As Pierre Brocheux (1983) argues for the Vietnamese case, peasants may cling to moral economy or engage in political economy depending on the general situation and what is at stake for them.

This complex variation of the peasant economy by rural strata and changing socioeconomic situations suggests that analyses of peasant protest must take note of similar complexities. The relatively well-to-do peasant presumably participates in protest in order to increase his share of the profits that the market creates, as Popkin's model predicts. The poorer strata, on the other hand, might protest simply to secure subsistence needs, as moral economists contend; and middle peasants whose interests are undermined by the state's excessive claims might become radicalized, as Wolf maintains. This recalls Charles Tilly's distinction between "offensive mobilization of the rich" and "defensive mobilization of the poor" (1978, pp. 69–78). Also, peasants' behavior should be different during depression years from what it is in more prosperous but otherwise similar years. Their demand for periodic tax adjustments in tight times, more in tune with calls for honoring the moral economy, could be foresworn during prosperous periods when market demands put them, as suppliers, in the driver's seat (Bowen 1988).

The nature of peasant protest also depends on class relations and power configurations. When the elite are powerful in a local setting, for instance, peasant behavior is more likely to be defensive. Weaker elite control will foster more offensive protest. And a noncultivating class that draws its income from industrial or commercial capital is less likely to provoke revolutionary movements than if it drew its income from the land, as Paige argues. Finally, state repressive power greatly influences the occurrence and success of radical movements, as Skocpol argues; when elite and state power suffices to make excessive the cost for any radical protest, peasants should favor more passive expressions of discontent (see Scott 1985).

To accommodate the multifaceted, complex nature of peasant protest, I begin analysis by identifying the conditions conducive to protest, rather than with any general theory of peasant political action. For example, market expansion, commercialization of agriculture, state repressive power, and certain forms of class relations denote structural conditions that bear on peasant protest. As Skocpol argues, the breakdown of the colonial state's repressive power is a precondition for social revolution. Also, a tenancy system may foster revolutionary zeal, as Paige claims. To be sure, as later chapters show, these structural factors are implicated in various forms of peasant protest in colonial and liberated Korea.

But these models do not pursue how any individual peasant or special stratum would behave given these structural conditions. They tend to assume that given X conditions, the result must be Y. Whereas some peasant protests occur in conjunction with particular kinds of class relations or structural conditions, the same form of protest (if any) clearly does not erupt *every* time these conditions obtain. Those models lack the intervening links between social structure and peasant action. As an integrated approach contends, peasant protest does not directly arise from structural conditions; deliberate and conscious efforts of peasants interact with such conditions. Any good explanation of peasant protest must supplement structural analysis with a social and political theory (or theories) of action.

Similarly, Charles Tilly (1978) argues that any good theory of collective action must combine the polity model with the mobilization model. For Tilly, the polity model explores structural and political forces such as class relations or power configurations among contenders. The mobilization model focuses on the process that organizes and mobilizes individual contenders into collective action. The models should indeed be combined, but Tilly wrongly limits the mobilization model to a utilitarian logic, as does Popkin. There are other forms of protest rationality (e.g., moral economy) in peasant society, and the utility of each must be evaluated, not assumed as universally operative, in probing peasant protest movements (see Shin 1992).

The second stage of analysis, then, focuses on how peasants react to structural conditions in *contingent* rather than deterministic ways. Scott's moral economy and Popkin's political economy can help clarify peasant political action given certain structural conditions. My approach differs, however, because starting with a general theory of peasant action cannot capture the dynamic relation between the changing sociohistorical circumstances and peasants' behavior. As discussed above, the peasantry is a differentiated class whose behavior cannot be generalized; also peasant rationality of protest may vary over time. How particular circumstances affect particular kinds of peasants in particular ways must be specified. The nature of peasant protest varies by stratum, structure, and time. As this study shows, structural changes such as agricultural commercialization affected different rural class structures in different ways, resulting in various forms of protest.

The following two chapters accordingly discuss social and economic changes in traditional and colonial Koreas as conditions tied to various forms of peasant activism. Subsequent chapters more rigorously explore each of these forms: tenant protest movements in the 1920s and 1930s (Chapters 4 and 7), the red peasant union movement in the 1930s (Chapters 5 and 6), "everyday forms of resistance" during the war years (Chapter 8), and the 1946 uprisings in liberated Korea (Chapter 9).

CHAPTER 2

Social Change and Land Tenure in Traditional Korea

The land tenure system in the early Chosŏn dynasty (1392–1910) was based on the notion of private ownership, contrary to an earlier historical view that state landownership prevailed (Duncan 1988; Palais 1982–83).[1] The so-called land allotment schemes of the dynasty—the rank-land system (*kwajŏnbŏp*) of 1391 and the office-land system (*chikjŏnbŏp*) of 1466—were simply grants of tax collection rights to people with official rank, not a system of national ownership and distribution. While some land belonged to palaces and state agencies, most was privately owned.

The general landholding pattern in the Chosŏn dynasty exhibited a high degree of unequal distribution. One study of several districts in the seventeenth and eighteenth centuries reports that about 10% of the landholders owned 40% to 50% of the registered land, while middle or poor peasants comprising about 60% of the rural population controlled only about 10% to 20%. In another case study, in one district 5.4% of the population, large landholders, owned 62.3% of the land (Kim Yongsŏp 1960). Also, social status and landholding displayed a high correspondence; most, if not all, of the larger landowners were *yangban*.[2]

Land cultivation followed one of three main avenues: the owner could cultivate the land himself, have his slaves farm, or rent land out to tenants. Tenants generally divided the crop on a fifty-fifty basis with the owner, and the owner owed 10% as *cho* to the state. Unfortunately, no reliable statistics assess the proportion of land cultivated by slaves, tenants, or the owner. But recent Korean historiography shows that slaves and tenants were the most important labor forces in the early Chosŏn dynasty. Especially in the dynasty's earlier years, slaves it seems were a pivotal labor force for officials. James Palais's (1984) review article on slavery in the Koryŏ dynasty (918–1392) notes two widely used criteria for determining whether a given society is a slave society. One assesses whether a certain proportion of the population, usually 30%, were slaves. For the early Chosŏn dynasty, only rough estimates postulate this figure.[3] The other criterion asks whether the political and economic elite are dependent on slave labor. In this respect, considerable evidence shows the importance of slaves to (especially) central officials, for grants of slaves usually accompanied land grants to high officials. For instance, in 1392 when the king gave Pae Kungnyŏm and Cho Chun 220 kyŏl of land, he also gave 30 slaves to each (Duncan 1988, p. 45). Whether the early Chosŏn was a slave society remains debatable, but slaves clearly constituted a major labor force for land cultivation.

The extent of tenancy in the early Chosŏn dynasty also lacks reliable documentation. Since tenants were classified as commoners and not a special class in the Chosŏn dynasty, their status went largely unspecified in official sources. Only some scattered historical documents yield a general sense of the extent of tenancy in the early period. For instance, Chŏng Ch'a-gong, a magistrate in P'yŏngsan of Hwanghae province, estimated that in 1458 about 30% of the population were tenants (Shin 1975, p. 56). Also Chŏng Yak-yong, a Sirhak (Practical Learning School) scholar, estimated that in the early eighteenth century 70% of the population in South Chŏlla province rented all or part of their land from others. Susan Shin's (1973) study of land tenure in the Chosŏn dynasty confirms that tenancy was widespread from the onset. While such sparse evidence cannot specify the relative use of tenants and slaves as a labor force in the early Chosŏn dynasty, in this period it seems that slaves played a more important role.

SOCIAL CHANGE IN THE LATE CHOSŎN DYNASTY

The land tenure system of the late Chosŏn dynasty showed both continuity and change compared with earlier patterns. Although private and highly unequal landownership perdured, the eighteenth and nineteenth centuries witnessed significant change: decline in the size of landholdings and unfree labor, increased tenancy, and the appearance of managerial farms and wage labor. Population growth and decline in the centrality of slaves as a labor force increased the importance of tenancy as a form of land tenure, whereas increased agricultural productivity and market growth promoted agricultural commercialization and, in turn, the appearance of managerial farms and wage labor. Population growth promoted agricultural involution, while agricultural commercialization facilitated social differentiation. Social change in the late Chosŏn dynasty is thus best depicted as ushering in social differentiation and agricultural involution.

Population Growth and the Peasant Economy

Population increase or decrease as a major factor of social change is widely discussed by demographers, historians, and economists, as well as sociologists (Boserup 1965; Geertz 1963; Goldstone 1991; Pak Sangt'ae 1987; Perkins 1969; Postan 1972). Dwight Perkins (1969) attributes increased agricultural productivity in China from the beginning of the Ming dynasty down to 1949 to population growth. According to Perkins, an expanded population drove migration into new frontiers and intensified labor use in cultivation. But increased agricultural output driven by an expanding population did not affect Chinese agriculture qualitatively. When new frontiers were saturated and land use intensification had reached something of a plateau in the twentieth century, crisis ensued (Perkins 1969, pp. 184-89).

By contrast, in Western Europe the population decline in the fourteenth century impelled the birth of Western capitalism, with its vast changes in agricultural practice. According to Postan (1972), decreased population in the fourteenth and fifteenth centuries drastically reversed the land/man ratio of earlier centuries. Labor force shortages in agriculture not only curtailed rent levels, but the lords' ability to restrict peasant freedom. In addition, demographic pressure stimulated technological innovation that increased agricultural productivity with less use of man power.[4] Geertz (1963) offers a third instance of population impacts, claiming that population growth was primarily responsible for economic backwardness in Java. He contends that surplus rural laborers unable to secure employment in industry remained in the countryside, where they sold their labor until its devaluation reduced their marginal return on land to zero and even subsistence was not possible.

The impact of population pressure on the peasant economy of the Chosŏn dynasty is at best speculative, primarily due to the paucity of reliable data on population and amounts of cultivated land. One source reports the 1807 Chosŏn population as 7,561,403 (see Ishi 1972, p. 62). Kwŏn T'aehwan and Sin Yongha (1977) estimate it as 18,383,000 in

1810, while Tony Michell (1981) assesses it as around 14 million. Such divergencies compel great caution in using these data.

Although the exact population of the Chosŏn dynasty remains uncertain, central to understanding the impact of population on land tenure is the direction of population figures—whether they are growing, falling, or relatively constant—rather than absolute numbers. Despite differences in absolute numbers, all three sources above report a similar general pattern of population change. According to Michell's estimate,[5] perhaps the best, population burgeoned from the fourteenth century (4–5 million) to the 1590s (about 10 million), followed by a decade of decline. From the early seventeenth century, population waxed again until the 1690s (about 12 million), followed by another decade of decline. Thereafter, population gradually increased until 1810 (about 14 million). After the mid-nineteenth century, population fluctuated until its early twentieth-century surge (Michell 1981, pp. 71–72).

Data on cultivated land also reveal large discrepancies, since much cultivated land in the late Chosŏn dynasty was not registered, to avoid taxation. One source sets the amount of cultivated land in 1803 at 845,900 kyŏl (see Pak Sangt'ae 1987, p. 107), whereas another estimates it at as much as 1,456,592 in 1807 (Susan Shin 1973, p. 75). As with population data, however, both studies present the same trend: the area of arable land increased steadily from the fourteenth to mid-eighteenth century, then perhaps decreased slightly. Accordingly, the land/man ratio decreased gradually from 0.25 kyŏl per capita in 1666 to .19 in 1807 (Shin 1973, p. 75), or rather rapidly from 0.11 kyŏl in 1592 to 0.05 kyŏl in the early nineteenth century (Pak Sangt'ae 1987, pp. 105–07).[6] That is, all estimates make fairly clear that per capita landholding was declining in the Chosŏn dynasty.[7] But declines in landholding do not necessarily imply peasant impoverishment.

Korean peasants responded to demographic pressure on land in three ways: crop specialization, technological innovation, and labor intensification. These responses are interrelated; in fact, the two former promoted the last.

Wide acceptance of cotton figured most importantly in crop specialization. First grown near Chinju in Kyŏngsang province in the late fourteenth century, cotton gradually spread into southern provinces and, by the early sixteenth century, into every province but Hamgyŏng and Kangwŏn. Its cultivation was encouraged by the growing, profitable market in Japan until the mid-sixteenth century and thereafter by the gradual (though limited) development of an internal market. By the end of the eighteenth century, cotton was sold in 258 local markets and income from a commercial crop such as cotton may have been twice that of grain (Shin 1973). In addition to cotton, commercial crops such as tobacco, silk, hemp, ginseng, vegetable oils, and sweet potatoes gradually appeared during the Chosŏn dynasty. Tobacco and vegetables were very profitable, and sweet potatoes, which thrived on land unsuited for grain, could supplement food shortages in poor seasons. Such crop diversification enabled the peasant to choose crops best suited to local growing conditions (in other words, to specialize) and could augment income.

In addition to crop specialization, better farming techniques and double cropping raised productivity. The technological innovation most consequential for Korean agriculture was rice transplanting (*iang*). Rice seeds raised in small nursery beds at the end of the second lunar month were transplanted into paddy fields vacated by the barley harvest. While this new method did not in itself raise yields, it enabled double cropping in the southern and central areas. According to Kim Yongsŏp (1970), double cropping was rare before 1600, but by the mid-eighteenth century it was widely practiced in the southern provinces (especially rice with barley). In addition to double cropping and transplanting, improved irrigation facilities and intercropping (planting a second crop between the rows of a first) increased late Chosŏn agricultural productivity.

Such specialization and innovation intensified labor use. Commercial crops like cotton and tobacco were labor intensive, and new technology such as transplanting required intensive labor during sowing. Small farms better exploited intensive labor than did large estates using unfree labor, since these innovations demanded specialized knowledge and skill, more attention to detail, and exercise of greater initiative and judgment. Weeding, seed selection, transplanting, intercropping, and other activities required the alertness, effort, and skill of individual workers to be effective. These changes in part explain a decline in unfree labor and a trend toward small farming, especially tenant farming, in the late Chosŏn dynasty.[8] Large landholdings as a unit of ownership did not disappear, but were slowly parceled into smaller tenant farms.

This development of new agricultural technology and intensified labor use with small farming resembles what happened in Tokugawa Japan and sharply contrasts with the Western experience.[9] In modern Western Europe (especially England) technological innovation facilitated mechanization, farm size growth, and social differentiation.

In short, in the middle to late Chosŏn dynasty, population increase, new technology, and crop specialization encouraged intensified labor use, which in turn reduced unfree labor and increased small farming, especially tenancy. But this trend toward small tenant farming is only part of the story. Market growth, both domestic and foreign, was another powerful force of social change.

The Growth of the Market and Social Differentiation

Little doubt exists that seventeenth- and eighteenth-century Korea featured markets. According to a report in 1726, 1,064 local markets (*chang*) served Korea. Another source sets the number at 1,061 in 1807 (Chŏng Sŏkchong 1972, pp. 153–54). Most local markets opened once every five days, and state control was minimal. Also, about 60% of the one million sŏk of grain consumed in Seoul each year was estimated to be provided by merchants from provincial markets. Some Korean historians even see a causal relationship between the development of the market, agricultural commercialization, and "sprouts of capitalism." But most Korean markets before the opening of ports to foreign countries in 1876 were local, and the lack of a coherent currency system prevented market integration.[10] After 1876, however, the market began to expand rapidly.

Traditionally the Chosŏn dynasty forbad private foreign trade. International trade was strictly tributary, primarily with China, and much less with Japan. Smuggling apparently increased in the late Chosŏn dynasty but fell far short of being an international trading system. However, the Kanghwa Treaty of 1876 cracked Korea's commercial isolation. Korea became not only a market for foreign manufactured goods but an exporter of grains—especially rice and beans—to Japan. From 1876 to 1900, foreign imports increased 23-fold and exports 15-fold, rice and beans constituting the main commodities (Table 2.1). Increases in grain exports to Japan drove up crop prices. From 1901 to 1910, the price of rice went up 79% and beans 64%. Furthermore, as Figures 2.1 and 2.2 show,[11] Korean agricultural prices became determined by the Japanese market. On the other hand, Korean handicraft industries such as cotton spinning and weaving lost ground to imports (Kimura 1990). Whether through free trade based on comparative advantage (Kimura 1990) or a typical core-periphery system, the Korean economy gradually was being integrated into the world (Japanese) market.[12]

Expanding markets undoubtedly facilitated commercialization of

TABLE 2.1
Korean Foreign Trade, 1876–1910
(1,000 wŏn)

		Exports		
Period	Imports	Rice	Beans	Total
1876–1880	421			440
1881–1885	1,616			1,385
1886–1890	3,288			1,392
1891–1895	5,531			2,460
1896–1900	9,950	268@	582@	6,770
1901–1905	21,170	35.3%	26.4%	8,019
1906–1910	37,710	38.0%	28.4%	14,469

NOTES: Figures are annual averages. @ is in 1,000 sŏk for 1895–99.
SOURCE: Miyajima (1974), pp. 216–17.

Korean agriculture. As discussed above, commercial crops such as cotton and tobacco were already being cultivated in the eighteenth century, partly in response to population pressures.[13] But the limited internal market could not transform Korean agriculture into a commercial enterprise. In the late nineteenth century, not only the older commercial crops (cotton and tobacco) but also the main subsistence crops such as rice and beans underwent rapid commercialization. As Table 2.1 shows, rice and beans constituted more than 60% of total exports in the late nineteenth and early twentieth centuries. The agents of this commercialization remain obscure, but it seems clear that not only landlords but also owner-cultivators and relatively well-to-do tenants and semi-tenants actively engaged in commercial trade. A 1910 survey shows that landlords sold 71.9% of their crops, and semi-tenants 42.2% (Miyajima 1974).[14] Miyajima Hiroshi's (1974) study further indicates that the landlord class led in rice commercialization, while upper semi-tenants and tenants led in the marketing of beans. Expanding textile imports depressed the cultivation of cotton, once a major commercial crop. Increasingly cotton was replaced by beans.

These markets provided burgeoning opportunities for landlords and some relatively well-to-do tenants and semi-tenants. Producers near port cities such as Mokp'o and Kunsan benefited especially from trade with Japan.[15] The landlord Yun family in Haenam county in South Chŏlla

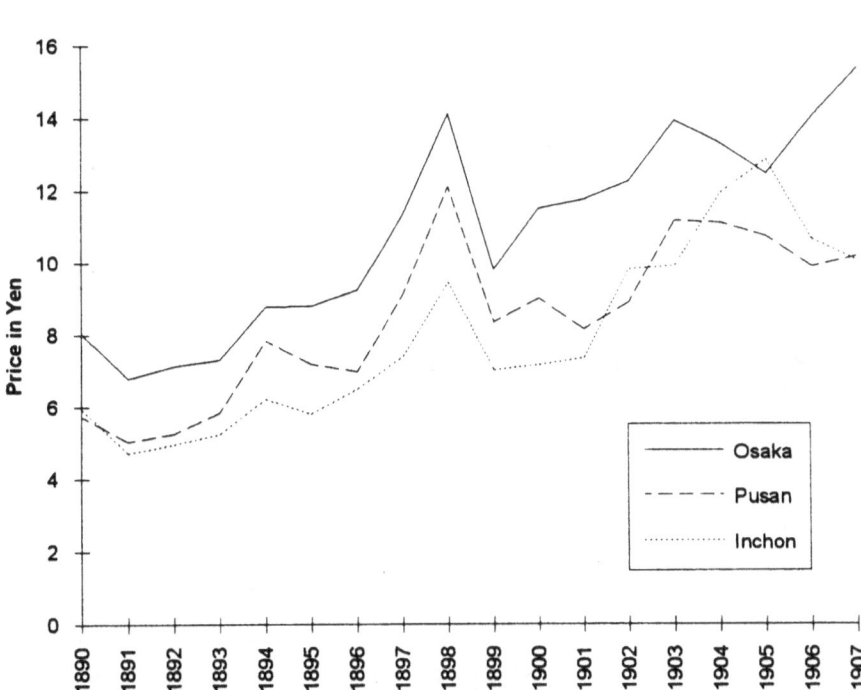

FIG. 2.1. Prices of rice in Korea and Japan, 1890-1907 (per sŏk in yen).
SOURCE: Kimura (1990), pp. 23-24.

province increased profits by exporting rice, geographically advantaged by proximity to Mokp'o, one of the two major ports of rice export to Japan. Its income rose significantly after the opening of Mokp'o in 1897, and its landholdings almost doubled between 1895 and 1919. The family not only leased lands to tenants but also cultivated land itself with wage laborers (Ch'oi Wŏngyu 1985). Kim Yongsŏp's (1972) study of the landlord Kim family of Kanghwa island in Kyŏnggi province, and Hong Sŏngch'an's (1986) case study of the landlord Yi family in Posŏng county of South Chŏlla province, show that expanding markets facilitated agricultural commercialization, significantly increasing their incomes.

30 *Social Change and Land Tenure in Traditional Korea*

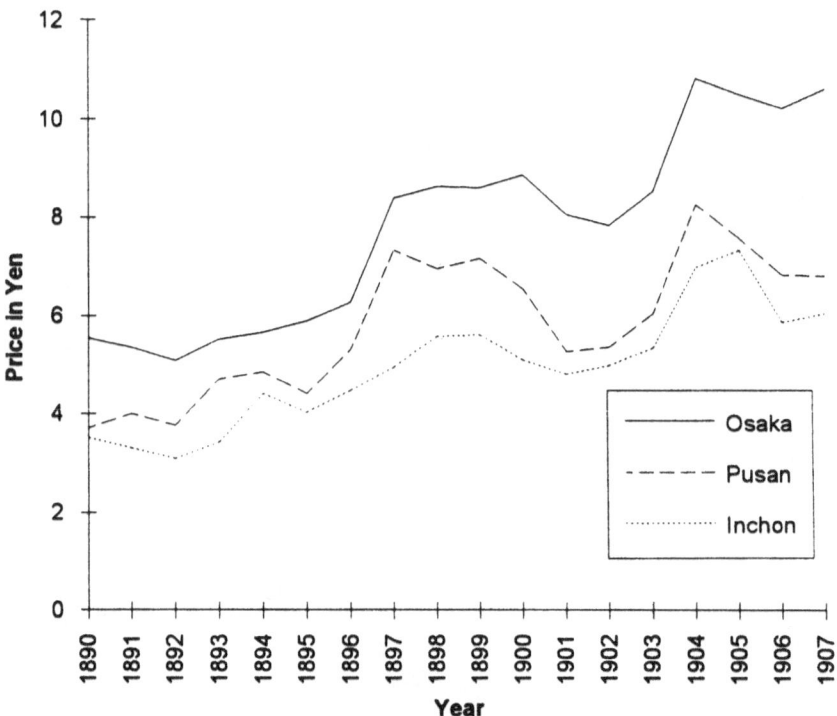

FIG. 2.2. Prices of beans in Korea and Japan, 1890–1907 (per sŏk in yen).
SOURCE: Kimura (1990), pp. 23–24.

While some relatively well-to-do tenants and semi-tenants who hired wage laborers also benefited from expanding markets and commercialization (Kim Yongsŏp 1970; Miyajima 1974), most of the poorer rural strata were becoming landless tenants and wage laborers and remained basically subsistence peasants (Kim Yongsŏp 1992). One survey finds that the landless tenant class sold almost no crops on the market (Miyajima 1974). In this way market expansion and increasing agricultural commercialization facilitated social differentiation of the Korean rural classes, into big landlords and some managerial farmers on the one hand and small tenants and wage laborers on the other. Yet whether increased commercialization and social differentiation suffice to indicate a capitalist mode of production in the late Chosŏn countryside remains to be examined.

Incipient Capitalism?

One of the most important tasks postwar Korean historiography pursued was to refute the so-called stagnation theory (*chŏngch'eron*), or colonial perspective (*singmin sakwan*), regarding Korean history. Japanese historians advanced stagnation theory as an explanation to justify their colonization of Korea, depicting it as a backward and stagnant society. To repudiate this colonial perspective, both South and North Korean scholars rigorously endeavored to show that capitalism "sprouted" in late Chosŏn society, long before the coming of (Japanese) imperialism, as evidenced by increased economic commercialization and development of capitalist wage labor. They further argued that Japanese colonialism destroyed such incipient capitalism, rendering Korea a "semi-feudal, colonial" society.

South Korean Kim Yongsŏp's (1970) series of analyses of land and tax registers, or *yang'an,* were influential in this nationalist historiography. He holds that internal urban market growth and technological innovations such as double cropping and transplanting brought commercial capitalism, led by "managerial farmers" (*kyŏngyŏnghyŏng punong*), as early as the eighteenth century in Korea. Unlike "feudal landlords," who increased yields by expanding holdings (cultivated by slaves and tenants), "managerial farmers" employed improved techniques to increase agricultural productivity and profit. But imperialist intrusion later skewed this path of development, reducing Korea to a "semifeudal, semicolonial" country and aborting capitalist "sprouts."

In the 1960s, North Korean historians also debated the origins of Korean capitalism. While primarily focusing on mining, paper, textiles, and shipbuilding, they in general agreed that capitalism had also infiltrated agriculture. Chŏn Sŏktam, for instance, claimed that free wage labor in the countryside was clear evidence of capitalist relations (see Ch'oe 1981 and Doe 1991).[16]

Although this argument for incipient capitalism has merit in showing that the Korean economy was not stagnant before imperialist intrusion and that emergent "managerial farmers" employed improved techniques using hired wage laborers, whether this development could have fostered agricultural entrepreneurs as a social class remains unclear. Also, the existence of free wage labor does not prove that a capitalist mode of production emerged in Korean agriculture. The incipient capitalism argument, while basically following a Marxist interpretation of historical development, concentrates mainly on production relations, to the neglect of "productive forces," the other factor crucial in the Marxist conception of a "mode of production."[17] In this regard, Philip Huang's (1985) criticism of using the same argument for North China applies also to Korea. Korean scholars, like their Chinese counterparts, tend to detect "capitalist sprouts" based on the appearance of supposedly capitalist relations between managerial farmers and wage laborers, assuming rather than demonstrating that advances in productivity accompanied such relations. In an overpopulated and unindustrialized society such as Korea, however, emergence of free wage labor does not suffice to prove qualitative change in modes of production, though it would seem to belie economic stagnation.

The presence of managerial farmers and wage laborers in late Chosŏn rural society did not signal differentiation into these two classes: small peasant farms remained the main unit of production if not of ownership. Modern Western Europe (especially England) saw a long-term process of social differentiation characterized by the rise of a capitalizing rural bourgeoisie and a proletarianized peasantry. Peasant society thus yielded to an industrial capitalist society. In Korea in the late nineteenth and early twentieth centuries, by contrast, social change did not end the small peasant economy, as in Russia (see Chayanov in Thorner et al. 1986) or in Java (see Geertz 1963). Rather, it simply fostered labor-employing but noncapitalizing managerial farms and partial proletarianization of an increasing proportion of peasants, most of whom remained tied to agriculture, working as both tenants and wage laborers, although some came to be employed in nonagricultural activities. This resembles what Huang (1985) calls "semiproletarianization" in describing early twentieth-century Chinese peasants, attributing it to population pressure and class relations, with more emphasis on the former. But in Korea the emphasis reverses, as will be shown below.

Involution, Social Differentiation, or Both?

Population growth brought a decline in landholding and a rise in tenancy rate, whereas the growth of agricultural productivity and markets introduced incipient capitalism in the late Chosŏn dynasty. The former nurtured an involuting process as the latter impelled social differentiation. Thus social change led to an involuted-differentiated peasant economy. Why did Korean society not become either involuted as in Java or differentiated as in Western Europe and Japan, but instead became both?

The first issue is why most managerial farmers did not transform into "agricultural capitalists." Previous scholarship blames colonialism as the main cause of this underdevelopment of capitalism. This is at best only a partial answer. The structural context of social change in the late Chosŏn dynasty, involving population pressures and class relations, must be examined as well. At that time, the landlord class remained sufficiently strong to quell any challenge to its social, economic, and political power, as the Taewŏn'gun's failure to restore state power at its expense in the 1860s attests (see Palais 1975). As Robert Brenner (1976) describes the grounds for enduring backwardness in Eastern Europe, so the strength of the landlord class was a main obstacle to Korean agricultural development. Furthermore, most managerial farmers increased their fortune not only through improved technology with hired labor, but perhaps more importantly through usury and commerce (Hong Sŏngch'an 1981, 1985). Interest on loans in rural Korea ran so high as to be more profitable than income from land.[18] Also, high rental rates may have discouraged managerial efforts to develop new technology and improve productivity: leasing land was as profitable as managing farms. Finally, cheap labor strongly deterred labor-saving capital investment by managerial farmers. Many in fact were becoming landlords rather than agricultural capitalists. A good example is Yi Kyesŏn of Naju in South Chŏlla province. Once a poor peasant, he invested wealth accumulated through commerce (as a rice dealer) in land to become a landlord (see Kim Yongsŏp 1992, pp. 129-72). In short, strong landlordism, based on usury and commerce, combined with abundant cheap labor to obstruct the development of large-scale managerial agriculture.

Such opportunities for landholders, of course, disadvantaged the poorer rural strata, who faced underemployment and the competition of excess labor. Lack of any substantial development of agricultural capitalism or industrialization in the late Chosŏn dynasty provided little outlet for surplus labor. Cultivation of a small amount of owned land, leased land, or both, for most poor peasants fell short of subsistence needs, often requiring them to sell their labor for supplemental income (Hŏ Chongho 1965, pp. 103-20; Kim Yongsŏp 1992, p. 167).[19] Conversely, wage labor alone also failed to support a family; moreover it garnered a village social status yet lower than that of tenants (Hŏ Chongho 1965, p. 115; Kim Yongsŏp 1992, p. 16). A typical poor peasant in the late Chosŏn dynasty owned little or no land, leased a small amount from others, and labored for wages. Many were compelled to hire out on farms in busy, crucial periods, at the cost of inadequate or untimely work on their own small farms (Ch'oi Wŏngyu 1985). For these poor peasants, survival, not optimal labor use, was the main concern.[20]

Thus population pressure and social stratification combined to form a tenacious, stagnant system, particularly vicious in human terms. Poor peasants became locked into dual dependence on family farming and hiring out, unable to do one without the other, since each provided below-subsistence incomes. Their cheap labor, in turn, helped maintain a nonproductive landlordism and stagnant managerial farming. In short, social change in the late Chosŏn dynasty involved the combined workings of involution, social differentiation, and semiproletarianization. An involuted-differentiated peasant economy and society emerged in which most peasants were partly proletarianized, forced to depend on a combination of family farming and wage labor for mere survival.

Comparisons with Western Europe put social change in late nineteenth-century Korea into perspective. The population decline in Western Europe during the fourteenth and fifteenth centuries created an agricultural labor shortage that stimulated technological innovation and expanded economic horizons. These and the growth of towns and the market divided peasants into capitalist farmers and wage laborers, modernized agriculture, and brought capitalist industrialization. Conversely, most Third World countries have witnessed agricultural involution. Clifford Geertz's (1963) well-known study of nineteenth- and twentieth-century Java shows how Dutch imperialism created a dual economy, in which modern export agriculture and a traditional subsistence economy coexisted. In the traditional sector, he claims, population growth without any substantial industrial development created a labor surplus forced to remain in the countryside as subsistence peasants. The involution led to a backward, underdeveloped economy in the presence of a modern agricultural sector, whereas social differentiation in Western Europe fostered capitalism.

If we consider these two models as ideal types, most other patterns of social change in agrarian societies lie somewhere in between. Philip Huang's (1985) study of social change in North China argues that the late nineteenth and early twentieth centuries brought both involution and social differentiation. Social change in Korea in the same period is also best described as "involuted social differentiation," but while the more determinative factor in North China was population pressure, in

Korea it was class relations. An important result of this involuted social differentiation in a small peasant economy was a rapid rise in the tenancy rate.[21]

LAND TENURE IN THE LATE CHOSŎN DYNASTY

The Prevalence of Tenancy

Unlike earlier periods, for the late Chosŏn dynasty the prevalence of tenancy is well-documented. For instance, Susan Shin's (1973) study of a 1720 district register in Namhae, an island off the southern coast of Kyŏngsang province, shows that among 962 registered households, 473 (49.2%) were landless tenants and 133 (13.8%) were semi-tenants. Kim Yongsŏp's (1960) study of the Kwangmu land survey (*yang'an*) of 1898–1904 shows that tenants constituted from as little as 11.5% in Sŏksŏng to as high as 93.7% in Onyang. If the data are excluded for Sŏksŏng, where landless tenants either went unrecorded or did not exist, the percentage of landless tenants and semi-tenants averaged 85.9%; that is, almost all farming families were renters of a portion of their holdings, but many also owned a part. As Susan Shin's (1975) study of tenant-landlord relations in the Chosŏn dynasty properly emphasizes, "such a substantial number of owner-tenants [semi-tenants] indicates the diversity of the tenant population." In addition, such semi-tenant prevalence signifies an important feature of late Chosŏn dynasty social change, the persistence of a small peasant economy despite market growth.

Other case studies of land tenure on private and state-owned lands show the same characteristics: high tenancy rate and persistence of a small peasant economy. For instance, the landlord Yun family in Haenam county of South Chŏlla province leased land to as few as 16 tenants and as many as 59 between 1872 and 1929 (Ch'oi Wŏngyu 1985, p. 301). The landlord Yi family in Posŏng county of South Chŏlla province between 1896 and 1931 leased to from 26 to 54 tenants (Hong Sŏngch'an 1986, p. 167). Another landlord, the Hong family in Kanghwa county of Kyŏnggi province, had 254 tenants as of 1908 (Hong Sŏngch'an 1981, p. 90). Tenants also frequently cultivated palace-owned lands, in addition to private land. For instance, a palace called Myŏngraegung owned land in over 91 locales. The number of tenants used to cultivate 11 of these holdings ranged from 14 in Chinch'ŏn of Ch'ungch'ŏng province, on 128 turak (1893); to 144 in Hŭnghae of Kyŏngsang province, on 702.1 (1891) (Yi Yŏnghun 1988, pp. 408–11). These cases all show that tenancy became the dominant form of land tenure in the late Chosŏn dynasty.

Not only did tenancy prevail in the late Chosŏn dynasty, but most tenants cultivated only a small amount of land. A landholding of 25 pu is generally considered to have been the minimum required to support an owner-cultivator peasant family, 50 pu for a landless tenant family. But most landless tenants were hard pressed to meet this subsistence level. For instance, of the 473 landless tenants studied by Susan Shin (1973) mentioned above, 332 (70%) leased no more than 25 pu. Also, of the 109 tenants of landlord Yi of Naju, 85 (78%) leased less than 50 pu (Kim Yongsŏp 1992, p. 166). Kim Yongsŏp (1960) estimates that in the districts he studied the after-tax income of 30% to 58% of farm households fell short of subsistence. The case studies of landlords mentioned above show the same small leaseholds for many tenants.

Tenant-Landlord Relations

Although tenancy characterized the Chosŏn dynasty, the dynasty conducted no systematic study of the tenancy system. Also, tenants did not leave known records of their relations with landlords. Therefore, the ensuing discussion of tenant-landlord relations relies on some case studies of landlords who recorded their land lease practices, and early twentieth-century Japanese surveys on tenancy customs. While regional variation occurred, a general picture of tenancy customs in the late Chosŏn dynasty emerges.

In traditional Korea, rent payments were usually either variable (*pyŏngjak*) or fixed (*tojo*). In the former arrangement (often called sharecropping), tenants and landlords most often shared crops on a 50/50 basis, whereas *tojo* fees were fixed, regardless of the harvest. In the Chosŏn dynasty *pyŏngjak* prevailed more commonly, although absentee landlords including palaces and government agencies customarily exacted fixed rent. Fixed rent was lower than 50% of crops, but was augmented by land tax responsibility.[22] Also, fixed rent was more popular in dry fields than in paddy fields. Transition from variable to fixed rent probably stemmed from the difficulties landlords had in measuring yields and preventing pilfering by tenants and stewards. The Myŏngraegung palace made this explicit in its instructions to stewards in 1774. "Because of difficulties in collecting rent from sharecroppers," the palace ordered one sŏk of grain to be collected for every mal of seed sown by the tenants (quoted in Susan Shin 1975, p. 60). Similarly, as mentioned above, fixed rent on privately owned land was customary when landlords lived far from holdings.

Rent was mostly collected in kind, only exceptionally in cash. When landlords lived at distances that made farm product deliveries difficult, or when they specifically required cash payment, rent was paid in currency (*taegŭmnap*) based on current crop prices. Such cash payment was not an uncommon practice on palace or government owned land such as Kungjangt'o or Yŏktunt'o.

Most tenancy contracts were oral, in some places followed by a written note from the landlord. The written contract was standard for the fixed rent arrangement, but again, this arrangement prevailed less than the variable form.

Finally, tenancy tenure was highly insecure. Some previous studies claim that before Japanese colonialism, tenancy was very stable, often lasting for a lifetime. Shin Yongha (1978) argues that unless the tenant failed to pay rent or utterly neglected farming, arbitrary transfer of tenancy was uncommon. This notion of a permanent tenancy right, he maintains, was based on patron-client relations as portrayed by moral economists, often influenced by Confucian ideology. Yet empirical evidence shows that permanent tenancy was exceptional, not the rule; tenure was very insecure in the late Chosŏn dynasty. For instance, Susan Shin's (1973) analysis of two palaces registered in Pup'yŏng of Kyŏnggi province reports that of their 22 holdings, all changed tenants between 1754 and 1771. Kim Yongsŏp's (1960) probe of landholdings of an institution in South Ch'ungch'ŏng province, Nogang sŏwŏn, shows that over a ten-year period, 31 of 37 fields changed tenants at least once. Hong Sŏngch'an's (1986) study of the landlord Yi family in Posŏng county of South Chŏlla reports that between 1896 and 1910, 28 of 37 fields, or 76%, did the same. Ch'oi Wŏngyu (1985) also shows that the landlord Yun family in Haenam county of South Chŏlla province changed tenants on 32 of 34 fields, or 94%, at least once over the ten years from 1881 to 1890. Among them, 15 shifted hands more than five times. These examples suggest that tenancy tenure was not as secure as some have argued.

To summarize, the most common tenancy arrangement in the late Chosŏn dynasty was a sharecropping rental arrangement with payment in kind. Also, most contracts were oral and tenure was very insecure. But again, tenancy customs varied across regions.

38 *Social Change and Land Tenure in Traditional Korea*

CONCLUSION: KOREA ON THE VERGE OF COLONIZATION

Nineteenth-century Chosŏn society underwent significant socioeconomic changes. Korean agriculture became increasingly commercialized with the growth of the market, managerial farmers and wage laborers emerged in the countryside, and "class" based on landholdings (i.e., landlords-tenants) began to supplant "status" (i.e., *yangban*-slaves) in rural authority relations. Despite all these changes in the countryside that perhaps weakened "feudal" social relations, the small peasant economy remained virtually intact. Capitalism as a mode of production did not replace the old social and economic order.

Further, the landed class still wielded powerful influence in local villages, despite sporadic peasant rebellions such as the Tonghak peasant wars of 1894. The state failed to inaugurate any reform—political, social, or economic—and faced competing imperial forces. In particular, Japanese influence on Korean society and politics substantially increased after victories in the Sino-Japanese War of 1894–95 and the Russo-Japanese War of 1904–5. Korea became a Japanese protectorate in 1905 and a full colony in 1910. The following chapter explores socioeconomic changes and land tenure in the early colonial years.

CHAPTER 3

Colonialism and Korean Agriculture
Growth without Development

Economic historians and historical sociologists have long argued about socioeconomic shifts in the Third World under colonial rule. One view claims that such rule, though objectionable on moral grounds, has often benefited indigenous societies. Marx's classical analysis of British imperialism as breaking the traditional economic structure in India represents this perspective. Conversely, most neo-Marxists, including Lenin and Mao, charge that imperialism or colonialism destroyed the potential for "incipient capitalism" in victimized countries and thus distorted their future development. Marx's interpretation of British rule in Ireland is along those lines.[1]

Such controversy about the nature of colonial rule also surrounds studies of Japanese colonialism in Korea (see Myers and Peattie 1984). Some Japanese and Western scholars maintain that the Japanese promoted Korean economic modernization, thus the colonial legacy was not necessarily negative for Korea. They cite the "educating and stimulating effect" on Korean society (Kimura 1990), or Korea's postwar economic development pattern (Eckert 1991), as evidence of a positive influence. In contrast, most Korean (South and North) economic historians blame Japanese colonialism for disabling indigenous development and for Korea's distorted, dependent development (Cho Kijun 1973).

While both views have some merit, the nature of Japanese colonialism in Korea changed over time and its impact in earlier years was limited. The Japanese did not radically alter land tenure, but accelerated economic forces already at work in the last decades of the Chosŏn dynasty. They neither introduced new crops nor built plantations using slave labor. They eschewed the large-scale, radical land reform undertaken in Taiwan. Earlier characteristics of land tenure (private ownership, highly unequal land distribution, prevalent tenancy, and semiproletarianization of the peasant) remained intact. Belying the nationalist view, land tenure patterns under early colonialism showed more continuity with those of the late Chosŏn dynasty than radical change. Since the cadastral land survey of 1910-18 is often regarded as a major means by which the Japanese consolidated early control over Korean agriculture, discussion turns now to its nature and impact to illustrate the nationalist fallacy.

THE CADASTRAL LAND SURVEY OF 1910-18

Japanese colonialism, through the land survey of 1910-18, is often alleged to have brought major land tenure changes that produced modern landownership and extreme inequality in rural Korea (In 1939; Pak 1933; Yi 1955). Pak Munkyu credits the survey with establishing the first Korean private landownership rights in Korean history. In addition, he charges that it allowed fraudulent claims by Japanese settlers and corrupt Koreans to land owned by illiterate and ignorant Korean peasants in rural villages who could not understand the notion of "reportism," and thus lost their landownership and became landless tenants. Another Marxist economic historian, In Chŏngsik, agrees that the cadastral survey served to legalize Japanese landownership claims under a new and alien system of private ownership rights. It enabled Japanese companies like Tōyō takushoku kabushiki kaisha (Oriental Development Company) to appropriate immense tracts of land. Later economic historians concur with this interpretation: the survey "legally" transferred landownership from exploited poor peasants (Cho Kijun 1973; Kim Chunbo 1970).

The survey did effectively identify the landholdings of the Yi royal family and government officials, and these lands reverted to the colonial government, often to be sold to Japanese land development companies such as the Oriental Development Company. But other arguments discussed above are empirically dubious. First, as the previous chapter discusses, private ownership, high inequality of landholding, and prevalent tenancy all characterized precolonial Korea. Yet, ironically, the nationalist interpretation of the land survey credits the Japanese with introducing the modern land system in Korea. Also, various case studies do not support alleged exploitation through the survey. For instance, in the Noksan district of Kimhae county the survey did not always favor large landowners, and reportism did not wrest land ownership from poor peasants: Cho Sŏggon (1988, table 8) shows that of 9,256 land parcels only 12, or 0.1%, went unreported. Also, among 26 members of the district survey committee established to confirm ownership and mediate any disputation, only 3 or 4 could be classified as landlords; 10 had no land in paddy or dry fields (1988, table 9). Further, only a few plots, less than 1% of the land, were disputed during or after the survey (1988, table 14).[2] Pae Yŏngsun's (1988) study of land tax reform and the survey supports Cho's claim of historical continuity in land tenure. Gragert's study of landownership change in four villages in the South Ch'ungch'ŏng, North Chŏlla, and Kyŏnggi provinces concurs: except for lands previously owned by palaces and government agencies, the survey brought little turnover of landownership (Gragert 1982, chap. 4).[3]

Other scholars charge that the cadastral survey deprived tenants of permanent tenure rights, *tojigwŏn*. The *tojigwŏn* customarily granted tenants exclusive cultivation rights that could be passed on through inheritance, gift, or sale, and were unaffected by land sale. The tenant paid rent lower than the usual 50%, and *tojigwŏn* could be sold at about one-third the land's value (Hŏ Chongho 1965). Sin Yongha (1979) claims that the land survey guaranteed landlords exclusive ownership and denied tenant cultivation rights such as *tojigwŏn*. While he concedes that private ownership prevailed in the late Chosŏn dynasty, he contends that the survey "destroyed the tenancy rights and other basic rights of the farmers . . . [and] gave complete protection to the private ownership of landlords" (p. 303), creating high tenancy insecurity. He further stresses that the undermining of tenure was primarily responsible for the tenancy disputes during the 1920s. Hŏ Chongho (1965) also argues that *tojigwŏn* had been a major means by which tenants and semi-tenants could accumulate capital and thus become owner-cultivators and that the survey blocked this upward mobility (see pp. 198–204).

While it is clear that the Japanese had no plan to destroy the landed class, that they maintained the landlord system, and that until the mid-1930s extended no legal protection to tenants (see Chapter 7), still the survey cannot be held solely responsible for insecure tenancy tenure or rural inequality. As the previous chapter discusses, even before Japanese rule, tenancy tenure was unstable and most of the rural poor had to work as tenants, wage laborers, or both. Also, *toji* tenure obtained in a relatively small area under limited geographic conditions. An extensive Japanese survey of tenancy customs primarily locates the *toji* tenure practice in sparsely populated northern areas or coastal districts that required considerable capital investment for constant cultivation (Chōsen sōtokufu 1930, vol. 2).[4] As Vlastos (1986) argues for the political economy of benevolence in Tokugawa Japan, the notion of *tojigwŏn* must be understood in the context of a larger socioeconomic structure in which permanent tenure served as a rational response to harsh environmental conditions. While the colonial government offered tenants no legal protection, charging that the land survey destroyed tenant rights seems to "exaggerate the role of *tojigwŏn* in premodern Korea by considering it the norm rather than a response to very specific economic conditions" (Shin 1975, p. 72).

The main purpose of the survey was to record for every land parcel in Korea details of ownership, quality, and value to secure colonial government revenue through land taxation. In fact the Korean government already had a similar, although less effective program at the turn of the century to identify ownership, productivity, and size of all agricultural fields (e.g., the Kwangmu yang'an [1896-1906]) in an ultimately futile effort to increase land tax revenue. Using their experiences in Taiwan as well as Japan, the Japanese introduced a modern registration system such as *t'oji taejang* and *t'oji tŭnggibu*, but had no radical plan to change land tenure.[5] Major accomplishments included exposing covert ownership and increasing government revenue through effective land taxation. Government statistics set the total area of registered cultivated land in 1910 at about 2.4 million chŏngbo (approximately 5.9 million acres). By 1919, after the survey, the total was 4.3 million chŏngbo, an 80% increase (Wada 1920). During the same period, land tax revenue swelled from 6 million yen to about 11.5, or by 91%. Until Korean industry began to develop in the 1930s, land tax constituted a major source of total colonial government revenue, about 30% (Chŏng T'aehŏn 1987).

In sum, the 1910-18 cadastral survey created an accurate land register, and secured government revenue and Japanese access to landownership. Private ownership, high inequality of land distribution, and insecure tenancy tenure, already prevalent in the late Chosŏn dynasty, were little affected. Whether the main purpose of Japanese colonialism was economic or strategic and political remains debatable (see Menzel 1986; Moskowitz 1974), but the Japanese did not implement radical measures to transform the Korean economy and society in early colonial years. Socioeconomic forces at work in the late Chosŏn dynasty accelerated, though under more direct government guidance. Of greatest significance were continuing market expansion and hastened agricultural commercialization, discussed in turn below.

TABLE 3.1
Indices of Agricultural Output and Labor Productivity
for Korea, Taiwan, and Japan, 1920–30

Country	Total Output			Labor Productivity		
	1910	1920	1930	1910	1920	1930
Korea	—	100	105	—	100	99
Taiwan	—	100	136	—	100	139
Japan	100	121	131	100	137	149

SOURCE: Hayami et al. (1979; tables K-1a, J-1, and T-1a in appendixes).

AGRICULTURAL GROWTH WITHOUT DEVELOPMENT

While it is often argued that the initial motives of Japanese imperialism in East Asia were not economic but political, strategic, or even psychological (see Menzel 1986), the Japanese never overlooked the importance of Korea as an agricultural source. As Moskowitz points out, they "had been interested in the potential of Korean agriculture even before the establishment of the protectorate [in 1905]" (1974, p. 77). Although Japanese penetration into the Korean economy since the opening of ports in 1876 had been rather gradual and steady, Japanese economic interests in Korea as a stable agricultural provider became more serious in the late 1910s. During and after World War I, Japan underwent rapid industrialization and faced rice shortages that culminated in the 1918 rice riots. Taiwan and Korea were logical choices for steady provision of agricultural crops, especially rice (Ohkawa and Rosovsky 1965).

In 1920 the Sanmai zoshoki keikaku (Program to Increase Rice Production) was launched, a major campaign for increasing Korean agricultural production. It encouraged use of chemical fertilizers and improved seeds, cultivation of new lands, and irrigation improvement. In addition, the colonial government required inspection of rice and beans to enhance quality and marketability. It already had established an agricultural experimental station in Suwŏn that pursued extensive research to improve seeds and disease control. In fact, Korean agriculture showed modest growth of 5% from 1920 to 1930 (see Table 3.1), an annual rate of 0.46% (see also Ban 1979, table 4–5a).

The growing demand for Korean agricultural crops (particularly rice) in Japan increased agricultural prices rapidly, stimulated exports, facilitated market growth, and encouraged commercialization. Crop prices increased almost fourfold from 1910 to 1920, and high prices persisted until the agricultural depression hit the Korean rural economy in the late 1920s (Suh 1978, p. 169). Exports to Japan also burgeoned until the late 1920s. During the 1921-25 period, the commodity trade balance between Korea and Japan significantly favored Korea, annually averaging 52 million yen, about 34% of the 1923 total government revenue (Choi 1970, p. 20; Suh 1978, p. 126).

Korean agricultural crops primarily fueled the trade surplus. Increased prices and exports further facilitated market growth. While local markets existed in Korea long before the Japanese arrived, the early twentieth century brought rapid market expansion. Colonial government statistics for 1910 report 980 markets in Korea, with total transactions worth about 50 million yen and involving principally agricultural products and livestock; by 1920 Korea had 1,214 markets with total transactions of over 103 million yen. The Japanese improved transportation and standardized market weights and measures (Myers and Saburo 1984). Port cities such as Kunsan, Mokp'o, Pusan, Chinnamp'o, and Wŏnsan grew rapidly (see *Annual Report on Reforms and Progress in Chosen,* 1917-18, pp. 82-83; 1921-22, pp. 157-58).

High prices, growing exports, and expanding markets promoted agricultural commercialization, particularly in southern provinces. Using colonial government statistics (*Chōsen tokei nempo,* 1909-11), Miyajima Hiroshi calculates rice and bean commercialization indices for Kyŏnggi, Ch'ungch'ŏng, Chŏlla, and Kyŏngsang provinces, assuming each household member consumed 0.7 sŏk of each crop and the surplus was sold on the market.[6] The indices, calculated by dividing the surplus by total production, show that rice was most commercialized in North Chŏlla (36.9% of the rice sold on the market), followed by South Ch'ungch'ŏng (33.8%) and North Kyŏngsang (30.5%). Beans were most commercialized in North Kyŏngsang (57.2%), followed by Kyŏnggi (47%) and South Ch'ungch'ŏng (38.9%) (see Miyajima 1975, table 2).

Miyajima further calculates an index for rice for various rural classes.[7] Using the same method outlined above, he estimates that in 1910 the landlord class commercialized 71.9% of their rice, the owner-cultivator class 58.8%, and the semi-tenant class 42.2% (Miyajima 1974). By 1937 the respective indices increased to 97.4%, 62.5%, and 71.7%. Even landless tenants commercialized 11.6% of their rice in 1937 (In Chŏngsik 1949, pp. 87-88).[8] Also, rice cultivation steadily increased, constituting 70.3% of total crops in 1935.

But mere increased output or commercialization does not necessarily presage agricultural *development*. Philip Huang (1990, p. 11) correctly distinguishes three patterns of agrarian change:

[F]irst, simple *intensification*, in which output or output value expands at the same rate as labor input; second, *involution*, in which the total output expands, but at the cost of diminished marginal returns per workday; and third, *development*, in which output expands faster than labor input, to result in increased marginal output per workday. Put differently, with intensification labor productivity remains constant, with involution it diminishes at the margins, and with development it expands. [emphasis in the original]

During the early colonial period, agricultural production increased at the cost of decreasing labor productivity; from 1920 to 1930, total output increased by 5%, but productivity decreased by 1% (see Table 3.1). This pattern sharply contrasts with those of both Taiwan and Japan (especially from 1910 to 1920), where labor productivity increased much faster than total output (Table 3.1). As Myers and Saburo state, "Korea ranked lowest of the three [Korea, Japan, and Taiwan] in agricultural productivity" (1984, p. 427). In Huang's (1990) terms, Korean agriculture *involuted* or at best *intensified*, whereas both Taiwanese and Japanese agriculture *developed*.

Together, increased labor input, increased crop area and double cropping, and crop diversification yielded increased output without development.[9] For instance, from 1920 to 1930, labor input increased by 8.1% and crop area by 9.2% (Ban 1979). Increased labor input despite a decreasing marginal return was of course abetted by a rural labor surplus. During the same period, an already excessive rural population grew by 5.5%. Also, from 1915 to 1927, paddy fields using double cropping increased from 17.0% to 23.1% (Keidel 1981). However, use of chemical fertilizers, a major method of increasing land productivity, was not popular until the 1930s, when Korea began itself to produce them (Ban 1979); in 1920, only 1,700 metric tons were used.[10]

Yet greater agricultural commercialization did not always benefit the peasantry. Based on early twentieth-century Chinese experiences, Huang (1991, p. 629) argues:

Commercialization is not always driven by capitalist enterprise. . . . It could as well be driven mainly by population pressure, by peasants marketing for survival more than for capitalist profit. Chinese peasants turned to commercialized crop production . . . which required much more intensive labor input . . . for expanded total output value, but at the cost of diminished marginal returns per workday. They did so in order to survive.

This description also approximates early colonial Korean agriculture. In addition, although from 1916–20 to 1926–30, rice production increased by 3.1 million sŏk, rice exports to Japan increased by 3.9 million sŏk. Thus, what Korean scholars call "famine export" forced Korean peasants to consume less rice and supplement it with inferior grains such as millet imported from Manchuria (see Suh 1978, tables 40 and 43). As I show below, many Korean peasants remained in poverty.

Thus early colonial Korean agriculture, despite both increased production and commercialization, did not show development. It typified growth without development, or "modernization without development" to use Norman Jacobs's (1985) term. Nevertheless, increasing penetration of capitalist relations into the rural economy further facilitated social differentiation of rural class structure, already at work in the nineteenth century, as the previous chapter discusses.

COMMERCIALIZATION AND SOCIAL DIFFERENTIATION

Past scholarship tends to present a simplified Korean rural class structure, one polarized into large, parasitic, absentee, backward, and regressive landlords and poor, exploited, landless tenants (An Pyŏngjik 1975; Kim Yŏngmo 1971). For instance, Kim Yŏngmo (1971) characterizes colonial-period Korean landlords as parasites exploiting the peasantry through high rents and usury. Im Pyŏng-yun (1971) portrays them as "stagnant landlords" (*chŏngt'aejŏk chiju*) in contrast to the "dynamic landlords" (*tongt'aejŏk chiju*) in Japan. Undoubtedly there were parasitic landlords in colonial Korea who exploited and impoverished tenants through high rents and usury, but evidence shows that rural class structure was much more diverse and complex than these studies describe.

As the colonial government recognized, landlords were of at least two types: (A) those who rented out all of their land and (B) those who rented out most of their land but cultivated a portion themselves (Chōsen sōtokufu 1929, p. 29).[11] Type A landlords tended to be larger, absentee landlords living in cities. They usually adopted neither agricultural commercialization nor land improvement, leaving land management to an agent, called *marŭm* or *saŭm,* though the term varied locally (see Sorensen 1990, pp. 47–50). Any investment in commercial and industrial enterprises was very limited, rental income and usury being their primary source of wealth.[12] In 1930, about 31% of landlords lived outside of their land's county (Chōsen sōtokufu 1930, vol. 2, pp. 78–79; 1934, p. 47). Between the mid-1920s and 1930 the number of landlord agents mushroomed from 18,785 to 33,195 (Chōsen sōtokufu 1929, pp. 237-38; 1934, pp. 115-16). Although their responsibilities varied by landlord, agents "typically took care of all aspects of managing tenants: selecting and removing tenants; setting, inspecting, and taking custody of sharecrops; inspecting tenanted land; investigating bad crop yield and making appropriate rent reductions; remitting taxes for the landlord; supervising repairs and improvement on the tenanted land; and dissolving, if need be, tenancy contracts" (Sorensen 1990, pp. 47-48). No comprehensive data portray the extent of parasitism in colonial Korea, but it seems safe to brand as "parasitic" the large, absentee landlords who lived off their rental income and usury without contributing to the agricultural economy.

Yet the reality of large, absentee, parasitic landlords tells only part of the story. As Sorensen points out, "the majority of landlords, in fact, were small, village residents," or Type B (1990, p. 43). Colonial government statistics for 1916 to 1926 show that the Type B landlord was three to five times more common than Type A and ascended substantially in number, from 50,312 in 1916 to 83,520 in 1924 (Chōsen sōtokufu 1929, pp. 28-29). Type B landlords themselves engaged in land cultivation or management and vigorously pursued commercialized export agriculture. According to a case study, the landlord Yun family in Haenam county not only tenanted but cultivated land (Ch'oi Wŏngyu 1985). The abundance of rural wage laborers made self-cultivation highly feasible. Landlord Yi in Posŏng county also combined self-cultivation with leasing. On leased land he introduced written contracts to preclude future disputes with tenants; he also sold rice directly to merchants in Mokp'o, a major export city, to maximize profits (Hong Sŏngch'an 1986).

The living standards of such landlords were not particularly high. Table 3.2 presents colonial government data on farm income balance (difference between income and expenses) for diverse rural classes in 1925. To be sure, landlords classified as "upper" in the table (those who owned more than 20 chŏngbo of land) enjoyed an affluence well above any other group. Yet they were only 0.3% of the rural population, or 5.6% of the landlord class. In contrast, the income balance for "lower" (less than 5 chŏngbo) and especially "tiny" landlords (less than 1 chŏngbo), together 76% of the landlord class, was comparable to, and often lower than, that of upper/middle owner-cultivators and even some semi-tenants (see Table 3.2).[13] While "lower" and "tiny" landlords may have supplemented farm with nonfarm income, they were far from rich, and "in terms of kinship and life style they would have been little different from other villagers" (Sorensen 1990, p. 44). These statistics, along

TABLE 3.2
Farm Income Balance (Difference between Income and Expenses),
by Rural Class, 1925

Class (by area, in chŏngbo)	Number of Households (Share)		Income Balance (wŏn per household)
Landlord:			
Upper >20	6,866	(0.3)	5,582
Middle <20	22,994	(0.8)	704
Lower <5	39,455	(1.4)	240
Tiny <1	52,670	(1.9)	47
Total/Average	121,985	(4.5)	545
Owner-cultivator:			
Upper >3	94,453	(3.5)	233
Middle <3	179,016	(6.6)	97
Lower <1	172,390	(6.3)	40
Tiny <.3	107,819	(4.0)	17
Total/Average	553,678	(20.3)	87
Semi-tenant (both owned and leased):			
Upper >3	98,628	(3.6)	91
Middle <3	263,747	(9.7)	44
Lower <1	329,431	(12.1)	7
Tiny <.3	225,605	(8.3)	−1
Total/Average	917,411	(33.7)	25
Landless tenant:			
Upper >3	88,226	(3.2)	16
Middle <3	233,029	(8.5)	−5
Lower <1	354,399	(13.0)	−20
Tiny <.3	298,084	(10.9)	−12
Total/Average	973,738	(35.6)	−11
Pauper	162,209	(5.9)	−4
Total/Average	2,729,021	(100.0)	47

SOURCE: Chōsen sōtokufu 1929, pp. 32, 38.

with examples mentioned above, suggest that landlords were not cut from one cloth; not every colonial-period landlord was a rich parasite who sat back and reaped surpluses. Landlords were diverse, many actively involved in land cultivation or management, and of frugal means.

The cultivator class was even more differentiated than the landlord class. While about two-thirds of the rural population rented all or part of their cultivated land from landlords (Table 3.2), not all of them suffered poverty or remained subsistence peasants. In particular, some semi-tenants and landless tenants actively pursued commercial agriculture. Government statistics report that some tenants leased extensive acreage and cultivated it with both hired and family labor (see Chōsen sōtokufu 1930, vol. 1, pp. 72–84). In South Chŏlla, for example, 22 upper tenants leased an average of 6.6 chŏngbo, with a range from 2 to 38.9, which was more than the land owned by most lower landlords. They used an average of two wage laborers in addition to five family members.

Cultivation of relatively large areas of leased land was not uncommon in Korea, especially in southern commercialized areas. Ch'oi Wŏngyu's case study of the landlord Yun family in Haenam county of South Chŏlla province shows that upper tenants began to appear after the late 1910s (see 1985, table 8). Hong Sŏngch'an's case study of the landlord Hong family on Kanghwa island in Kyŏnggi province shows the same trend; while in 1908 only 13 tenants leased more than 25 turak, in 1926 the number of relatively large tenants was 53 (see 1981, tables 10 and 20). Robust prices and expanding markets in the early colonial years provided such large semi-tenants and upper tenants a good opportunity to become owner-cultivators. As Table 3.2 shows, upper tenants and most semi-tenants had a surplus in 1925. According to government statistics, 97,800 semi-tenant and tenant households became owner-cultivators from 1913 to 1923 (Kang T'aehun 1988).

While an economic boom in the late 1910s, which brought increased commercialization, certainly enhanced upward mobility for large, relatively well-to-do tenants and semi-tenants, the poorer rural population advanced little. They stalled at subsistence, cultivating leased plots and/or working for wages. Cultivation income alone could not meet family needs (see Table 3.2) and outside employment was crucial. But colonial Korea before the mid-1930s had little industry to absorb rural surplus labor.[14] A Marxist economist, In Chŏngsik, describes their plight: "Poor peasants cannot support their family with income from their own farming. They have to supplement their income by selling their labor" (quoted in Kang T'aehun 1988, p. 179). Ohno Tamotsu, a Japanese author, agrees: "The percentage of peasant households who have to work outside as wage laborers is on the increase. Incomes from their own farming are not sufficient to survive and thus it is necessary to supplement with outside employment" (quoted in Kang T'aehun 1988, pp. 179–80).

Table 3.3 shows the extent of the peasants' dual dependence on land and wage labor for income. In 1913, 13% of peasants worked as wage

TABLE 3.3
Percentage of Households Required to Supplement Income
with Outside Employment, by Province, 1926 and 1930

Province	1926	1930
South Chŏlla	24.8%	47.0%
North Chŏlla	18.3	48.1
South Kyŏngsang	20.8	39.7
North Kyŏngsang	18.6	29.7
South Ch'ungch'ŏng	18.2	50.7
North Ch'ungch'ŏng	15.7	38.2
Kyŏnggi	13.3	41.7
Hwanghae	11.1	27.6
Kangwŏn	11.6	32.8
South P'yŏngan	15.0	24.4
North P'yŏngan	14.0	22.3
South Hamgyŏng	13.1	33.2
North Hamgyŏng	13.6	24.5
Average	16.0	35.4

NOTE: Percentage in 1926 is for all rural households; in 1930, for tenant households.
SOURCES: Chōsen sōtokufu 1929, pp. 26–27, and 1934, p. 70.

laborers; but by 1926 the figure was 16.0%, and by 1930, 35.4%. Also, 1933 wage income on the average constituted 33.5% of total tenant household income (Chōsen sōtokufu 1940b, p. 10). Dual dependence on family farm and wage income was higher in southern areas such as Chŏlla and Ch'ungch'ŏng provinces (Table 3.3). According to a 1930 government survey, 22,622 tenants hired 81,862 wage laborers, usually termed *koji*, at various times of the year (Chōsen sōtokufu 1930, vol 2, pp. 41–45).[15] Most of the *koji* were of course poorer tenants. According to another survey, in North Chŏlla where *koji* use was popular, only 29% of them were exclusively wage laborers: most were poorer tenants and semi-tenants (Yun Sujong 1990).

Thus the rural class structure's broad differentiation into big landlords and some managerial farmers using hired labor, on the one hand, and landless tenants and wage laborers, on the other, continued into the early colonial years. Yet so did its great diversity: neither social differentiation of the rural population into agricultural capitalists and wage laborers nor a complete involution occurred in colonial Korea. This diversified class structure was closely related to various forms of rural conflict, as subsequent chapters will show. But first, tenant-landlord relations in the early colonial years will be considered.

TENANT-LANDLORD RELATIONS IN COLONIAL KOREA

Tenancy, a major feature of late Chosŏn dynasty land tenure, as the previous chapter discussed, continued to prevail throughout the colonial period until abolished by postwar land reform. By the time the cadastral survey was completed, 77.2% of the rural population were reported to lease part or all of their cultivated land. Like most other features of social change and land tenure, tenant-landlord relations altered little from the late Chosŏn to the early colonial period. Most rent remained paid in kind by a variable arrangement (*t'ajo*), the contract was typically oral, and tenancy tenure was highly insecure. A trend toward fixed rental payment with a written contract might seem suggested, especially in the South: as of 1930, 32% of rent was paid at fixed rates and 27% of tenant contracts were written (Chōsen sōtokufu 1930, vol. 1, pp. 15, 117). However, considering that in 1930 agricultural depression brought substantial change in land tenure, such figures indicate remarkable continuity of tenancy customs from the late Chosŏn to the early colonial period. Furthermore, even in 1930, 93.9% of the rent in paddy fields and 92.1% in dry fields was paid in kind (Chōsen sōtokufu 1934, pp. 76–77). Rental rates averaged around 50%, and tenancy tenure was insecure. Table 3.4 shows the rental rate in 1926 by province ranged from 33.3% (for "tiny" tenants in Kyŏnggi) to 68.8% ("lower" tenants in Kyŏnggi), averaging slightly under 50%. The rate was somewhat higher in southern commercialized areas. But again, no rapid increase in rental rate from the late Chosŏn to the early colonial period emerges: traditional tenant-landlord relations perdured.

Also, the power of landlords was undiminished. They not only benefited from increased commercialization and growing rice exports to Japan, but often actively collaborated with or at least passively supported Japanese colonialism (Ch'oi Wŏngyu 1985; Hong Sŏngch'an 1985). To colonize Korea, the Japanese needed support, which the landlord class provided. Hong Sŏngch'an points out: "In early colonial years, the Japanese knew that security measures alone would not suffice to establish a colonial system. They needed a permanent ruling structure to appease anti-Japanese sentiments developed through peasant wars and nationalist uprisings; thus they were in search of a social class with which to ally. In the early 1910s the landlord class met their need" (1992, pp. 55–56).

TABLE 3.4
Rental Rate (Percentage of the Crops), by Province
and Size of Leased Land, 1926

Province	Size of Leased Land			
	Large	Medium	Small	Tiny
South Chŏlla	44.8%	43.8%	46.0%	46.2%
North Chŏlla	46.7	42.0	42.4	43.4
South Kyŏngsang	48.1	47.4	46.9	46.2
North Kyŏngsang	47.2	48.3	47.4	48.3
South Ch'ungch'ŏng	51.7	51.2	50.9	51.6
North Ch'ungch'ŏng	42.4	44.0	47.0	51.0
Kyŏnggi	55.3	60.0	68.8	33.3
Hwanghae	49.0	49.1	49.9	51.4
Kangwŏn	50.1	50.0	51.6	50.0
South P'yŏngan	49.8	50.0	50.0	50.0
North P'yŏngan	47.1	50.0	48.3	50.0
South Hamgyŏng	49.4	48.3	49.7	49.8
North Hamgyŏng	50.4	50.0	50.0	48.6
Average	48.6	48.8	49.9	47.7

SOURCE: Chōsen sōtokufu 1929, pp. 220–21.

As a step toward using Korean landlords as a social basis of their colonial rule, the Japanese established landlord associations (*chijuhoe*) in the country and eschewed any lessening of the landlords' economic power in the early years. In addition, Tsurumi points out, the colonial government in the 1910s "sought to win the *yangban* class by tolerating their traditional academies [such as] *sŏdang*" (1984, p. 299). Also, land remained a very attractive investment, far more profitable than other investments. As late as 1929, the rate of return from paddy and dry field investments amounted to 8.2% and 8.8% respectively, whereas stock investments yielded 7.1% (Chang Siwŏn 1980). Robust rice prices (especially in the early colonial years) and high rental rates were the primary reasons for the higher land profits. Landlords also accumulated fortunes by lending money to poorer peasants at exorbitant interest rates.

Market expansion, strong agricultural prices, and increased commercialization boosted the Korean rural economy in the early colonial years. But benefits from a booming economy did not accrue evenly to all the rural strata. The group of upper-class landlords prospered most, followed by some commercializing owner-cultivators, semi-tenants, and tenants. Most landless peasants remained at subsistence, forced to supplement their income by wage labor. For upper semi-tenants and tenants, high rental rates strongly impeded upward mobility, and for poorer tenants such rates and insecure tenancy tenure threatened survival. Both had much to lament. The powerful landlord class would not lower rental rates or provide more secure tenancy tenure unless forced to do so. Encouraged by the moderation of colonial policy after the March First nationalist movement in 1919, poorer as well as relatively well-to-do tenants and semi-tenants began to assert their grievances against landlords. Landlord strength was fatally attenuated after liberation, but this would not have been possible without the continuous challenges from tenants and semi-tenants throughout the colonial period—struggles discussed in the following chapters.

CHAPTER 4

Tenant-Landlord Conflict, 1920–32

Ideology or Interest?

"Family-sized tenancy" was common in nineteenth- and early twentieth-century East Asia and Southeast Asia, and its conduciveness to rural conflict has been studied extensively (Marks 1984; Mitchell 1968; Paige 1970; Smethurst 1986; Stinchcombe 1961; Waswo 1977; Wiens 1980; Zagoria 1974). For instance, Stinchcombe (1961) argues that of his five types of land tenure systems, family-sized tenancy is the form most likely to produce intense class conflict (the other four types are the hacienda system, family smallholding, plantation agriculture, and capitalist agriculture with wage labor). Citing evidence from diverse regions including Asia, Europe, and Africa, he stresses that conflicts over how the crop is shared between tenant and landlord, the immense social distance separating them, the peasants' technical knowledge, and the leadership of wealthier tenants combine to produce political and class conflict (see Chapter 1).

Korea is no exception in this regard. As discussed in previous chapters, the country had a long history of tenancy from the fourteenth century to the postwar land reforms (Kim Yongsŏp 1970; Shin 1973).[1] Tenancy-related disputes were a prevalent form of rural conflict that became a major policy issue not only for the Japanese colonial government but also for the American military government and the Rhee government (Chōsen sōtokufu 1929; Cho 1964). Especially during colonialism, tenancy disputes were a "constant phenomenon" nationwide in rural society. The 20 years from 1920 to 1939 witnessed 140,969 disputes involving 397,254 tenants, landlords, and agents (Chōsen sōtokufu 1934, p. 122; 1940a, pp. 26–27).

Most of the many studies that have attempted to explain the causes and consequences of tenancy disputes in colonial Korea overemphasize (1) their defensive posture, a product of the extreme rural poverty and inequality, and (2) their ideological motivation, such as anticolonialism or socialism (Asada 1973, pp. 149-275; Cho Tonggŏl 1979; Hŏ Changman 1963; Kwŏn Tuyŏng 1979). Certainly these factors merit consideration, but they are only part of a phenomenon that demands closer scrutiny. Dispute agendas were primarily reformist rather than revolutionary; their principal concerns were rooted in concrete economic interests, not political or ideological issues. Also, emphasizing only the defensive aspect of tenancy disputes leaves unaddressed the many differences in form and nature of the disputes.

While tenancy disputes arose throughout colonial Korea, some changes in their nature over time and their frequency across the nation are evident. In the early to mid-1920s, disputes mounted by tenants were offensive, large in scale, well organized, and often successful, whereas in the depression years they became defensive, isolated, and unsuccessful. Also, most disputes prevailed in southern commercialized areas such as the Chŏlla and Kyŏngsang provinces. This chapter addresses the several issues raised above—dispute motivation, character, forms, variation over time and place—by looking at the land tenure system and rural class structure from 1920 to 1932.[2]

AN EMPIRICAL OVERVIEW OF TENANCY DISPUTES

Although landlord and tenant disputes were not unique to the colonial period (Kim Yongsŏp 1972; Shin 1973, pp. 91-95), they had previously been a relatively minor form of rural conflict.[3] But such disputes changed in frequency and intensity after 1920: their number, as recorded by the colonial government, swelled from 15 in 1920 to 176 in 1924; and in 1923 these disputes occurred in 11 of the 13 provinces. They increased to 726 in 1930 and numbered 667 in 1931.[4] During the 13 years from 1920 to 1932, a total of 4,804 disputes were recorded, involving 74,581 landlords and tenants (Chōsen sōtokufu 1934, p. 122). Thus tenancy disputes became a key policy concern for the colonial government, which devoted substantial time and money to investigating their causes and consequences.[5]

The major forms of dispute varied from a simple verbal argument to more radical protests involving violence and arrest, and the number of participants ranged from a few peasants to several thousand tenants and landlords. As Table 4.1 shows, in the early 1920s disputes were not fre-

TABLE 4.1
Summary of Tenancy Disputes (Annual Average), 1920-32

	1920-22	1923-26	1927-29	1930-32
(1) Disputes	22	186	763	566
(2) Participants	145	31	6.2	16.5
(3) Causes:				
Tenancy rights	21%	67%	47%	58%
Rent	47	22	49	34
Land taxes	11	5	0.2	5
Other	21	6	4	3
(4) Price indices				
(1920-22 = 100)	100	103	89	56

SOURCES: Chōsen sōtokufu 1929, pp. 58-61; 1940a, pp. 21-24, 26-27. Suh (1978), p. 169.

quent but were large in scale (i.e., the annual average from 1920 to 1922 was 22 disputes involving 145 tenants and landlords per case), whereas the depression years brought more frequent conflicts but at a substantially reduced scale (i.e., the annual average from 1927 to 1929 was 763 disputes engaging only about 6 tenants and landlords per case).[6] The tenants mainly demanded tenancy-right guarantees and rent reduction. From 1920 to 1922, rent fueled 47% of the disputes, followed by tenancy rights (21%) and land taxes (11%) (Table 4.1). After the mid-1920s, more than half of the disputes involved tenancy rights.

Geographically, most disputes occurred in southern commercialized areas. In the 13 years from 1920 to 1932, as Table 4.2 shows, 4,396 of the disputes (91% of the total cases), involving 55,552 tenants, landlords, and agents (74% of the participants), occurred in six southern provinces. These were colonial Korea's most commercialized areas, with modern land relations. In these six provinces, compared with other areas, paddy fields were more dominant (57% versus 34% in central areas and 13% in northern), as suits rice, a major commercial crop; as were fixed rent (44% versus 34% and 13%) and written contracts (45% versus 17% and 7%) (Table 4.2).

TABLE 4.2
Disputes and Related Rural Economic Indicators, by Province

Province	(1) Disputes 1920-32	(2) Participants 1920-32	(3) Paddy Fields 1926	(4) Rent 1930	(5) Contracts 1930
Southern					
S. Chŏlla	716	14,188	49%	36%	60%
N. Chŏlla	1,740	6,969	71	45	74
S. Kyŏngsang	642	11,772	61	47	49
N. Kyŏngsang	117	10,624	49	30	30
S. Ch'ungch'ŏng	1,069	6,740	66	31	34
N. Ch'ungch'ŏng	112	5,259	44	77	22
Subtotal	4,396	55,552			
(Average)	(732)	(9,259)	(57%)	(44%)	(45%)
Central					
Kyŏnggi	264	4,480	52	24	11
Hwanghae	78	7,301	24	35	20
Kangwŏn	21	1,069	25	42	20
Subtotal	363	12,850			
(Average)	(121)	(4,283)	(34%)	(34%)	(17%)
Northern					
S. P'yŏngan	19	675	17	23	16
N. P'yŏngan	19	4,564	19	6	4
S. Hamgyŏng	7	940	12	17	7
N. Hamgyŏng	—	—	5	5	1
Subtotal	45	6,179			
(Average)	(11)	(1,545)	(13%)	(13%)	(7%)
Total	4,804	74,581			
(Average)	(369)	(5,737)	(38%)	(32%)	(27%)

NOTE: Column headings are as follows: (1) Number of disputes; (2) number of participants; (3) percentage of cropland in "paddy fields" (indicating the degree of commercialization of agriculture); (4) and (5) percentage of "fixed rent" and "written contracts" (indicating the degree of modernization of land relations).
SOURCES: (1) Chōsen sōtokufu 1940a, pp. 8-9; (2) 1934, p. 122; (3) 1929, p. 5; (4) 1930, 1:117; (5) 1930, 1:15.

PREVIOUS EXPLANATIONS OF KOREAN TENANCY DISPUTES

As noted above, most studies of Korean tenancy disputes emphasize their defensive and ideological nature (Asada 1973, pp. 149-275; Cho Tonggŏl 1979, pp. 97-157; Chu Ponggyu 1981; Hŏ Changman 1963; Kang Hundŏk 1981; Kang Chŏngsuk 1983; Kwŏn Tuyŏng 1979; Um 1984). They argue that Japanese colonialism inaugurated extreme poverty and inequality, and with the rapid polarization of rural class structure, starving peasants harboring tenancy grievances swelled the nationalist and/or communist movements. For example, Kwŏn Tuyŏng (1979) characterizes colonial-period tenancy disputes as anticolonial and nationalist movements of starvation-driven poor peasants led by nationalist leaders. Asada (1973) interprets disputes similarly, though he stresses socialist influence. This anticolonial, nationalist, or socialist interpretation of the disputes reflects two influences: (1) a moral economy approach to the devastating impact of capitalism on peasant villages (Scott 1976); and (2) a Marxist view of a starving peasantry as a revolutionary force.[7]

While a "pauperization-revolution" thesis has some merits, it is only a partial explanation.[8] First, these studies oversimplify rural class structure and capitalism's impact on peasants. Portraying that structure as polarized into large parasitic landlords and poor landless tenants, they then overplay the potential for revolution. As the previous chapter revealed, however, rural colonial Korea comprised noncultivating landlords (Type A), small landlords who hired a significant amount of labor (Type B), owner-cultivators dependent on household laborers, semi-tenants, landless tenants, and agricultural laborers.[9] Furthermore, agricultural commercialization diversely affected these different rural strata, transforming some upper tenants/semi-tenants into owner-cultivators, while abandoning many poorer tenants to a struggle for subsistence (Kang T'aehun 1988; Miyajima 1974). Upper tenants/semi-tenants therefore had different motives from those of poorer tenants for mounting tenancy disputes, as specified below.

Second, these studies overgeneralize to other periods the character of tenancy disputes during the depression years: the "desperation of the poor." As delineated above, disputes in the early to mid-1920s differed in many ways from those of the depression years, begging explanation of how variation in the socioeconomic situation shaped these differences.

Third, the studies cited above stress the reactions of peasants to external conditions—their frustrations—as the spark that ignited an explosion. Whether they speak of peasants' pauperization through colonial changes or, as do moral economists, of landlords' abandonment of traditional ways of supplying social and economic insurance, these scholars maintain that peasants rise up only when something has been done to them or taken away from them. Yet to interpret tenancy disputes simply as defensive or reactionary actions ignores their frequently forward-looking nature, aimed at securing better terms of trade from exploiting landlords.

Fourth, to say that tenancy disputes were anticolonial, nationalist, and/or revolutionary movements has scant empirical support. In the early to mid-1920s at least, they were primarily reformist efforts to lower rents and improve tenancy conditions, and only secondarily sought abstract goals such as destroying an inequitable land tenure system or obtaining political independence. Viewed as reformist, these disputes were quite efficacious: many peasants indeed gained favorable outcomes, such as rent reductions.

TENANT-LANDLORD DISPUTES, 1920-26

That tenants took the initiative in launching disputes during the 1920s is generally agreed.[10] For example, in December 1921, 2,250 tenants in the Talsŏng county of North Kyŏngsang province demanded that their landlords pay, rather than pass on to them, the landowner taxes established by the colonial government in 1914. The following December, 1,600 tenants in Sunch'ŏn county of South Chŏlla province mounted massive rent reduction disputes with landlords (see Ōwa 1982). In August 1923, 1,000 tenants on Amt'ae island of the same province took up the same issue for almost a year (see Cho Tonggŏl 1979, pp. 126-35; Pak Sundong 1986). October 1924 saw about 500 tenants in the Bungnyul district of Hwanghae province, north-central Korea, rally against the district branch of the Japanese-owned Oriental Development Company, seeking rent reduction and guaranteed tenancy rights (see Cho Tonggŏl 1979, pp. 135-51).

This assertiveness did not presage revolution, as some writers maintain, but clearly revealed important changes in rural authority relations. Tenants no longer meekly accepted subordinate status, but now collectively confronted landlords, demanding that their grievances be heard. From 1920 to 1926, 808 disputes occurred, averaging 40 participants (both tenants and landlords) per dispute. Especially in the early years (1920-22), disputes engaged large numbers, averaging 145 (see Table 4.1). These large, offensive movements in the early to mid-1920s sharply contrast with later disputes during the depression years, more frequent but smaller in scale. What does their relatively offensive and collective nature suggest?

Most studies of tenancy disputes during the colonial period detect roots in rural inequality and poverty (Cho Tonggŏl 1979, pp. 97-157; Kwŏn Tuyŏng 1979). They argue that colonial agricultural commercialization and the land survey rapidly polarized the rural class structure, relegating most of the rural population to frequent subsistence crises despite increased agricultural production. But statistics for the early 1920s depict no radical, rapid polarization of rural class structure into two classes, big landlords and poor tenants. Colonial government data, for instance, show that between 1918 and 1927 landless tenants averaged 41.0% of the total rural population and semi-tenants 35.7%. This was only a 2.4% increase in landless tenants and a 2.1% decrease in semi-tenants compared to 1913-17 (Chōsen sōtokufu 1929, pp. 28-29; 1940a, p. 139). As these figures and previous chapters suggest, the process of rural differentiation begun in the nineteenth century did not diminish in the early years of Japanese colonialism. Furthermore, despite rapid population growth, the average acreage per peasant household increased steadily up to 1924 (Chōsen sōtokufu 1940a, p. 138). Again, these statistics show that the rapid polarization of rural class structure in the depression years was not presaged by early colonialism.

Gragert's (1982) analysis of shifts in landownership during the colonial period confirms this argument.[11] Analyzing three types of local land registers (*yang'an, t'oji taejang,* and *t'oji tŭnggibu*) from four villages in South Ch'ungch'ŏng, North Chŏlla, and Kyŏnggi provinces, he claims that private landownership in Korea predated the Japanese colonial administration and that no significant transfer of landownership occurred at its outset. On the contrary, he argues, landownership and tenure configurations changed only gradually through the early years. Large-scale landownership transfers began only with the massive economic dislocation caused by worldwide economic depression, 1930-35. Hong Sŏnghŭp's (1985) analysis of colonial land tenure changes in a village of South Ch'ungch'ŏng province reaches the same conclusion. Colonial government statistics also show that the percentage of landless tenants and of leased land increased to 50.6% and 56.6%, respectively, between 1930 and 1935 (Chōsen sōtokufu 1940a, p. 139). Thus, evidence contradicts arguments that colonial policy, especially the land survey of 1910-18, radically altered the land-tenure system and thereby rural class structure. Dramatic changes in fact came only in the late 1920s. This still leaves open the description of peasants' economic conditions in the early to mid-1920s.

TABLE 4.3
Income Balance of Tenant Class, by Province, 1925
(wŏn per household)

Province	Semi-Tenants Income/Expenses/Balance	Landless Tenants Income/Expenses/Balance
Southern		
S. Chŏlla	531/530/ 1	542/523/ 19
N. Chŏlla	623/601/ 22	421/494/ 73 (−)
S. Kyŏngsang	855/814/ 41	664/694/ 30 (−)
N. Kyŏngsang	801/781/ 20	692/710/ 18 (−)
S. Ch'ungch'ŏng	645/620/ 25	555/558/ 3 (−)
N. Ch'ungch'ŏng	606/540/ 66	502/476/ 26
Central		
Kyŏnggi	611/501/110	523/514/ 9
Hwanghae	379/364/ 15	349/340/ 9
Kangwŏn	520/490/ 30	429/434/ 5 (−)
Northern		
S. P'yŏngan	363/325/ 38	313/309/ 4
N. P'yŏngan	493/443/ 50	456/444/ 12
S. Hamgyŏng	601/583/ 18	405/409/ 4 (−)
N. Hamgyŏng	602/529/ 73	646/510/136
Average	587/548/ 39	500/494/ 6

SOURCE: Chōsen sōtokufu 1929, pp. 35–36.

As already mentioned, Korean rural society witnessed an economic boom in the late 1910s. Growing Japanese demand after World War I boosted Korean rice prices and exports of rice to Japan. Crop prices increased by 128% from 1910-17 to 1918-27, and crop exports to Japan increased by 62% from 1919 to 1926 (Suh 1978), heavily favoring Korea's commodity trade balance with Japan. But these overall statistics convey little about the economic situation of the poor rural stratum, the tenants. Most studies argue that despite increased agricultural production and prices, extreme inequality in rural class structure denied tenants their share of the growing economy. Therefore, the poor stratum's welfare is examined more closely below.

Data on income balance per household (the difference between income and expenses), as surveyed by the Bureau of Social Affairs in the

TABLE 4.4
Living Standards, per Capita, 1912-40

Annual Average	(1) Rice Consumption (sŏk)	(2) Daily Food Availability (calories)	(3) Expenditures (yen, 1934-36 prices)
1912-1915	0.64	2,133	61
1916-1920	0.61	2,206	61
1921-1925	0.53	2,033	92
1926-1930	0.47	1,924	88
1931-1935	0.46	1,812	83
1936-1940	0.54	2,033	87

NOTES: Column (3) figures are for 1910-14, 1915-19, 1920-24, 1925-29, 1930-34, and 1935-38 (instead of the groupings used for the other two columns).
In Column (2), the calorie estimate is based on the three major crops: rice, barley, and millet.
SOURCES: Columns (1) and (2): Suh (1978), pp. 86-87. Column (3): Ho (1984), p. 398.

Government-General in 1925, offer a picture of rural living standards. Table 4.3 shows the income balance of semi-tenants and landless tenants by province. Clearly, many peasants suffered poverty; landless tenants in six provinces averaged expenses in excess of income. But this negative balance averaged less than one-twentieth of the peasant's income, and tenants in the other seven provinces showed surpluses. Semi-tenants evinced income deficits in no province, and Table 4.3 data likely overstate tenant and semi-tenant poverty. As Keidel (1981, pp. 45-49) convincingly argues, the data do not account adequately for farm income in kind (produce not sold but rather consumed on the farm). Because a greater proportion of total produce is generally consumed on small farms than on larger, more commercial ones, the results from a survey of cash receipts and incomes tend to present a more negative economic picture than is warranted for the poorer stratum.

Considering that these data are for 1925, not a very productive year (marred by drought in 1924 and a large flood in 1925), the claim that in the 1920s the rural poor suffered extreme poverty seems unjustified. Also, if desperate poverty was the major cause of tenancy disputes, they should have been more frequent in North Chŏlla province, where income deficits were highest. Instead only three disputes erupted. More than half of the disputes in 1925 flared in South Chŏlla province, where tenant household income averaged a surplus (Chōsen sōtokufu 1940a, pp. 8-9).

Since rice had been a major Korean crop and the peasants' preferred diet for generations, the decline of per capita rice consumption is frequently used to indicate their deteriorating economic condition. As column 1 in Table 4.4 shows, per capita rice consumption fell steadily, to be supplemented by less preferred grains, especially Manchurian millet. An overall measure of peasants' diet, in per capita calories, also dropped gradually (column 2).

That both per capita rice consumption and calories declined during the colonial period, however, does not prove that most tenants suffered terrible poverty.[12] Column 2 captures only 70% of the total food consumed, and the population figures used to calculate both measures are not standardized for age and sex, so food availability is probably understated. During the colonial period, the population increased steadily and the average age fell.[13] A population with more children presumably requires fewer calories per person (Ho 1984, pp. 378-80). Also some peasants may have reduced their food intake to save money for long-term investments such as their children's education.[14] That despite a decline of food consumption, per capita total expenditures increased in the early 1920s supports this theory (column 3). Certainly rural Korean society knew poverty, but some scholars may have exaggerated its extent and depth. Poverty, after all, is relative. In the nineteenth century, famine was a notorious specter in rural society.[15] The point is not that Korean tenants lived well, but that desperate poverty is not a satisfactory explanation for the tenancy disputes in this period (1920-26).

What alternatives to the pauperization thesis might explain the tenancy disputes of the early to mid-1920s? Did they fester because of tenants' "relative deprivation" or their "rising expectations," as some theorists argue (Davies 1962; Gurr 1970), or because of their "moral outrage," as moral economists contend (Scott 1976)? Does Popkin (1979) correctly claim that the rational peasant detected new political openings that could turn trade terms in his favor through collective action?

First, it should not be assumed that only poor tenants disputed with their landlords. While poor tenants were the majority of plaintiffs, upper tenants and semi-tenants with some surplus also participated, with middle peasants (owner-cultivators) often organizing and directing the disputes (Asada 1973).[16] Asada (1973) and Cho Tonggŏl (1979) aver that this co-participation indicates that both poor tenants and relatively well-to-do upper tenants/semi-tenants shared the same plight; that is, they suffered landlord exploitation. This, Asada (1973) argues, is because rural class structure, as Marxists would predict, was rapidly polarizing into virtually two classes. But as argued above, rural class structure was diversified; thus understanding tenancy disputes requires an approach that considers that various tenant strata participated in disputes for different reasons: lower rents and more secure tenancy rights promised upper tenants/semi-tenants a step toward becoming owner-farmers, and poorer tenants a lessening of their poverty. In South Chŏlla and Kyŏngsang provinces, where most tenancy disputes erupted in the early 1920s, the percentage of owner-cultivators increased steadily up to 1926. In contrast, in North Chŏlla and Kyŏnggi provinces, which witnessed only a few disputes, the percentage of owner-cultivators dropped (Chōsen sōtokufu 1937, pp. 153-55).

A notable characteristic of the early to mid-1920s tenancy disputes is that they prevailed not in areas with strong landlords, but in places with relatively strong middle peasants (owner-cultivators). From 1920 to 1926, as Table 4.5 shows, 48% of the disputes occurred in South Chŏlla and South Kyŏngsang provinces, engaging 41% of the total participants. But these provinces had relatively weak landlords and a high ratio of owner-cultivated land. In South Chŏlla province, for instance, upper landlords (over 20 chŏngbo; Table 3.2) constituted only 3.8% of the landlord population; more than half of the land (58.4%) was owned by owner-cultivators. In contrast, in North Chŏlla and South Ch'ungch'ŏng provinces, with stronger landlord power (e.g., in both provinces upper landlords constituted more than 11%), far fewer disputes occurred (see Table 4.5).[17] This evidence belies the pauperization-revolution thesis that class conflict is more intense in areas with large, absentee, and parasitic landlords. Tenancy disputes in at least the early to mid-1920s cannot simply be attributed to exploitation by landlords or extreme peasant poverty. As a sociological theory of collective action—"resource mobilization theory"—argues, not the mere existence of oppression, but the recognition of it or perception of possible redress, constitutes the prime factor for collective action such as tenancy disputes (Tilly 1978).[18]

Thus tenancy disputes between 1920 and 1926 were not simply defensive reactions of desperately poor tenants, but conscious efforts by rational peasants to turn trade terms in their favor through collective action. This point is illustrated by the nature of tenancy disputes: they were large in scale and well organized, but reformist rather than revolutionary. The change in colonial policy in 1920 from militaristic to much more moderate was especially enabling to active peasant organization

TABLE 4.5
Disputes and Rural Power Structure

Province	Number of Disputes	Number of Participants	Strength of Landlords	Extent of Middle Peasants
S. Chŏlla	210 (26%)	7,996 (25%)	3.8%	58.4%
S. Kyŏngsang	176 (22%)	5,327 (16%)	6.3%	40.7%
N. Chŏlla	40 (5%)	1,687 (5%)	11.3%	25.9%
S. Ch'ungch'ŏng	209 (26%)	1,685 (5%)	11.4%	37.4%

NOTES AND SOURCES: The data for the number of disputes and participants (1920-26) come from Chōsen sōtokufu 1934, p. 122. Strength of landlordship is measured by the percentage of big landlords with over 20 chŏngbo among landlords in 1925 (Chōsen sōtokufu 1929, p. 33). Extent of middle peasants is measured by the percentage of owner-cultivated lands in 1928 (Chōsen sōtokufu 1940a, pp. 121-22).

and mobilization. After the March First nationalist movement in 1919, the first nationwide nationalist movement for independence, the Japanese lessened repression: Koreans enjoyed some freedom of speech and organization, more opportunity to hold official positions, promises of better education, and even gestures toward some autonomy in local administration. These changes were strictly limited and calculated to serve colonial purposes, but this so-called cultural policy allowed peasants some leeway to organize tenant unions and engage in collective action such as tenancy disputes (see Baldwin 1969 and Robinson 1988).

The first organization of subordinate groups (representing not only peasants but also workers) was the Korean Workers Mutual Aid Association (Chosŏn nodong kongjehoe) established in Seoul in April 1920. Albeit organized by intellectuals, it expressed concern for tenant welfare in its treatise "All Tenants, Unite!" reminiscent of Karl Marx's "Workingmen of All Countries, Unite!" in *The Communist Manifesto* ([1888]1987) (see Chapter 5 for intellectual discourse on the peasantry in colonial Korea). The tract stressed that "tenants' welfare cannot be improved by expecting benevolent action from landlords, but only through tenants' collective action" (quoted in Kim Chunyŏp and Kim Ch'angsun 1963-76, vol. 2, p. 69). The association published an official journal, *Kongje* (Mutual Aid), and organized at least 47 branches in the early 1920s (Sin Yongha 1987, chap. 6).

With the association's help tenant unions sprang up in the countryside, especially southern areas, and mounted aggressive disputes against landlords. In March 1922, in Chinju of Kyŏngsang province, a southern county of Korea, the association helped tenants organize a union to rally effective collective action against landlords. In December 1922, the association's Koesan branch supported tenant protest that demanded rent reduction and land tax payment by landlords. The association was also behind organization and mobilization for collective disputes in Sunch'ŏn county (December 1922); Yŏsu county (April 1923); Ch'ŏngnyang, P'unggi, Sunch'ang, and Talsŏng counties (all in December 1923) (see Sin Yongha 1987, pp. 432–45).

Establishment of the Korean Worker-Peasant League (Chosŏn nonong ch'ŏng dongmaeng) in April 1924 further facilitated tenant organization. The league actively supported tenant unionization and disputes, and a total of 181 worker/peasant organizations were affiliates (Lee 1978, p. 24). By September 1926, 83 peasant unions with 11,938 members appeared in South Chŏlla province, the center of 1920s disputes (Asada 1973, p. 182). Unlike some radical intellectuals who anticipated that tenant organization and disputes would foment revolutionary movements, tenants seemed to consider unions a pragmatic base from which to negotiate with landlords. The main issues in unions and disputes were concrete, such as rent reduction, secure tenancy rights, and greater member solidarity. Also, as Alavi (1965) points out for Russia, China, and India, in Korea the middle peasants (owner-cultivators) provided tenant union leadership. Pak Pogyŏng, for example, a major player in unionizing Amt'ae island tenants, was a middle peasant educated in a Christian school.

The main tactics of tenant unions included the threat of noncultivation, refusal to harvest, and withholding rent. Tenants sought collective negotiation with their landlords to obtain reduced rents, more secure land tenure, and better contract terms. In Sunch'ŏn county of South Chŏlla in 1922, for instance, the tenants demanded that (1) rent be 40% of crops, (2) landlords pay the land tax and public dues, and (3) tenancy rights not be transferred arbitrarily (Ōwa 1982). Closer examination of these three goals shows neither desperate reaction nor revolutionary terms.

First, tenants aimed to lower the customary 50% rental rate to 40%. This goal is well explicated by the socioeconomic changes of the early 1920s, which produced a strong rural economy, as discussed earlier. Hong Sŏngch'an's study of harvest documents (*ch'usugi*) of landlord Yi in Posŏng county shows a slight rate decrease between 1915–20 and 1921–26, from 12.85 tu per turak to 12.79 in paddy fields. Yet since crop prices substantially increased during the same period, landlords' rental income swelled from 580.8 yang per turak to 778.9, or by 34%.

Such demands as lower rent embodied tenants' and landlords' conflicting interests in the expanded economy. On Amt'ae island, tenants also demanded and achieved rent reduction from 50% to 40% (Cho Tonggŏl 1979, pp. 127–32).

Second, in the 1920s landlords increasingly adopted fixed rental arrangements in order to avoid disputes (Eckert 1991, p. 22). Customarily, when tenants paid fixed rent (a rate generally lower than for sharecropping), they also paid the land tax (Chōsen sōtokufu 1930, vol. 2). But the Land Tax Law of 1914 decreed that landowners owed the tax. Landlords wanted to reinstate the older custom, to which the tenants of course objected.

Finally, demand for more secure land tenure was not the result of desperate poverty. Moral economists argue that peasants close to the margin prefer security over the risk of maximizing profits (Scott 1976, pp. 13–55), a claim used to characterize tenancy disputes in Korea as defensive reactions to preserve subsistence rights. But indications are that demands for more secure tenancy in Korea were not simply based on tenants' subsistence needs; such security could allegedly boost their land utilization and productivity, and hence their profits (*Tonga ilbo* 23 November 1923). Tenant union demands for land improvement were common in the early 1920s (Ōwa 1982).

Again, such detailed analysis of tenant demands suggests neither peasant desperation nor revolutionary zeal. Tenants did not pursue abolition of private landownership or destruction of the tenancy system. Occasionally revolutionary slogans like "Land for the tiller" or "Class struggle" appeared, but the cultivators themselves sought lower rents and better tenancy terms. Disputes can therefore be considered progressive, reformist movements to shift the terms of tenancy in favor of the tenants.

As reformist efforts, then, did these movements succeed or fail? Table 4.6 presents outcomes from 1920 to 1926. Tenants prevailed only 29.3% of the time, but this exceeded landlord victory (12.9%) by two and one half times. The most frequent resolution was "compromise" (31.1% of the cases). The pauperization-revolution thesis interprets compromise as a tenant defeat: compromise gained the peasants no truly improved living situation and only delayed the revolutionary moment. But in a reformist context, compromise may signify success. A demand for rent reduction of 30% that settles for 20% can hardly be deemed a failure (Hŏ Changman 1963, pp. 57–59). Also, as Sunch'ŏn county and Amt'ae island tenancy disputes show, colonial government mediation in this period often favored tenants (Ōwa 1982), basically to prevent constant

TABLE 4.6
Results of Tenancy Disputes

Outcome	1920-26	1927-32
Tenant victory	29.3%	14.7%
Tenant defeat	12.9	13.8
Compromise	31.1	41.6
Unresolved	26.7	29.9

SOURCES: For 1920-26, Chōsen sōtokufu 1929, p. 61. For 1927-32, Chōsen sōtokufu 1940a, pp. 43-44.

rural turmoil and interruption of agricultural production. The government had to keep tenants producing the rice needed for Japan. Finally, traditional rural society subordinated tenants to landlords through economic and extra-economic means. That tenancy disputes in the colonial period often brought tenant victory implies significant change in Korean rural authority relations. As Hong Sŏngch'an's study of landlord Hong on Kanghwa island of Kyŏnggi province shows, "increase in cultivated land per tenant and decrease in tenancy transfer in the 1920s were largely due to increased power of the tenants and weakening of landlord authority" (1981, p. 108).

In summary, tenant movements from 1920 to 1926 were reformist in character and quite successful as such. Effective disputation made some upper tenants or semi-tenants into owner-cultivators and yielded poor tenants some relief from poverty, largely due to favorable opportunities during the economic boom of the late 1910s and a moderate colonial policy in the early 1920s. But the late 1920s and early 1930s paint a much different picture of rural economy and society.

TENANT-LANDLORD DISPUTES, 1927-32

The economic boom of the late 1910s and mid-1920s was short-lived. When agricultural prices in Japan began to fall in 1926, Korean prices followed suit. By 1927, the price of brown rice was 22% off that of 1925, and by 1931 was only 39% of the 1925 price (Suh 1978, p. 158). Agricultural commercialization had brought temporary prosperity for Korean peasants in the first half of the 1920s, but collapse of the world market was a severe blow to Korean agriculture. Furthermore, export concentration on one crop—rice—worsened the impact, for rice prices

TABLE 4.7
Income Balance, by Class, 1931
(yen per household)

Class	Income	Expenses	Balance
Owner-cultivators	679	701	−22
Semi-tenants	392	473	−81
Landless tenants	297	327	−30

SOURCE: Figures are from an Agricultural Association of Korea investigation sponsored by the Government-General of Korea, reprinted in Lee (1936), p. 272.

plunged deepest. As discussed above, increased agricultural commercialization raised the ratio of rice to the total agricultural crops to 70.3% by 1935 (Hori 1976).

The falling prices of agricultural products in general and rice in particular placed most peasants, including owner-cultivators, in debt. According to a survey by the provincial government of South Kyŏngsang, among the 26,160 farm households investigated in 1932, 62.3% were in debt, averaging 107 yen (Lee 1936, p. 235). Given an average income of 297 yen in 1931, debt was more than one-third of total annual income (Lee 1936, p. 272). Table 4.7 shows the differences between income and expenses in peasant households (income balances) in 1931, as investigated by the Agricultural Association of Korea (Chosŏn nonghoe). Unlike 1925 (see Table 3.2) in 1931 even owner-cultivator expenses exceeded income. Spring was the worst season for poor peasants. They had paid rents and taxes the previous autumn and were frequently out of food by spring. Starvation was common. The *Tonga ilbo* (Far Eastern Daily) in Seoul described this spring poverty under the title "A Starving Hell" (24 March 1932):

Despite the sowing season ahead, countless impoverished peasants are drifting away from their villages.... Conditions are none other than a living hell.... Peasants have been depending on grass roots and tree bark for their sustenance, but even such stuffs have now been exhausted.... There is no other way for them than to go out and beg. They live because they cannot die.

Heavy debt and declining living conditions rapidly polarized rural class structure. Of the total rural population, 43.8% were landless tenants in 1927, but 52.7% were by 1932 (Chōsen sōtokufu 1940a,

TABLE 4.8
Average Debt, by Class, 1930
(yen)

Class	Debt per Household	Debt per Capita
Landlords (Type B)	768.54	99.03
Owner-cultivators	207.93	32.05
Semi-tenants	188.53	28.13
Landless tenants	86.71	16.08

SOURCE: Lee (1936), p. 235.

p. 139). During the same period, the percentage of semi-tenants decreased to 25.4% from 32.7%, and of the owner-cultivators to 16.3% from 18.7%. Concurrently, the percentage of big landlords (Type A) increased to 1.1% from 0.8%. Gragert's (1982) analysis of landownership in four villages shows the same pattern.

The nature of disputes changed in the altered economic climate brought on by depression. While the number of disputes increased, their scale decreased, and transfer or cancellation of tenancy rights became a more frequent cause (Table 4.1). Also, the ratio of landlord to tenant participation increased, from $\frac{1}{18}$ in 1927 to about $\frac{1}{9}$ in 1931 (Chōsen sōtokufu 1940a, pp. 26–27). These changes indicate a shift in tactics. In the depression years of the late 1920s and early 1930s, tenants mounted small-scale, defensive disputes to protect cultivation rights and thus their livelihood, instead of the large, aggressive disputes of the more prosperous 1920s, aimed at reducing rents and improving tenancy conditions. Hit hard by falling rice prices and threatened with eviction, marginal tenants became the motivating force behind the small-scale antilandlord movements.

A notable change during the depression years was the increase in disputes initiated by small landlords (Type B). The plunge in agricultural prices sharply reduced landlord income from the sale of rice collected as rent payment, yet the land taxes remained essentially unchanged. Large landlords, able to accumulate reserves of rice and money during prosperous years, simply reduced unnecessary expenses. But many small landlords, especially with less than 5 chŏngbo of land and little in the way of savings and rice reserves, were hard hit by declining agricultural prices and found themselves deeply in debt. Table 4.8 shows the average amount of debt per household and per capita by rural class in 1930, drawn from a 1930 colonial government survey covering 13 provinces and 1,249 farm households. Small landlords (Type B) carried the heaviest debt, per capita debt three times that of owner-cultivators (99.03 vs. 32.05 yen). Only with difficulty could they maintain their already frugal way of life. Concern frequently centered simply on having enough to eat.

These smaller landlords employed three principal strategies to alleviate their distress, all of which led directly or indirectly to tenancy disputes.[19] One exploited increased land competition among tenants, canceling existing tenancy contracts and re-leasing at substantially higher rents to new tenants. For instance, in 1932 landlord Yi in Posŏng county of South Chŏlla province increased rent, on average, from 13.14 tu to 18.19 tu per turak or by 38% by changing tenants (Hong Sŏngch'an 1986). A second strategy was to resume or expand self-cultivation by evicting some tenants totally or reclaiming some land from them. In 1930 in North Ch'ungch'ŏng province, 17 small landlords (with average lands of only two chŏngbo) resumed cultivation by evicting 84 tenants (Chōsen sōtokufu 1930, vol. 2, pp. 232-33).[20] Eliminating these tenants' share of the crop assured them of their own food supply. Finally, some sold small land parcels; in most cases, prospective buyers wanted to change tenants. All three strategies threatened tenants: already hard-pressed, they were apt to protest, demanding the right to continue cultivation.

The defensive nature of depression-era disputes is illustrated by examining dispute issues. As expected, most addressed transfer or cancellation of tenancy rights. For example, in 1932 the percentage of eviction disputes was 72% (Chōsen sōtokufu 1940a, p. 22). In earlier years, the percentage of disputes due to *threat* of eviction ran high (see Table 4.1), but the threat was tactical, used to discourage tenants who demanded rent reduction.[21] But evictions in the depression years involved more than bluff. Official colonial government statistics show that 17% of the land involved in tenancy disputes from 1927 to 1932 reverted to landowners (Chōsen sōtokufu 1940a, pp. 44-45). Landlord expropriation was especially high in 1930 at 28.9% of returned lands.[22] Also, as Table 4.9 shows, 70% of leases in 1930 lasted no more than one year.[23] Thus, that tenancy rights was the main issue in the depression years does not mean that tenancy disputes developed into "struggles to obtain a fundamental solution of land problems," as some scholars argue (see Chi Sugŏl 1993, p. 45); it reflects the defensive nature of tenancy disputes, often a struggle to survive.

Furthermore, increased land eviction intensified competition among tenants. Kim Pyŏngsun's article in *Nongmin*, entitled "How to Prevent

TABLE 4.9
Lease Duration, 1930

Duration in Years	Peasant Households	
	Number	Percent
1	327	70
1-3	59	13
4-5	49	11
6-8	4	1
9-10	10	2
11-15	5	1
16-30	11	2
Total	465	100

SOURCE: Lee (1936), p. 166.

Tenant Transfer" (1932, 3[12]: 7-8), lamented this heightened competition:

As small landlords resumed the cultivation, it became much more difficult to lease land. In order to lease new land from a landlord, the tenant often had to offer gifts like chicken, wine, and vegetables, etc. On the other hand, the current tenants had to accept an increased rental rate just to keep the land leased.

Chosŏn ilbo also reported that in Haman county of South Kyŏngsang province disputes between current and new tenants intensified (28 May 1932). In Taesan district of Ch'angwŏn county, current tenants refused to yield their leased lands to new tenants (*Nongmin* 1933, 4[7]: 45). As mentioned above, landlords often changed tenants in order to increase rental fees, and this practice ignited fierce competition among tenants, impeding collective action. Piven and Cloward's study of the American labor movement of the depression years reveals a parallel phenomenon (1977, p. 98):

First and most obviously worker solidarity was influenced by market conditions. Workers could join together in strikes and slowdowns more readily when business prospered and when the demand for labor was strong. But during periods of depression, men and women were laid off, wages were cut, and hours were lengthened. Defensive strikes and riots sometimes erupted during depressions, but they usually had little effect.

Not only did employers find it easier to resist strikes when trade was slow and there was less to be lost by halting production, but with jobs scarce, workers were forced to undersell each other in the scramble for employment. Workers' associations which emerged during boom times were unable to resist these forces; they were usually simply wiped out when the market fell.

In addition to such market conditions, changes in colonial policy in the late 1920s that restricted involvement of outside organizations in tenancy disputes greatly impeded organized collective action against landlords.

Thus depression-era tenancy disputes were defensive struggles by poor tenants to ward off starvation and landlord eviction—that is, to preserve subsistence. Korean tenants, like Scott's (1976) peasant, frequently invoked traditional practices, such as the custom of easing rents in hard times, to justify their subsistence demands. According to a survey on tenant customs by Chosŏn nongminsa (Institute of the Korean Peasant), peasants often complained that landlords "lost their benevolent roles" (*Chosŏn nongmin* 2[10]: 13) and became "exploiters" (*Nongmin* 1932, 3[4]: 1). Yet little evidence suggests that they wanted to revert to traditional tenure practices. As Vlastos (1986) argues for the Tokugawa peasant protests, to mitigate immediate hardship, Korean tenants also used the right to subsist and the benevolent role of the landlord to justify their protest, but usually unsuccessfully. Between 1927 and 1932, tenants prevailed in only 14.7% of the disputes, far below the 29.3% between 1920 and 1926 (see Table 4.6); about half ended in tenant defeat or were unresolved; compromise rose to 41.6% from the previous 31.1%. However, unlike the early 1920s, depression-era compromise could not be considered a tenant victory. Tenants compromised in most cases by yielding their rent reduction demands in return for noneviction. Many who were even less fortunate had to leave home villages for Japan or Manchuria (see Chapter 8).

CONCLUSION: DEFENSIVE STRUGGLES OR FORWARD-LOOKING EFFORTS?

Previous studies of colonial Korea's tenancy disputes that stress their defensive and ideological nature require reexamination. Unsubstantiated contentions that rural class structure was extremely polarized leads them to overestimate the "potential for revolution" (Sorensen 1990). But, as shown above, a differentiated class structure bred diverse forms of tenant protest. Especially in the early to mid-1920s, disputes were primarily offensive, forward-looking tenant efforts to improve contracts with landlords. Upper tenants and semi-tenants aspired to become owner-cultivators, while poorer landless tenants hoped to relieve some of their poverty through these collective actions. Favorable socioeconomic and political conditions afforded many victories. The depression, however, brought greater class polarization, and tenancy disputes became much more defensive, often a matter of survival.

Disputes from 1920 to 1932 were reformist and practical rather than revolutionary or ideological. Though peasants were often susceptible to ideological appeals such as anticolonialism, nationalism, or socialism, their primary concerns were concrete and economic, such as rent reduction and secure tenancy contracts. They sought not revolution but limited changes and reforms that would improve terms of trade with landlords (1920–26) or minimize adverse market effects (1927–32). In short, Korean peasants were neither a "sack of potatoes" nor a "true revolutionary force." They were rational actors turned politically active for diverse motives of self-interest—offensive in the early to mid-1920s and defensive in the depression years—as suited the impact of socioeconomic and political conditions upon them. This view supports the integrated approach to peasant protest outlined in Chapter 1.

While most depression-era tenancy disputes met with defeat, in the long run they weakened landlord power. Troubled by increasing rural unrest, the colonial government undertook legal measures to protect tenant rights and limit landlord power—for example, the Tenant Arbitration Ordinance of 1932 and the Agricultural Lands Ordinance of 1934. Accordingly, disputes after 1933 were more often individual law suits than collective action, as Chapter 7 shows. Moreover, while tenant-landlord conflict continued, the 1930s witnessed a new, much more radical form and target of collective peasant protest, explored in Chapters 5 and 6.

CHAPTER 5

The Red Peasant Union Movement, 1930-39, Part I
An Overview and Critique

Colonial Korea's socioeconomic and political situation rapidly altered in the late 1920s. The economic depression had devastated the rural economy and cast most peasants into heavy debt. More than half of the rural population suffered "spring poverty," many forced to leave home villages to survive, many migrating to Manchuria or Japan as laborers. Also, the government tightened its relatively moderate "cultural policy" through a series of security laws, particularly the Peace Preservation Law (Ch'ian yujibŏp) in 1925. That law greatly restricted political activity, impeding the involvement of outside organizations in tenancy disputes (see Suzuki Ikuo 1989, pp. 177-358). As discussed in the previous chapter, depression-era tenant protests against landlords in the form of disputes increased in number but decreased in scale and often met defeat.

Despite (or because of) worsening socioeconomic and political circumstances, a new form of peasant protest appeared in the late 1920s. Unlike tenancy disputes, which prevailed in southern commercialized areas, "red peasant union" protest centered in the northeastern region of the peninsula and involved a much broader spectrum of the peasantry.[1] Also of note, this protest did not erupt in areas with high tenancy rates but in regions with a high ratio of owner-cultivators, such as the Hamgyŏng provinces. In addition, protest often directly confronted local colonial government officials. Unlike reformist disputes, this new type became radicalized and often violent. The peasants organized red peasant unions with help from radical nationalists or communists, unions capable of mobilizing large numbers of the peasantry, including middle peasants (owner-cultivators).

Why did these protests turn radical? Why did the nature of protest change from antilandlord to antistate or from class conflict to state-society conflict? Why were radical protests more frequent in the northeastern area with relatively good economic conditions and less landlord exploitation? What role did communists or radical intellectuals play? How did the movement affect Korean social and political conditions?

Discussion of the red peasant union movement of the 1930s is divided into two parts. This chapter presents an overview, past interpretations of the movement, statistical evidence, and the role of intellectuals in the movement. Chapter 6 explains the roots, process, and politics of the movement from the sociohistorical perspective that Chapter 1 specifies.

OVERVIEW OF RED PEASANT UNION PROTEST

The center of protest shifted from southern commercialized areas to the northeastern region in the late 1920s and early 1930s. Among the 69 known red peasant unions (*chŏksaek nongmin chohap*) from 1930 to 1939, 22 (about one-third) appeared in the Hamgyŏng provinces (see Appendix 1). Most of the active, well-organized, and large-scale unions operated in the Northeast. For instance, the Yŏnghŭng red peasant union, active from 1930 to 1933, had 12 branches and about 18,000 members.[2] Given that Yŏnghŭng county had 22,658 households in 1937 and assuming that unions drew an average of one person per contributing household, the union organized about 80% of the county's households (Hida 1982b). The Chŏngp'yŏng red peasant union, also well known, boasted 4,602 members as of late 1930, or about 36% of the county's households (Chōsen sōtokufu, Keimukyoku 1931, p. 9). Both unions were located in South Hamgyŏng province. Also, the Myŏngch'ŏn red peasant union, the most long-lived, operated in North Hamgyŏng province (see Appendix 1).

Protest demands and targets also differed significantly from those of the 1920s. Tenancy disputes had focused on landlords and primarily sought secure tenancy contracts and rent reduction. Red union protests in the 1930s included the same demands, but more often confronted local government officials directly, decrying tax policy and the local government's interference in village affairs through such tactics as raids on night schools. Also, ideological and political slogans such as "anticolonialism" or "national liberation" appeared more frequently than in earlier tenancy disputes. In May 1931, for example, 2,000 peasants of Hongwŏn county in South Hamgyŏng province protested against the county government for increasing household taxes to finance construction of a county government office building. Peasants demanded

TABLE 5.1
Number of Koreans Arrested and Prosecuted
for Violation of the Peace Preservation Law, 1926–35

Year	Arrested			Prosecuted		
	Cases	Persons	Average	Cases	Persons	Average
1926	45	356	7.9	27	157	5.8
1927	48	279	5.8	32	135	4.2
1928	168	1,415	8.4	98	494	5.0
1929	206	1,271	6.2	106	443	4.1
1930	252	2,661	10.6	140	690	4.9
1931	180	1,708	9.5	99	651	6.6
1932	254	4,381	17.2	159	1,011	6.4
1933	205	2,007	9.8	115	539	4.7
1934	145	2,065	14.2	84	518	6.2
1935	135	1,478	10.9	76	437	5.8
Total	1,638	17,621	10.1	936	5,075	5.4

SOURCE: *Shisō ihō* 8 (September 1936): 58–60.

that instead the tax be reduced, since most peasant households were already suffering economically from the depression (*Shisō ihō* 3(12): 29). November 1931 brought red peasant union protest in Samch'ŏk county of Kangwŏn province against a new tax to finance construction of a provincial road; about 2,000 peasants attacked the local government office (*Chosŏn ilbo*, 2 December 1931). In August 1931, the Chŏngp'yŏng red peasant union denounced local government interference in its night schools, which totaled 59 and taught radical thought such as Marxism. The Yŏnghŭng union protested for the same reason in October 1931. That protests increasingly concerned government interference in night schools suggests that Japanese police raids were frequent.

The protests led by red peasant unions against the local government often featured violence and arrests. When the Hongwŏn red peasant union members attacked the county office with sickles and sticks, 500 were arrested. In July 1930, several hundred peasants from Tanch'ŏn county attacked a district office to resist the forest association fee: police gunfire killed 13 and wounded 26 (*Chosŏn ilbo*, 21–22 July 1930). Protests in Myŏngch'ŏn county brought prosecution of 578 union members (Kim Chŏngsuk 1958). The Chŏngp'yŏng and Yŏnghŭng red peasant unions saw several hundred members arrested in 1931. Most arrests and prosecutions invoked the notorious Peace Preservation Law. As Table 5.1 shows, its use mushroomed from 1928, peaking in 1932. In 1927 it detained only 279 persons, but in 1928 it detained 1,415, and in 1932, 4,381. In 1932, 1,011 among the arrested were prosecuted. This was also the year red peasant union activities peaked (*Shisō ihō* 8[11]).

PAST SCHOLARSHIP ON PEASANT RADICALISM IN COLONIAL KOREA

North Korean scholars predominate in the study of the "red peasant union movement" form of radical peasant protest, for more than geographical reasons (most radical protest in the late 1920s and 1930s flared in the northeastern region of the peninsula): political motives led them to seek to root their regime's legitimacy in national liberation struggles during the colonial period. Kim Chŏngsuk (1958), for instance, interpreted the Myŏngch'ŏn red peasant union activities between 1934 and 1937 as "anticolonial, revolutionary struggles," only completed in the post-1945 era. A year later, however, such an interpretation was severely criticized as giving the movement undue credit. In an effort to derive the regime's legitimacy strictly from Kim Il Sung's armed struggles in Manchuria, North Korean scholars stress the "factional" and "provincial" character of the red peasant union movement, which allegedly hindered the national liberation movement (Kim Yŏngsuk and Kim Hŭiil 1959). It became orthodoxy that the regime's legitimacy is traced solely to Kim Il Sung and his fight against the Japanese. Most important studies on radical peasant protest in the colonial period appeared in *Yŏksa kwahak* (History and Science) in the late 1950s and early 1960s, when factional debates within the Workers' Party (Nodongdang) of North Korea were at a peak and Kim Il Sung was finally able to establish his power firmly.

Japanese scholarship on the subject commenced in the early 1970s. Influenced by North Korean scholarship, it also interprets red peasant protest as anticolonial and nationalistic. Asada Kyoji's *National Revolutionary Movements under Japanese Imperialism* (1973) represents this approach. Later works, however, view the protest as a response to particular peasant conditions. For instance, Namiki's (1983) case study of the Hongwŏn red peasant union protest finds it rooted in concrete economic interests; as it became increasingly political and ideological, it lost peasant support.

South Korean scholarship on red peasant protest lagged behind North Korean and Japanese studies. Kim Chunyŏp and Kim Ch'angsun's five-volume *History of Korean Communist Movements* (1963-76) simplistically explains the red peasant union protest as the result of the so-called December Theses issued by the Comintern. Cho Tonggŏl's *History of Peasant Movements under Japanese Colonialism* (1979), a major work on peasant protest in colonial Korea, mentions the red union movement in only a brief six pages (pp. 165-70). Not until the 1980s did younger scholars begin to deal thoroughly with red peasant union protest.[3] Some recent works view the organization of red peasant unions primarily as a response by radical nationalists and communists disappointed with the failure of 1920s reformist efforts (Yi Chongmin 1989; Yi Chunsik 1984, 1993). They also use a new term, "revolutionary peasant union movements" (*hyŏngmyŏngjŏk nongmin chohap undong*), instead of the conventional "red peasant union movements," emphasizing their revolutionary character (Chi Sugŏl 1993; Yi Chunsik 1993).[4]

Works in English on this subject are also limited. Yoo Se Hee's (1974b) doctoral dissertation, "The Korean Communist Movement and the Peasantry under Japanese Rule," is a major work on radical peasant protest, but no further work has ensued. Suh Dae-Sook's *The Korean Communist Movement, 1918-1948* (1970) and Scalapino and Lee's two volumes on *Communism in Korea* (1972) discuss red peasant union protest only in passing. Lee Chong-Sik's *The Korean Workers' Party* (1978) devotes one chapter to colonial peasant movements as background for the North Korean agrarian revolution.

The four main arguments these works proffer to explain peasant radicalism are evaluated below, following some statistical evidence correlating peasant radicalism with other key socioeconomic, demographic, and religious variables.

STATISTICAL EVIDENCE

To correlate peasant radicalism with possibly relevant key socioeconomic, demographic, and religious variables can be very useful. But the most readily available information on the dependent variable, the extent of radicalism in red peasant union protest, provides data only on the *presence* of red peasant unions in a given county. Yet some of them mounted highly active and sustained radical protests, whereas the police demolished others in the very process of organizating. Therefore some indicator of peasant radicalism, taking into account intensity, scale, and duration of union activities, is desirable. The index of peasant radicalism in each county used here assigns a value of one for the mere existence of a red peasant union, two for evidence of protest, three for protest with violence, and four for particularly rebellious activity (see Appendix 1 for the assigned scales). The scaling is somewhat arbitrary and subjective, but it allows correlation of the index with other socioeconomic, demographic, and religious variables. It appears to measure peasant radicalism reasonably well, since it highly correlates with the number of red peasant unions for 13 provinces ($r = .89$, $p < .01$). Table 5.2 presents correlations of the peasant radicalism index and of the number of red peasant unions with other key variables for 13 provinces, controlling for the size of the rural population. Although the correlation coefficients are based on a small number of cases (13 provinces) and results in Table 5.2 are thus only suggestive, they greatly assist in identifying factors conducive to peasant radicalism.

The 17 key factors postulated here (in italics) to relate to peasant radicalism are:

- Level of "rural poverty," measured by the percentage of peasant households (1) suffering from *spring poverty* (*ch'un'gunggi*) and (2) requiring part-time *wage labor* to supplement their income, both in 1930.
- "Rural class structure," gauged by the percentage of (3) *tenant households* and (4) *owner-cultivator households*, both in 1930.
- Degree of the influence of "returnees" to home villages, depicted by the number of (5) *returnees* to home villages from Manchuria in 1934 and (6) *Korean students in Japan* in 1925.
- Intensity of "tenant protests," assessed by the number of (7) *tenancy disputes* and (8) *dispute participants*, both between 1928 and 1932.
- Intensity of "labor activism," measured by the number of (9) *labor disputes* and (10) *labor dispute participants*, both from 1921 to 1929.
- "Village power structure," measured by number of (11) *clan villages* (*tongjok purak*) in 1930. The existence of clan villages indicates that village affairs were strongly influenced by local elites, mostly former *yangban* and landlords.
- Degree of "community solidarity," assessed by the percentage of villages having (12) *mutual aid associations* (*tonggye*) in 1930. These associations enhanced communal solidarity in traditional rural society.
- Impact of "population," conveyed by (13) *population change* from 1927 to 1932 and (14) *population density* per square kilometer in 1930.
- "Education" level, measured by the 1930 (15) *literacy rate*, that is, the percentage of the rural population who read and wrote Korean, Japanese, or both.

TABLE 5.2
Correlations of Peasant Radicalism Index
with Key Variables, Across 13 Provinces

	Correlations	
Variable	With Radicalism Index	With No. of Red Unions (1930-39)
1. % of spring poverty (1930)	-.40*	-.35
2. % of wage laborers (1930)	-.15	-.05
3. % of tenant households (1930)	-.71***	-.61**
4. % of owner-cultivator households (1930)	.59**	.49**
5. No. of returnees (1934)@	.59**	.51**
6. No. of Korean students in Japan (1925)@	.30	.44*
7. No. of tenancy disputes (1928-32)@	-.25	-.23
8. No. of participants (1928-32)@	-.53**	-.53**
9. No. of labor disputes (1921-29)@	.15	.12
10. No. of participants (1921-29)@	.28	.28
11. No. of clan villages (1930)@	-.36	-.31
12. % of mutual aid associations (1930)	.50**	.40*
13. Population change (1927-32)@	.21	.19
14. Population density (1930)	-.26	-.13
15. Literacy rate (1930)	-.10	-.25
16. No. of Christians (1931)@	-.29	-.34
17. No. of Ch'ŏndogyo believers (1932)@	.18	.02

NOTE: @ indicates partial correlation coefficients controlling for the rural population.
$*p < .10. **p < .05. ***p < .01.$
SOURCES OF MEASURES: red unions (Yoo 1974b, pp. 144-45); spring poverty and wage laborers (Chōsen sōtokufu 1934, pp. 69-70); tenant households and owner-cultivator households (Chōsen sōtokufu 1940a, pp. 140-53); returnees from Manchuria (Yi Hyŏngch'an 1988, p. 218); Korean students in Japan (Yoo 1974a, pp. 288-89); tenancy disputes and dispute participants (Chōsen sōtokufu 1934, p. 122); labor disputes and dispute participants (Chōsen sōtokufu 1933, pp. 144-45); clan villages (Yi Kwanggyu 1990, p. 250); mutual aid associations (Pak Myŏnggyu 1987, p. 565); population change (Chōsen sōtokufu 1940a, pp. 140-53); population density (Yoo 1974b, p. 203); literacy rate (Yoo 1974b, p. 262); Christians (Yoo 1974b, p. 261); Ch'ŏndogyo (Chōsen sōtokufu 1933, p. 126).

- "Religion," captured by the number of (16) *Christians* in 1931 and (17) *Ch'ŏndogyo* (Tonghak) believers in 1932.[5] (See Table 5.2 for sources of measurement.)

Among these 17 factors, as Table 5.2 shows, *owner-cultivator households, returnees* from Manchuria, and *mutual aid associations* show statistically significant positive correlations with peasant radicalism, whereas correlations for *spring poverty, tenant households,* and *tenancy dispute participants* are negative and statistically significant. Demographic, educational, and religious factors show no significant correlation with radicalism. Analogous results appear in correlations with the number of red peasant unions. These findings receive closer treatment by comparison with studies discussed below.

Poverty and Peasant Radicalism

Poverty, or "pauperization," is frequently claimed to be the radicalizing element for subordinate classes. Marxists argue that the starvation-driven poor, be they working class (Marx) or peasant (Mao), with nothing to lose but their chains, join radical or revolutionary movements. Moral economists also, as Chapter 1 discusses, contend that the penetration of capitalism into peasant villages brings radicalizing subsistence crises. Most works on Korean peasant radical protest in the 1930s have adopted this kind of pauperization-revolution thesis (Asada 1973; Kim Chunyŏp and Kim Ch'angsun 1963-76; Ko Chŏngsu 1958a; Yi Chunsik 1984). They assume the presence of certain structural conditions (i.e., rural poverty) and accordingly ask what turned a potentially explosive situation into radical protest. For North Korean scholars, Kim Il Sung's influence sparked that kind of protest (Kim Chŏngsuk 1958). For Kim Chunyŏp and Kim Ch'angsun (1973) and Lee Chongsik (1978), resolutions issued by the Comintern and Profintern were incendiary. Yi Chunsik (1984) and Yi Chongmin (1989) cite as pivotal the radical intellectuals' recognition of the importance of the peasantry as a political force and their subsequent efforts to raise peasants' consciousness. These works harbor no doubt that poverty was a necessary condition for peasant radicalism. Even Japanese authorities attributed peasant radicalism to rural economic impoverishment and peasant ignorance (Chōsen sōtokufu, Keimukyoku 1933, p. 48).

Most depression-era Korean peasants indisputably suffered subsistence crises, as the next chapter demonstrates. Yet, to show that poverty prevailed in rural Korea is different from arguing its responsibility for peasant radicalism. Accordingly, a key question still to be explored is whether peasant radicalism succeeded in areas with the worst economic situations.

To probe the possible effect of poverty on radicalism entails examining the economic situation of the rural strata from a comparative perspective. One available indicator of the rural poor's situation is the percentage of rural households that suffered from the notorious spring poverty. As mentioned above, spring was the worst season for most Korean peasants. In 1930, for instance, about 47% of rural households suffered from spring poverty (Appendix 2, column no. 1). Among the tenants, 68% so suffered (Chōsen sōtokufu 1934, p. 69). Clearly, poverty prevailed in rural Korea in the early 1930s. But as to the question at issue here, peasant radicalism was not most prevalent in the areas hit hardest economically. For instance, South Ch'ungch'ŏng province, where nearly 70% of the peasant households suffered spring poverty, sponsored no red peasant union. North Ch'ungch'ŏng and North Chŏlla provinces show the same pattern. The northeastern region, such as the Hamgyŏng provinces, witnessed the most radical and sustained red peasant unions, yet had relatively good peasant living conditions. In fact, as Table 5.2 shows, on average across regions spring poverty is negatively related with radicalism ($r = -.40, p < .10$).

The proportion of rural household heads who supplemented their income with wage labor is another indicator of peasant living conditions in the early 1930s. As Chapter 3 shows, many poor peasants could not support their families with farm income alone and thus required additional, outside work. While the correlation coefficient with peasant radicalism is not statistically significant, it is negative ($r = -.15$). This negative relationship is illustrated by South Ch'ungch'ŏng and North Chŏlla provinces, which had little radical activity yet the highest percentage of peasant households supplementing their income as wage laborers (Appendix 2, column no. 2).

These two poverty indicators reveal that poverty alone cannot adequately explain peasant radicalism in the early 1930s. In fact, the two appear to be inversely related. Whether the land tenure system of tenancy was responsible for peasant radicalism is examined below.

The Tenancy System and Peasant Radicalism

The family-size tenancy system has long dominated land tenure processes in Asian countries, and its conduciveness to peasant radicalism has been an important issue in studies of peasant protest and historical change. As Chapter 1 indicates, for instance, both Stinchcombe (1961) and Paige (1975) claim that tenancy systems provoke revolutionary movements.

While Korea has shared this traditional method of land allocation since the fourteenth century, peasant radicalism has not varied with the tenancy rate. As the previous chapter shows, tenancy disputes prevailed in the southern commercialized areas, where the tenancy system was most dominant, but these tended to be reformist rather than revolutionary. Radical protest, as it turns out, flared in areas with a high ratio of owner-cultivators, such as the Hamgyŏng provinces. Even among the six highly commercialized southern provinces, the three (South Chŏlla, North and South Kyŏngsang) with relatively high ratios of owner-cultivators showed higher peasant radicalism than the other three (North Chŏlla, North and South Ch'ungch'ŏng) with high ratios of tenants (see Appendix 2, column nos. 3 and 4). Table 5.2 also shows on average across regions that peasant radicalism has a negative relationship with the ratio of tenant households ($r = -.71$, $p < .01$) but a positive one with that of owner-cultivators ($r = .59$, $p < .05$). Therefore, Wolf's (1969) argument that middle peasants (owner-cultivators) are more likely than landless tenants to be radical seems to hold for Korea.

Some studies have attempted to link the tenancy disputes of the 1920s to red peasant union movements in the late 1920s and early 1930s (Asada 1973; Ko 1958a). Asada (1973) argues that the red peasant union movement emerged from peasants' growing class and national consciousness raised by tenancy disputes in the 1920s. Yet red peasant union protest was not most prominent where tenancy disputes were strongest in the 1920s, the southern commercialized areas, but where almost no disputes erupted.[6] Table 5.2 shows negative correlations of peasant radicalism with both the number of, and number of participants in, tenancy disputes between 1928 and 1932 ($r = -.25$, n.s.; $r = -.53$, $p < .05$), indicating that tenancy disputes and the red peasant union movement were distinctive types of protest in colonial Korea.

Migration and Peasant Radicalism

Exposure to a new social environment is often seen as crucial in breaking peasant ties to tradition and stimulating new forms of political participation (Deutsch 1961). Such is said to provoke peasant radicalism, especially when peasants return to their home villages after having worked in the industrial sector or where revolutionary movements have developed (Cumings 1981b). Yoo Se Hee (1974a) thus argues that the main reason for strong peasant radicalism in the Hamgyŏng provinces was that many of their peasants had migrated to Manchuria in the 1910s and then returned in the depression years with radical ideas such as communism.[7] Between 1910 and 1931, he contends, about 46% of the migrants to Manchuria came from the Hamgyŏng provinces, and during the same period about one-third of these migrants returned to their home villages, thus provoking the peasant radicalism so concentrated in that area (1974a, p. 74). Table 5.2 shows a significant positive correlation between peasant radicalism and the number of returnees from Manchuria in 1934, controlling for the size of the rural population ($r = .59$, $p < .05$). The number of Korean students in Japan in 1925 also has a positive, though nonsignificant, relationship with peasant radicalism ($r = .30$). In addition, as the next chapter shows, some evidence suggests that returnees to their home villages from Japan, Manchuria, or China often provided peasant union leadership (see Appendix 3 for details).

While returnees may have played an important role in organizing and directing peasant unions, their number was small. More important, left unexplored is why local peasants proved susceptible to agitation by a few—usually educated—returnees, a question the next chapter examines.

Workers' Strikes and Peasant Radicalism

Marxists contend that, while successful social revolution in agrarian society requires alliance with the peasantry, leadership belongs to the workers (see Chapter 1). The December Theses issued by the Comintern to Korean communists in 1928, as discussed below, espoused such a view. Accordingly, some works seek to explain the red peasant union movement as due to labor activism such as workers' strikes or labor disputes (Hŏ Changman 1963; Kim Chŏngsuk 1958; Ko Chŏngsu 1958b; Yi Chunsik 1989).

Labor disputes flared frequently in the 1920s and increased in the 1930s. However, their geographical distribution did not correspond to that of peasant radicalism. Labor movements mobilized in the South P'yŏngan, Kyŏnggi, South Kyŏngsang, South Ch'ungch'ŏng, and Hamgyŏng provinces; among them only South Kyŏngsang and the Hamgyŏng provinces witnessed strong peasant radicalism. Also, South Chŏlla and Kangwŏn, strong in peasant radicalism, sponsored no significant labor activism. In short, as Table 5.2 shows, no significant relationship appears between peasant radicalism and the number of either labor disputes or participants in them in the 1920s ($r = .15$, n.s.; $r = .28$, n.s.).

Wolf describes the effect of labor movements on peasant radicalism as rather indirect: "It is probably not so much the growth of an industrial proletariat as such which produces revolutionary activity, as the development of an industrial work force still closely geared to life in the village" (1969, p. 292). Indeed, some evidence suggests that peasants who had taken mining or industry jobs to support their families but lost them during the depression stimulated peasant radicalism as they returned to their villages. But in colonial Korea most significant peasant immigration into cities or industrial regions such as the Kangwŏn and Hamgyŏng provinces occurred *after* the depression, during extensive industrialization (Eckert 1991; Suh 1978).

Although some influence by labor movements on peasant radicalism cannot be denied, it appears minimal. Again, a better explanation considers what it was about the peasants' actual socioeconomic situation that might have radicalized them. However, before the sociohistorical perspective specified in Chapter 1 is enlisted to account for the red peasant union movement, the role of intellectuals in the movement, frequently emphasized, is treated below.

INTELLECTUALS AND PEASANTS

The role played by intellectuals in peasant rebellions and revolutions is well explored by many scholars.[8] According to Migdal (1974), for instance, a prerequisite for peasant revolutionary movements is the existence of "outside leadership and direction": peasant participation is "preceded by the development of an organizational superstructure by students, intellectuals, and disaffected members of the middle class" (p. 232). Similarly, Eric Wolf's analysis of peasant wars in six countries emphasizes "a fusion between the 'rootless' intellectuals and their rural supporters" (1969, p. 289). Jenkins agrees that "the political role of the peasantry therefore depends on the actions of other groups . . . such as urban organizers or a revolutionary party" (1982, p. 512). Also, as discussed earlier, some works (e.g., Kim Chunyŏp and Kim Ch'angsun 1973; Lee 1978) stress the role of Korean radical intellectuals after the December Theses of 1928 in their explanations of the red peasant union movement. Hence a brief discussion is warranted on the subject of Korean intellectuals in the early twentieth century with regard to their perception of the peasantry and its role in social change.

A major event in Korean intellectual history of the twentieth century was the March First independence movement, the first nationwide nationalist movement for independence. It began 1 March 1919 in Seoul and P'yŏngyang, Korea's two largest cities, with nationalist leaders who declared Korean independence and led street demonstrations. The movement quickly suffused the country and lasted several months. While some violence erupted, such as the killing of Japanese officials, and 19,525 were arrested, the movement embraced nonviolence in order to achieve recognition of Korean sovereignty by foreign countries (Baldwin 1969). It by no means urged social revolution. This movement was the first nationwide political mobilization, involving about one million Koreans, but fell short of its primary goal, political independence from Japan.[9]

The failure of the nationalist movement in 1919 divided Korean intellectuals into two groups: moderate "cultural" nationalists and radicals. The former deemed Korea not yet ready for independence and saw any radical revolutionary movement as visionary. They stressed gradual reform, education, and economic development as a base for future independence. Their gradualist approach to national development and independence is well illustrated by Yi Kwangsu's "Minjok Kaejoron" (Treatise on the Reconstruction of the Nation), which argued for reforms "within limits" (Robinson 1988). An Ch'angho similarly advocated "unembarrassed gradualism" that stressed "the necessary reconstruction of the national character and spiritual strengthening of the Korean people" (Gardner 1979, p. 393). Accordingly, cultural nationalists supported reformist programs such as creation of the National University (Minnip taehakkyo), the Korean Language Research Society (Chosŏnŏ yŏn'guhoe), and the Society for the Promotion of Native Production (Chosŏn mulsan changnyŏhoe).

As Michael Robinson shows, however, these gradualist movements were basically elitist and not specifically designed to benefit the masses, the peasantry.[10] Although "not without concern and empathy for the masses," they stressed "the need first to work with an elite who could then diffuse to the bulk of people" the "values" necessary for modernization and independence (Gardner 1979). They considered the masses uneducated and superstitious, rather than a political force that could be mobilized for independence or national liberation movements.[11] Increasing pauperization of the rural economy they attributed to peasants' personal ignorance and superstition rather than to colonial social and economic structure. For them, peasants were not historical agents of social change, but simply "objects" to be taught and enlightened if rural poverty was going to be eradicated.

The contending intellectual contingent comprised radicals influenced by socialist ideas. The success of the Russian Revolution in 1917 and the

Soviet Union's emergence as champion of oppressed peoples throughout the world generated tremendous excitement among those disappointed with Western liberalism and cultural nationalism. Korean nationalists abroad in Japan, China, and Siberia, relatively free as they were to read and discuss radical ideas and join groups professing Marxist-Leninist principles, were especially attracted to a new vision of social and political development, one that offered insight into the causes of Korea's colonial subjugation.[12] They impugned cultural nationalists' class interest, charging that the ultimate result of cultural nationalism would be perpetuation of imperialist oppression. For the radicals, underdevelopment and colonialization were structurally based, the result of Japanese imperialism, not of Koreans' ignorance or inferior national character. They espoused a materialist view of history and saw class struggle as the engine of social change. But like most other East Asian socialists, Korean radicals had difficulty applying the orthodox view of class struggle within capitalist society to their own country's situation due to Korea's lack of industrial development. Given the proportionally insignificant proletariat class, for instance, they substituted more general and vague categories such as "propertied" (*yusanja*) and "propertyless" (*musanja*) for bourgeoisie and proletariat. This formula pitted "the small minority of the rich, comprised of capitalists, landlords, and elements of an urban leisure class, against the overwhelming majority of poor Korean peasants and laborers," regardless of many other criteria for class distinction (Robinson 1988, p. 121).

While intellectual radicals espoused the importance of mass mobilization for national liberation from Japan, they could not fully escape their movement's elitist character. Their main activities were limited to "speculation" and "debate over the nature of Korean society," at meetings held largely in Seoul and a few other cities. But the easy dissolution of the Korean Communist Party by Japanese police in the mid-1920s challenged the primarily intellectual nature of the early national liberation movements. Radicals began to recognize the centrality of grassroots mobilization of peasants and workers.[13]

Promulgation of the December Theses is frequently cited as the turning point in the thought and strategy of Korean radicals and communists.[14] In December 1928, the Sixth Comintern Congress in Moscow investigated the Korean situation and ordered reconstruction of the Korean Communist Party based on worker and peasant membership:

The revolutionary movement in Korea is passing through a severe crisis.
... Japanese imperialism is intensifying its assault upon your country. ...

But the Communist movement, torn by inner disputes, cannot be . . . the leader of struggle, so long as the closest connection is not established between the individual revolutionaries and the working masses. . . . The proletariat of the colonial countries, in alliance with the broad masses of peasants, enters the political arena as an independent political factor which must have the hegemony in the revolution. . . . [But] there can be no victorious national liberation struggle without an unfolding of the agrarian revolution. . . . [T]he peasant problem . . . is of greatest importance for Communist activity in Korea. Only by bringing the peasants under their influence, only by appealing to them by means of intelligible and popular slogans and demands, will the working class and its vanguard be able to accomplish a victorious revolution in Korea. . . . In the sphere of work among the peasants, the Party must become more active among the tenants and half-tenants. [Quoted from Suh 1970, pp. 243–49]

The theses criticized the party's elitist character and enjoined a proletariat/peasant alliance under working class leadership. They recognized the agrarian nature of Korean society and urged Korean communist leaders to organize and mobilize the peasantry, particularly landless tenants and semi-tenants. In September 1930, the Profintern specified further the need to organize peasant unions. Kim Chunyŏp and Kim Ch'angsun (1963–67, vol. 3), Suh (1970), and Lee (1978) all hold that a series of Comintern and Profintern resolutions were primarily responsible for peasant mobilization and radical protest.

While such resolutions powerfully redirected the strategy of Korean communists, some radicals already had recognized the class nature of Korean society and the importance of worker and peasant mobilization. Thus early radicals, finding proper class analysis of Korean society difficult, used vague terms such as "propertyless" to identify the revolutionary force in the national liberation movement. But they soon began a finer articulation of the movement's class nature. Following Marxist orthodoxy, they deemed the proletariat the main revolutionary class and rejected both petty bourgeois (elitist) and populist views of revolution. Writing on 28 March 1928, Ko Kyŏnghŭm, under the alias Kim Yŏngdu, stated: "They [populist intellectuals] argue for liberation of all the people. Doesn't this slogan represent the petty bourgeois character? They do not ask for liberation of the proletariat, but of all the people. . . . This is not an orthodox Marxist view of revolution. . . . All the serious problems of Korea can only be solved by the proletariat" (translated from Pae Sŏngch'an 1987, pp. 215–16).[15]

This approach rejects as quasi-Marxist the populist view of revolution, which includes all oppressed people as the revolutionary class.[16]

The writer reserved this role for the proletariat: peasants and other subordinate groups can support the revolution, but never lead.

In an article published in a radical journal, *Leninjuŭi* (Leninism),[17] a leader in the Korean Communist Party, An Kwangch'ŏn (alias Sagong P'yo), presented a similar view:

> Korean revolutionary movements have not yet begun. The revolutionary movement must be carried out through mobilization and organization of the workers. . . . But the workers and peasants are not yet mobilized for the movement and petty bourgeois intellectuals make up the majority of the national liberation front. . . . A fundamental weakness in our liberation movement is a lack of strategy for agrarian revolution. [Translated from Pae Sŏngch'an 1987, p. 99]

His is the orthodox Marxist stance: the proletariat is the revolutionary engine, but the agrarian character of Korean society requires a "strategy for agrarian revolution." He further contended:

> Peasants are of critical importance in the current stage of the Korean revolution. It is impossible to think of any bourgeois-democratic revolution without participation of the peasantry. Without taking peasant problems seriously, without fighting for peasant demands, the revolution cannot succeed. The crying demand by the peasantry, a fundamental revolution in the land tenure system, must be the basis of a Korean revolution. [Translated from Pae Sŏngch'an 1987, p. 109]

Published in 1929, this article was actually written in mid-August 1928, some four months before promulgation of the December Theses. An Kwangch'ŏn indisputably recognized the peasants' centrality in the "Korean revolution." Like Ko Kyŏnghŭm, however, he saw the proletariat as the revolutionary class and the peasantry as a vital but subordinate ally:

> The leading class in the Korean revolution must be the proletariat. . . . The Korean proletariat is still weak. . . . Korean peasants are powerful in numbers. But this does not mean that the peasantry is the revolutionary class. They are no more than remnants from the old feudal landlord system. They cannot organize themselves for revolution. Only when led by the proletariat can they be revolutionary. [Translated from Pae Sŏngch'an 1987, p. 108]

Thus Korean radicals and communists were developing a more sophisticated analysis of Korean class structure and the unique problems for activism it posed in the late 1920s, even before the more fully elaborated exposition in the December Theses appeared. Already they embraced the orthodox Marxist-Leninist view of revolution: the proletariat must lead and the peasantry be secondary allies, and among the peasantry the rich peasants could not be trusted, requiring that most attention go to organizing the rural poor, especially landless tenants and semi-tenants.

In summary, then, three points should be stressed. First, to view the December Theses as pivotal (because critical of the revolutionary movement's elitist character and cognizant of its need to focus on class issues) is only partly accurate. Although the theses undoubtedly provided Korean communists with a clear theoretical outline of the revolution, by the mid-1920s some radicals and communists had already emphasized the class nature of the national liberation movement in colonial Korea.

Second, while radicals and communists began to organize and mobilize rural peasants in the countryside, they did not expect a peasant revolution. They envisioned a proletariat-led social revolution that must enlist the peasantry solely as an allied, subsidiary force.[18]

Third, among the peasantry, Korean communists and radicals focused on landless tenants and poor semi-tenants. This approach was in line with Marxist theory: "Those who have nothing to lose but their chains are the most revolutionary." But such orthodoxy excluded the revolutionary potential of the middle peasant (owner-cultivator) with something to defend, well illustrated in the 1930s red peasant union movement.

Thus, although not to be discounted, the role of intellectuals in peasant radical movements was limited. Again, their view of the peasantry reflected the orthodox Marxist-Leninist theory of class and revolution and was often contrary to what transpired in 1930s Korea. For instance, peasant radicalism prevailed in areas with a high ratio of owner-cultivators. In Snow and Benford's (1988) words, their "diagnosis" and "prognosis" of the situation was "distant from the everyday experiences of potential participants [peasants]." Also, as is shown in the next chapter, movement concerns were primarily local, and leadership often came from the peasants themselves. Furthermore, focusing on intellectuals cannot explain how and why peasants perceived the current situation as unjust or accepted the intellectuals' articulation of interests. Accordingly, the next chapter explains the red peasant union movement from the peasants' vantage point.

CHAPTER 6

The Red Peasant Union Movement, 1930–39, Part II
History from Below

In *Peasants, Politics, and Revolutions,* Joel Migdal criticized two popular assumptions found in studies of peasant revolutionary movements: in one, peasants are seen as not having revolutionary tendencies "prior to the coming of the outside leaders"; the other assumption considers peasants "so impatient or frustrated with the current state of events that the mere appeal to revolution will spark loyalty and support" (1974, p. 238). Korean intellectuals in the 1920s and 1930s held similar convictions—cultural nationalists espousing the former view, and radicals the latter. Cultural nationalists deemed peasants to be backward-looking and conservative, "objects" to be educated and enlightened, while radicals stressed the peasants' revolutionary potential. But different as these two attitudes are, they both oversimplify the peasantry.

Chapter 3 revealed peasant heterogeneity and the effects of structural factors, such as colonialism and capitalism, on peasant radicalism as mediated through this differentiated class structure. But simply to examine radicalizing structural conditions such as rural poverty or exploitation—or the intellectuals' recognition of peasant revolutionary potential—does not adequately explain the peasant protest movement. As Migdal indicated, "village specific problems" that "various segments of the peasantry seek to solve" must be examined. Accordingly, this chapter approaches the Korean red peasant union movement of the 1930s from the sociohistorical perspective that relates the land tenure system and differentiated rural class structure to peasant political action. Socioeconomic conditions are discussed first.

CAPITALISM AND PEASANT IMPOVERISHMENT

Most studies of peasant politics emphasize the transformative effect of the world market on agrarian relations (Migdal 1974; Paige 1975; Scott 1976; Wolf 1969). For instance, James Scott (1976) argues that the world market dramatically altered Southeast Asia's agrarian system during the early twentieth century, reducing peasants' subsistence margin and rendering them increasingly vulnerable. This vulnerability took two forms: subsistence crises in an absolute sense and income fluctuations. The combination proved disastrous for peasants, especially smallholders.

Korean peasants in the late 1920s and early 1930s confronted an analogous situation. Since the late 1910s, favorable agricultural prices and strong encouragement by the colonial government had accelerated agricultural commercialization. By the early 1930s rice constituted over 70% of all agricultural production, and more than 40% of it went to Japan. Korean and Japanese markets had become closely linked: peninsular rice prices were affected directly by market conditions in Osaka and Tokyo.

Chapter 4 discussed the severe blow dealt the burgeoning Korean agricultural economy by the worldwide agricultural depression of the late 1920s. In 1927, brown rice fetched prices 22% lower than in 1925, which by 1931 were only 39% of the 1925 price (Suh 1978, p. 158). Plunging agricultural prices, of rice particularly, threw most peasants into subsistence crises. An article in *Chosŏn ilbo* (Korean Daily) of 27 March 1932 asked:

> How can the hunger-stricken peasants live? In Tŏgwŏn county [South Hamgyŏng province] alone, there are twenty thousand starving peasants. Over two thousand have wandered away, because they would not wait for death by staying at home. The irrational economic system in Korea has cursed the peasant class to such an extent that the villages are devastated. . . . In Kongju county, South Ch'ungch'ŏng province, the whole population is in a hopeless plight. . . . The peasant-tenants were deprived of such farm products as they had by merciless landlords and by iron-hearted usurers in the early autumn. They have been suffering from lack of food. By eating grass roots and tree bark they barely escaped imminent death. . . . They have to wander away from the villages with their little children on their backs and in their arms. Words fail to describe the perilous circumstances of these hungry peasants.

Korean newspapers and magazines printed many such accounts.[1] A local correspondent of *Tonga ilbo* (Far Eastern Daily) reported:

Around Changsŏng county, South Chŏlla province, soil fertility is said to be of top quality. On the other hand, the living situation of the peasant-tenants is extremely poor. It is reported that the number of peasants who are struggling on the death line is over 90% of the total population of the county. Many of the peasants have reached the point at which death by starvation is inescapable. The whole county is wrapped in deep fear. They have managed to live until now by eating grass roots and tree bark, but even these are gone. The wives of the peasants went out to the fields to gather grass roots, but often they were mercilessly chased away by the landlords. Not only that, they were weeping and crying because the landlords snatched away the baskets which they had brought to gather the roots. [Quoted from Lee 1936, p. 172]

Such abject misery has been captured in Tawney's famous passage characterizing the Chinese peasant of the early 1930s as "standing permanently up to the neck in water, so that even a ripple is sufficient to drown him" (1966, p. 77). By the late 1920s and early 1930s most of the Korean rural population hovered at subsistence. A colonial government publication reported that 46.5% of the rural population in 1930 suffered the notorious spring poverty (see Appendix 2, column no. 1); for tenants the percentage was 68 (Chōsen sōtokufu 1934, p. 69). Also, more than one-third of the rural population had to supplement their income with wage labor (see Appendix 2, column 2). Clearly this poverty was detritus from the crumbling world (Japanese) market. For instance, the Korean harvest in 1930 was large, the best in over two decades, but plummeting agricultural prices dropped the actual income of most peasants well below subsistence.

Thus, integrating the Korean rural economy into the world market (via Japan) facilitated agricultural commercialization, but sudden depression hit that economy hard. Most studies cited in Chapter 5 attribute radicalism in the red peasant union movement to peasant impoverishment. Indisputably poverty prevailed in rural Korea in the late 1920s and early 1930s, but whether poverty itself radicalized the Korean peasantry is questionable. Although peasant radicalism and the world market's devastating impact on the rural economy appear significantly linked, the correlation's mediating mechanisms remain to be specified. As Robert Marks convincingly argues (1984, pp. 283-84) in explaining peasant radicalism in South China during the 1920s:

[T]he irruption of the capitalist world market into China created socioeconomic conditions favorable for rural revolution. The reason was not . . . that imperialism caused the peasants' standard of living to fall, creating the rural impoverishment and misery that fueled revolutionary movements. Rather, it was because imperialism changed the rural social structure in certain ways. Just as the fact of a bad harvest only made its impact felt through existing social relations, so too . . . the impact of [China's integration into the world market] . . . was determined by the class structure. . . . The outcome of that [class] struggle . . . was determined not by imperialism but by factors which affected the strengths and weakness of the contending classes.

Accordingly, since Chapter 1 contends that the world market's effects on rural economy and society varied across a differentiated Korean rural class structure (as described in Chapter 3), how such differentiation mediated market effects on peasant radicalism must be considered.

THE WORLD MARKET, THE STATE, AND RURAL CLASS STRUCTURE

Worldwide depression in the late 1920s and early 1930s accelerated polarization of rural class structure. Chapter 4 showed how land was amassed by a few big landlords while many small owners and part owners became landless tenants. Falling agricultural prices crushed middle peasants (owner-cultivators) who had borrowed from rural credit societies or commercial banks at high interest rates. According to a 1931 investigation, the annual interest rates ranged from 7% to 40% for mortgage credit and 7% to 70% for personal credit, with averages of 15% and 30% respectively (Lee 1936, p. 238). The main rural credit organizations in colonial Korea were "rural credit co-ops" (kŭmyung chohap), although individual lenders were more numerous. In 1930, rural credit co-ops numbered 600, with 639,705 members and loans totaling 101,568,035 yen, the equivalent of 42% of the government budget. On average, members borrowed 158.77 yen, an increase of 54.69 yen or 53% over 1928 (Lee 1936, pp. 243-44). The members' growing indebtedness was a result of the agricultural depression, affecting small owners and part owners as well as tenants. A 1932 survey of 374 households in 31 villages in 10 counties of 5 provinces (South and North P'yŏngan, Hwanghae, South Chŏlla, and South Ch'ungch'ŏng) records that 68% fell into debt (Table 6.1). Among them, the owner class incurred the heaviest debt, although the ratio of indebted households was higher for tenants; per capita debt for owner-cultivators was 42.02 yen, or 42% of income, whereas for landless tenants it was 16.53 yen, or 33% (Table 6.1). Owners and part owners, so heavily burdened, regressed into part owners and landless tenants. Tenancy rates acceler-

TABLE 6.1
Indebtedness, by Class, 1932

Class	No. of Households Indebted/Not Indebted		Debt per Household (wŏn)	Debt as % of Income	Debt per Person (wŏn)
Owner-cultivators	63	73	283.50	42%	42.02
Semi-tenants	61	27	175.59	45	27.11
Landless tenants	116	20	96.70	33	16.53
Wage laborers	14	—	85.35	—	23.90
Total/Average	254	120	161.36		26.52

SOURCE: Lee (1936), pp. 236, 272.

ated significantly during the depression years, as did rural class polarization.[2]

The above discussion suggests that the depression hit small landowners harder than tenants. This was mainly because owners converted their produce to cash for taxes and farming needs such as seed and fertilizer. The fallen prices of rice and other crops reduced cash returns significantly, necessitating that money be borrowed to cover farming overhead.[3] A 1931 survey reports that 38% of rural credit co-op loans to peasants went for fertilizer and farming tools. Landowners also owed land taxes, their main cash expenditure. By contrast, tenants generally paid rent in kind. As of 1930, for instance, 93.9% of rent in paddy fields and 92.1% in dry fields was paid in kind (Chōsen sōtokufu 1934, pp. 76–77). Thus in a relative sense, the depression affected tenants less than owners. Gragert's analysis of four southern villages confirms that the depression found small landowners the most vulnerable (1982, pp. 290–325).

Despite increasing rural impoverishment, however, land taxes were not eased. The 1914 tax rate was 1.3% of land value, the same as in Japan. In 1922, during agricultural prosperity, upward revisions distinguished rural from urban land: tax rates rose to 1.7% for the former, compared to a 0.95% level for the latter, increasing the rural burden by more than 30% (*Annual Report on the Administration of Chōsen*, 1928–29, p. 40). The depression, however, occasioned no tax reduction, but rather an increase. The colonial government's average land tax revenue during 1930–32 increased by 5% compared to 1925–27 (*Annual Report on the Administration of Chōsen*, 1927–28 and 1932–33). In contrast,

TABLE 6.2
Tax Burden, by Class, for Four Selected Provinces
(wŏn)

Province	Owners	Semi-Tenants	Landless Tenants
South Chŏlla	28.6	10.3	1.6
Kyŏnggi	51.8	12.9	1.1
South Kyŏngsang	74.7	35.4	2.9
South P'yŏngan	12.5	11.0	.6
Average	41.9	17.4	1.5

SOURCE: Pak Myŏnggyu (1987), p. 562.

Japan reduced land tax rates to 1.0% from 1.3%. Again, Korean land taxes encumbered small landowners much more than landless tenants. As Chapter 4 shows, the transfer of tax to tenants was a major impetus for tenancy disputes in the early 1920s, and by later in the decade most landlords were paying their own land tax. Tables 6.2 and 6.3, showing tax burdens by class, make this clear.

Table 6.2 outlines the general tax burden by class for four selected provinces, surveyed by the semi-official Agricultural Association of Korea (Chosŏn nonghoe) in the early 1930s. Landowners incurred the heaviest burden (an average of 41.9 wŏn per household), followed by semi-tenants (17.4 wŏn) and landless tenants (1.5 wŏn). Table 6.3 displays the same class pattern for the payment of various taxes and public dues. For owner-cultivators, payment of various taxes, on average, amounted to 51.8 wŏn, or 35% of cash expenditures and 10.2% of total expenditures. For semi-tenants, payments were 12.9 wŏn, or 10.9% of cash expenditures and 2.9% of total expenditures. Landless tenants paid little taxes, only 1.2 wŏn.

Such heavy tax burdens could easily be expected to arouse discontent among small owners faced with the depression, and new taxes or rate hikes by local governments often provoked radical protests. The point is not that landless tenants were better off than owners, but that the depression eroded the position of owners more seriously.[4] As Eric Wolf (1969) argues, middle peasants or landowners were the stratum "relatively the most vulnerable to economic changes wrought by commercialism" (p. 292).

Public dues demanded by certain semi-official rural organizations (i.e., the Irrigation Association, the Forestry Association, and the Agri-

TABLE 6.3
Burden of Tax and Public Dues, by Class, 1933
(wŏn per household)

Burden	Owners	Semi-Tenants	Landless Tenants
Tax			
land tax	10.2	3.7	—
provincial tax	26.6	5.1	0.7
district tax	15.0	4.1	0.5
total	51.8	12.9	1.2
as % of cash expend.	35.0%	10.9%	1.2%
as % of total expend.	10.2%	2.9%	0.3%
Public dues	14.4	4.4	1.1
Total all burdens	66.2	17.3	2.3
as % of cash expend.	44.7%	14.2%	2.3%
as % of total expend.	13.1%	3.7%	0.5%

SOURCE: In Chŏngsik (1939), pp. 135-36, 148.

cultural Association) further extorted cash from owner-cultivators, fully 9.7% of their cash outlays in 1933. A brief discussion of the Irrigation Association (Suri chohap) will help to clarify the nature of public dues and why they came to burden owners.

When the Japanese launched the rice increase plan in 1920, the colonial government pursued three methods of land improvement: (1) better irrigation, (2) changing dry fields to paddy fields, and (3) developing uncultivated lands (Pak Kyŏngsik 1986). The first was particularly critical since Korean agriculture was regularly devastated by natural disasters such as drought and flood. By 1934, as a result, 192 irrigation associations were responsible for 93% of the 131,000 chŏngbo of land reclaimed or improved since 1920 (Pak Kyŏngsik 1986). In principle an irrigation association's jurisdiction required approval by "not less than two-thirds of the area to be included in the association area." In reality, landowner consent was implicitly coerced by the government, and individuals often had little choice in the matter (Lee 1936, p. 127).

Such associations were funded by the colonial government and loans obtained from sources such as the Industrial Bank of Chosen, usually incurring a 25-year payback. Local association members bore responsibility for debt repayment. Theoretically, increased yields, hence profits, would exceed fees charged for association debts. In reality, the reverse often occurred. In 1931 the average fee per chŏngbo was 61.6 yen, more than the increased profit. This fee became a greater burden for landowners during the depression years. In 1932, Kenkichi Nishimura, an agricultural expert, described "this cursed irrigation work":

> Irrigation on a large scale was the heart of a policy of increasing rice production. . . . The work of irrigation cannot go on if it must be carried [out] by so huge an amount of borrowing at a high rate of interest. It is only natural that the projects are in this embarrassing position when the price of rice is as low as it is today. . . . In spite of this unfortunate condition, the association goes on charging fees varying between 6.11 and 6.97 yen per *tan*, a high rate. [Quoted from Lee 1936, pp. 127–29]

Many small landowners who could not pay the fee had to borrow more money at high interest rates or sell part or all of their land. The Irrigation Association, chartered to improve land quality and productivity, became a "cancer of Korean rural economy." Such usury was most pernicious during the depression (Chang Hyŏnch'il 1935; see also Table 6.3). That many red peasant unions resisted irrigation associations is therefore no surprise. Among the 69 red peasant unions, apparently 9 refused to pay the irrigation fee and 3 challenged the Forest Association fee. In both cases they attacked local government offices.[5]

Unlike the tenant-landlord conflicts of the 1920s, discussed in Chapter 4, depression-era dissent led by red peasant unions often targeted local government offices. Small landowners who had become tenants or stood to lose land were the main participants. In short, the nature of peasant protest changed from class conflict in the 1920s to state-society conflict in the 1930s. Tilly (1975) shows that protest in eighteenth- and nineteenth-century Europe issued from modern state-building efforts and that taxes were a main point of tension. In Korea, early Japanese modern state-building sparked little radical reaction, but when rural economic depression struck, state tax levies inflamed peasants.

Thus the devastation wreaked by the world market on the rural economy during the depression had a complex effect on peasant radicalism, since it altered both rural class structure and the peasants' relations with the state. New discontent and grievances festered among peasants, especially small landowners. But, as resource mobilization theorists argue, the mere existence of oppressive conditions or discontent does not prompt collective action; grievances must be organized and mobilized (Gamson 1975; Oberschall 1973; Tilly 1978), "objective interests" translated into "subjective interests." Therefore, discussion of how depression-era peasant discontent was organized and mobilized for radical protest is taken up next.

ORGANIZATION AND MOBILIZATION OF THE PEASANTRY

In "Toward a Theory of Revolution," James Davies (1962) using a psychological approach, claims that revolutionary movements are likely "when a prolonged period of objective economic and social development is followed by a short period of sharp reversal"; during the reversal, people feel "relatively deprived," experience "a mental state of anxiety and frustration when manifest reality breaks away from anticipated reality," and thus participate in political movements to vent such stress (p. 6). For Davies, therefore, revolutionary or political movements are primarily the psychological expressions of frustrated and angry people. Similarly, Ann Waswo's (1974) analysis of tenancy disputes in prewar Japan argues that rising expectations during the 1910s due to wartime economic growth provoked rural unrest in the 1920s when economic recession hit. The Korean situation of the late 1920s and early 1930s appears analogous to the reversal scenario that Davies and Waswo describe, for the Korean economy plummeted after a relatively prosperous mid-1920s.

But identifying discontent and grievance far from explains protest movements. Organization and mobilization must evolve. The red peasant union movement was more than psychological venting by frustrated small owners; it was a conscious and deliberate social and political action to defend and improve their interests in times of economic crisis. To understand how peasant discontent and complaints were organized and mobilized into the red union movement, the following first examines union leadership.

Some Characteristics of Union Leadership

While the role of peasants in national liberation movements was hotly debated among Korean radicals, and the December Theses must have influenced their views on Korean revolution, peasant mobilization was localized. By 1926 the Japanese had already crushed the Korean Communist Party, and neither Sin'ganhoe, a major national organization of radical nationalists and communists, nor Chosŏn nongmin ch'ong tongmaeng (General League of Korean Peasants), a major national organization of peasants, was effective in mobilizing the peasantry. In the late

1920s and early 1930s this fell to young local leaders, usually modestly educated, whose main occupation was agriculture.

A look at the origin, education, age, occupation, and experience abroad of union leaders as described in various documents of Japanese courts helps to portray the red peasant union leaders.[6] For instance, on 14 December 1933, 41 union leaders of Chŏngp'yŏng county were convicted of violations of the powerful Peace Preservation Law. They had resisted night school closures, taxes, and Agricultural Association fees (*nonghoebi*), and attacked policemen. Thirty-three of them, or 80%, were engaged in agriculture, and most were reasonably well educated (*Shisō geppō* 3[10]).[7] Two were newspaper reporters. Of particular interest, all convicted leaders were born in the county. While some had studied abroad and returned with some knowledge of radical ideas and experience with labor movements (Yi Tongsŏn, Hwang Sŏnghwan, and Chu Tugi attended colleges in Japan, and Han Pongjŏk had some experience with labor movements there), they had preserved close ties to home villages. The leaders were young, ranging in age from 19 to 33, averaging 25.8 (see Appendix 3).

The leaders of the Munch'ŏn union in South Hamgyŏng and the Uljin union in Kangwŏn province repeat this portrait. All 11 union leaders convicted on 22 April 1935 in Munch'ŏn county were peasants with at least an "ordinary" (elementary) school (*pot'ong hakkyo*) education and from the county, as were the 14 convicted on 12 July 1935 in Uljin. Four leaders (Yi Ujŏng, Yun Tuhyŏn, Chu Chinhwang, and Chŏn Yŏngkyŏng) had traveled to Manchuria. The Peace Preservation Law stood behind conviction of 20 Yŏnghŭng county red peasant union members on 12 July 1934. Again, they were young, averaging 26 years of age, while 16 (80%) were peasants. Two leaders, Ch'ae Such'ŏl and Kim Kilgu, had Japanese labor movement experience, and Kim Kyŏnghwan had been in Manchuria (see Appendix 3 for details on these and other counties).

To recapitulate, most red peasant union leaders were young peasants with some elementary education. Some returned to home villages with exposure to radical thought and experience in labor movements in Japan, Manchuria, and Russia; but even so, most were of local origin and engaged in agriculture. Further, little evidence suggests direct orders from Seoul or any national organization, or that activities in any one county were coordinated with those of others. As emerges below, union activities were primarily in response to local conditions.

Unions were organized at the county level, but size and endurance ranged from incipient ones demolished by the police to those strong enough to develop district-level subbranches. Most peasant unions in southern areas were short-lived, whereas northeastern unions were stronger and longer lasting. Organization took two forms: (1) remodeling existing organizations such as tenant unions, branches of the Sin'ganhoe, or youth leagues, and (2) establishment of entirely new units. Red peasant unions in Yŏnghŭng, Hongwŏn, Chŏngp'yŏng, Tanch'ŏn, Pukch'ŏng, and Sŏngjin built upon preexisting organizations (*Kōtō keisatsu hō*, vol. 2, p. 17; Chōsen sōtokufu 1933, p. 48). For instance, the Chŏngp'yŏng peasant union was formerly the Chŏngp'yŏng branch of the Peasant League, while the Tanch'ŏn union incorporated the Peasant League, the branch of Sin'ganhoe, and the Youth League (Hida 1982a; Yi Chunsik 1984). Newly created unions emerged in Suwŏn, P'yŏngt'aek, Naju, Ponghwa, Yŏngju, Kimch'ŏn, Kowŏn, Munch'ŏn, and P'ungsan (Chōsen sōtokufu 1933, p. 48). Although sometimes organized with help from outside entities such as the Comintern, Profintern, the Chinese Communist Party, or Korean communist groups in Manchuria (Yoo 1974b), these unions were, for the most part, the result of local leaders' efforts to address peasant grievances.

The Main Issues of Red Peasant Unions

As we have seen, the main issues in tenancy disputes were reformist and economic ones such as rent reduction and secure contracts. But issues in radical protests broadened to include both economic and political demands. For instance, the Chŏngp'yŏng red peasant union sought the following goals (Chōsen sōtokufu, Keimukyoku 1931, pp. 6–7):

1. rent reduction
2. permanent tenancy contracts
3. legalization of the right to dispute
4. freedom of assembly, speech, and publication
5. abolition of all oppressive laws
6. abolition of fixed agricultural prices
7. removal of agricultural agents
8. investigation of government-official corruption
9. cessation of closed courts, torture, and unwarranted arrest
10. Agricultural Association reform
11. reforms in Regulations on Land Improvement
12. protection of "fire-field" farmers
13. cessation of forced seed distribution
14. landlord payment of fertilizer and seed costs as well as land taxes

15. fixed wages
16. abolition of feudal practices for employees
17. abolition of feudal constraint on women and youths
18. rural educational improvement
19. admission to all committee meetings
20. cessation of discrimination against Koreans in education
21. cessation of Japanese immigration
22. alliance with the working class
23. organization of class-based unions
24. establishment of departments of youth and women
25. organization of self-defense units
26. organization of peasant unions in other, yet unorganized areas

Also, the Munch'ŏn red peasant union chose the following main goals (*Shisō ihō* 3 [June]: 31–33):

1. rental rate reduction
2. abolition of indirect tax on daily necessities
3. landlord payment of all taxes
4. destruction of debt documents
5. a bidding system in marketing agricultural crops
6. cessation of preharvest sale of crops
7. increased wages for agricultural laborers
8. abolition of the water tax
9. cessation of forced trials of arrested leaders
10. mandatory education for all Koreans
11. worker employment insurance
12. dissolution of reactionary organizations
13. organization of self-defense units
14. autonomy of peasant organizations
15. freedom of assembly, speech, and publication
16. abolition of the Peace Preservation Law
17. release of all imprisoned workers and peasants
18. support for families of the imprisoned
19. dissolution of reformist organizations
20. support for the left in labor unions
21. cessation of imperialist wars
22. support for Soviet Russia
23. support for Chinese communists
24. withdrawal of the Japanese army
25. overthrow of Japanese imperialism
26. complete Korean independence

27. land redistribution to peasants
28. union control of the Rural Revitalization Council

Again, the main demands were both political and economic. Political issues ranged from abolition of authoritarian laws, to freedom of speech, publication, and meetings, to the overthrow of Japanese imperialism. Economic concerns broadened to include the interests, not only of tenants, but of owner-cultivators and wage laborers. For instance, abolition of the water tax or irrigation fee, destruction of debt documents, abolition of fixed prices, and reform of the Agricultural Association were issues more oriented toward owner-cultivators. Such issues, along with complaints against corruption of local officials and police, reflect the growing discontent of Korean peasants, especially owner-cultivators, with colonial government agricultural policy. This broader spectrum of economic issues and their political expression significantly departs from earlier tenancy disputes, primarily confined to rent reduction and secure tenancy tenure concerns expressed through class conflict.

Political Consciousness and Peasant Mobilization

Scholars of collective action and social movements well indicate the importance of political consciousness in collective action (Hirsch 1990; Klandermans 1984; Klein 1984, 1987; McAdam 1982; Mueller 1987; Piven and Cloward 1977). For instance, Doug McAdam's analysis of the civil rights movements of the 1950s and 1960s stresses the need to "distinguish objective social conditions from their subjective perception . . . [because] segments of society may very well submit to oppressive conditions unless that oppression is collectively defined as both unjust and subject to change" (1982, p. 34). Marx called the transformation of objective to subjective interests the process of becoming a real class or "class-for-itself" (Balbus 1971); this must occur before any political collective action can take place. In E. P. Thompson's (1978) parlance, the impact of a production mode on class relations is always first mediated by human experience and interpretation. The conversion of objective into subjective interests, or the interpretation of imperialism's effect on rural class relations, entails fostering political consciousness. Therefore, proper understanding of radical rural protest requires examining how peasant political consciousness in the late 1920s and early 1930s was marshaled.

Documents on red peasant unions make clear that the two main avenues taken to raise consciousness were education and publication.

Night schools were especially important. Traditionally education was highly regarded in Korean society and a main route to government posts. But most subordinate groups, including peasants, were excluded from formal education. Accordingly, when union leaders opened night schools, peasant response was enthusiastic. For instance, by late 1930, the Chŏngp'yŏng red peasant union boasted 37 night schools with 54 teachers and 1,203 students (Chōsen sōtokufu, Keimukyokyu 1931, p. 26). Given a total of 1,627 ordinary schools (*pot'ong hakkyo*) with 471,083 students in Korea in 1929 (about 7 schools with 2,000 students per county) (*Annual Report on the Administration of Chōsen*, 1928-29, p. 86), that one union sponsored so many night schools indicates the great strength of peasant interest.[8] Although the exact number of such night schools cannot be determined, various Japanese court documents indicate their popularity in other red peasant unions as well (see Appendix 1). Peasant adults and children were taught about why they were impoverished and the nature of imperialism and Marxism-Leninism. For instance, Japanese police found in Chŏngp'yŏng county the radical publications *Musanja sinmun* (Newspaper of the Propertyless), *Chŏksŏng* (Red Star), *Hyŏntangye* (Present Stage), *Marŭk'ŭsŭ juŭi* (Marxism), *Sajŏk yumulnon* (Historical Materialism), and so on, most probably used as textbooks (Chōsen sōtokufu, Keimukyoku 1931, pp. 27-28).[9]

Union leaders also organized "reading circles" (*toksŏhoe*) which studied radical publications. For instance, Japanese court documents show prosecution of Pak Insun of Munch'ŏn county and Kim Hŏnsik of Yŏnghŭng county for organizing "reading circles" to promote "communist thought" (*Shisō ihō* 3: 44; 4: 39).[10] Also popular were plays satirizing rural impoverishment and the colonial government's agricultural policy. These satirical dramas had titles such as "Peasants" and "Fire-field Farmers" (in Pukch'ŏng county), and "The Unemployed" and "Forest Association" (in Chŏngp'yŏng county). Night schools and reading circles as well as drama performances became major targets of Japanese raids, which provoked radical peasant protest. Japanese court documents also accused event organizers of "raising dangerous consciousness." This heightening of political consciousness through education and publication turned the peasant discontent, prompted by the depression, into actual radical protest in the late 1920s and early 1930s.

THE PROCESS OF PEASANT PROTEST

While the main slogans of red peasant unions addressed both political and economic issues, and the latter were broadened to represent interests of all the subordinate rural strata (e.g., tenants, owner-cultivators, and wage laborers), not all issues cited provoked *actual* protest. Although such revolutionary slogans as those demanding the overthrow of Japanese imperialism and the establishment of Korean independence could have reinforced protesters' determination and sense of legitimacy, they alone rarely impelled actual protest. As Marks properly points out in explaining peasant radicalism in South China in the 1920s, "purely political slogans . . . can't arouse the masses. Only economic demands necessarily close to the masses can mobilize them for an uprising" (1984, p. 241).

While Marks's comment holds true for Korean peasant radicalism, economic issues such as tenancy also rarely provoked actual radical protest, even though they almost always enjoyed preeminence on lists of union grievances. That top priority probably reflected the orthodoxy declaimed in the December Theses (see Chapter 5), and embraced by radicals and communists, that landless tenants were to be mobilized as major allies in the proletariat-led national liberation movement. What really ignited radical protests was primarily the interference of police in village affairs, such as night school raids, or dissatisfaction with the local government's agricultural policy, such as increased taxes.

Discerning that night schools were the peasants' main instructors in radical ideas, the Japanese took rigorous disruptive measures. For instance, the Japanese police closed 30 night schools and 5 public meeting places in Chŏngp'yŏng county from August to December 1930 (Chōsen sōtokufu, Keimukyoku 1931, p. 26). According to Japanese court documents, this interference inflamed passions, causing violence. During one incident on 6 August 1930, about 80 peasants with stones and clubs attacked 2 policemen attempting to arrest night school leaders. Night school closure in Yŏnghŭng county in September 1931 also provoked peasant radicalism, leaving one red peasant union member, Hwang Chaebo, fatally wounded by Japanese police (Hida 1982b). In September 1931, radical response to Japanese subversion of Hongwŏn county night schools resulted in one wounded and 100 arrested (*Chosŏn ilbo*, 20 September 1931). Protests in Munch'ŏn and Hamju in South Hamgyŏng province, and Sŏngjin in North Hamgyŏng province, all contested Japanese interference in night school operations (see Appendix 1). Clearly peasants saw night school raids as an undue intrusion in village affairs and accordingly protested severely.

The second main focus of radical protest—taxes, debt, and semiofficial organization fees—bore on the heavy economic burden of peasants already ravaged by the depression, especially small owner-cultivators. Accordingly, most radical protest targeted local government officials, police stations, and semi-official organizations that faithfully served colonial policy. In May 1931, about 2,000 members of the Hongwŏn red peasant union descended upon the county office, demanding a reduction in the household tax: As of 27 May, members had paid only 100 yen of the 20,000 owed. In addition, in September 1931, union members attacked close to 70 rich peasants and landlords in 13 villages and burned debt documents (*Chosŏn ilbo*, 5-6 September). In 1911, the colonial government had placed full control of forests under the Forest Association, run by forest owners. In July 1930, faced with falling agricultural prices, 200 Tanch'ŏn red peasant union members entered the district office to demand reduced Forest Association fees (Yi Chunsik 1984). Also, the Chŏngp'yŏng red peasant union sponsored frequent public speeches encouraging boycotts of taxes and public dues, and members indeed refused to pay Agricultural Association and Stockraisers Association fees.

The Agricultural Association, one of the main semi-official rural organizations, was established in 1926 to mitigate growing rural unrest, and was controlled by government officials and rich landlords. As of November 1930, only 10% to 40% of the fees due in Chŏngp'yŏng county had been paid (Chōsen sōtokufu, Keimukyoku 1931, p. 37). In October 1931, the Yŏnghŭng red peasant union stormed the Inhŭng district office, burning tax-related documents. This attack primarily embodied their complaint against taxes imposed to build a new district office, and it considerably disrupted revenue flow. Three members were killed and more than 500 arrested (*Chosŏn ilbo*, 31 October 1931). Among the 217 prosecuted, 20 were convicted (see *Shisō geppō* 4[5]: 14-44). Peasant protests in Haman, Kosŏng, and Ulsan in South Kyŏngsang province; Samch'ŏk and Kangnŭng in Kangwŏn; Kangsŏ in South P'yŏngan; Kowŏn, Hamhŭng, and Anbyŏn in South Hamgyŏng; and Sŏngjin and Onsŏng in North Hamgyŏng, all related to taxes, debt, or Irrigation Association fees (see Appendix 1). This evidence makes clear that most red union peasant protest of this period targeted local government offices or semi-official rural organizations, a significant change from previous, milder class conflict into radical state-society confrontation.

Since small owner-cultivators were the most severely affected by the depression and thus were the main protest contingent, a significant positive correlation emerges between owner-cultivator class size and peasant radicalism in Table 5.2. Actual cases gleaned from the most radical counties bear out this correlation. The Chŏngp'yŏng red peasant union had 4,602 members as of late 1930, 52.3% either owner-cultivators or semi-tenants. Class origins in other unions are not known, but considering that most radical protests flared in counties with a high ratio of owner-cultivators, it seems fair to assume that owner-cultivators were the main participants. For instance, in Tanch'ŏn county, even in 1932, about 80% of the households were either owner-cultivators or semi-tenants; in 1933, in Myŏngch'ŏn county, 82% were owner-cultivators or semi-tenants and only 12% were landless tenants (Kim Chŏngsuk 1958, p. 12). These numbers far exceeded the national average of 42% owner-cultivators or semi-tenants and 53% landless tenants in 1932 (Chōsen sōtokufu 1940a, p. 139).

Also, as discussed above, most union leaders were themselves peasants. Although there is little information on their class backgrounds, the leaders often boasted at least a modest education, and some of them had even studied abroad, suggesting relatively well-to-do origins. A 1930 government report attests that only 6.75% of the population could read and write both Korean and Japanese, and another 15.01% only Korean, leaving 76.37% illiterate (see Appendix 2, column no. 15).[11] Given such a high rate of illiteracy, the leaders' guidance of publication and education suggests that few came from the poorest families, the landless tenants.[12] Therefore, since unions excluded rich landlords, most leaders probably came from the owner-cultivator class (Chi Sugŏl 1993).[13]

THE POLITICS OF PEASANT PROTEST

These findings add to the ongoing debate in the literature on peasant protest and revolution that explores which peasants are most inclined toward radicalism and why. As Chapter 1 discusses, Stinchcombe (1961) and Paige (1975) consider that landless tenants are most likely to be radicalized, whereas Scott (1976) and Wolf (1969) claim that radicalism occurs more often among smallholders. The Korean experience unequivocally supports the latter proposition; peasant radicalism prevailed in areas with a high ratio of owner-cultivators. While Scott and Wolf agree about class susceptibility, they offer quite different reasons for it. For Scott, the key to smallholders' radicalism is cultural autonomy, whereas for Wolf the social and ecological power structure proves crucial. Scott (1977, p. 289) avers:

[W]e are often likely to find the strongest resistance to capitalism and to an intrusive state among the more isolated peasantries with entrenched precapitalist values. While the values that motivate such peasantries are thus hardly socialist values in the strict, modern use of that word, their tenacity and the social organization from which they arise may provide the social dynamite for radical change. The situation of immigrant workers and landless day laborers . . . may well seem more appropriate to strictly socialist ideas, but their social organization makes them less culturally cohesive and hence less resistant to hegemony.

Wolf, on the other hand, claims that since landless tenants or laborers are usually closely tied to or dependent upon landlords, they cannot rebel unless outside forces mobilize them. Much greater "tactical leverage" to engage in radical protest is normally possessed by smallholders or tenants who live in communal villages outside direct landlord control, and by peasants who live in geographically marginal areas relatively inaccessible to governmental authorities. He concludes: "But, ultimately, the decisive factor in making a peasant rebellion possible lies in the relation of the peasantry to the field of power which surrounds it. A rebellion cannot start from a situation of complete impotence" (1969, p. 290). Thus, for Wolf, the resource for smallholders' rebellion is not cultural, as Scott argues, but the material and organizational advantage their situation offers for collective protest against outside oppressors.

Combining both Scott's and Wolf's theoretical discussions helps explicate why actual protest was more successful and sustained in the northeastern region of Korea, especially the Hamgyŏng provinces, despite the potential for protest in other areas with a high ratio of owner-cultivators: South Chŏlla and both Kyŏngsang provinces. While owner-cultivators in both the northeastern region and the three southern commercialized provinces felt growing discontent during the depression of the late 1920s and early 1930s, the former enjoyed a cultural cohesiveness and tactical advantage in translating grievance into actual protest. The northeastern provinces, including both Hamgyŏng and Kangwŏn, remained the most backward and therefore the most traditional, thus providing the "social dynamite" for radical protest that Scott cites. Historically, Korean mainstream politics excluded them, and increasing market penetration into their villages during the 1920s seemed to fail to convert their cultural traditionalism.[14] The Japanese complained that the people of this region were "violent and unruly" in character, fiercely nationalistic, and resistant to authority. Scalapino and Lee go one step further, claiming that "these areas, where living was hard and dangerous and the central government only a distant rumor, had undoubtedly bred a militant political subculture" (1972, p. 200). Whether exaggerated or not, this description suggests that northeasterners had a deeply imbedded character and tradition.

The presence of *tonggye,* the village mutual-aid associations, reveals the relative traditionalism of various areas. The village *kye* was popular in rural colonial Korea, especially in the northeast; and where present, the village *kye,* vestige of the early Chosŏn dynasty, comprised most village peasant households.[15] Members not only helped each other financially on such occasions as weddings and funerals, but exchanged labor in the busy season, thus enhancing communal solidarity (Kim Kyŏng'il 1987).[16] Table 5.2 shows a positive significant correlation between the proportion of a province's villages with *tonggye* and peasant radicalism ($r = .50$, $p < .05$). This finding suggests that precapitalist values, preserved through voluntary mutual-aid associations such as *tonggye,* contributed to radicalizing and mobilizing the peasantry when market forces hit the rural economy.[17] As Chirot and Ragin (1975) argue for the 1907 Romanian peasant rebellion, it seems that traditionalism agitated by market forces ignited peasant radicalism.

Perhaps more significant than cultural autonomy was the northeastern region's "tactical leverage" in social power relations. The three southern provinces with weak red peasant union movements (North Chŏlla, South and North Ch'ungch'ŏng) had a strong tradition of *yangban* influence over local politics, exemplified by the large number of clan villages (see Yi Kwanggyu 1990, chap. 7). According to a colonial government survey in 1930, Korea had 15,000 clan villages (*tongjok purak*), among which 1,685 were particularly well known (Suzuki 1943, p. 512). Of the latter, 619 (37%) lay in the three southern provinces, but only 171 (10%) were in the three northeastern regions (Kangwŏn, South and North Hamgyŏng) (Suzuki 1943, pp. 392–93).

Local communities in such clan villages displayed what Barrington Moore, Jr. (1966) called "conservative solidarity": rich peasants or landlords who controlled village resources and organizational levers dominated peasant smallholders or tenants. A fairly strong negative correlation between the number of clan villages and peasant radicalism supports Moore's thesis, controlling for rural population size for the 13 provinces ($r = -.36$, $p < .15$; see Table 5.2). In the famous clan villages, powerful local elites, mostly former *yangban* and landlords, hindered peasant mobilization for actual protest (Chi Sugŏl 1993).[18]

Furthermore, the northeastern region, bordering Manchuria, was so mountainous as to hinder Japanese search and seizure of activists. The Myŏngch'ŏn red peasant union even built mountain caves to hide from the police (Kim Chŏngsuk 1958). Activists in the border region could easily cross over into Manchuria, where anti-Japanese armed struggles were active. In short, northeasterners had both "reason" and "capacity" for radical protest.

Finally, the northeastern political opportunity structure favored peasant protest. According to Charles Tilly (1978), "the level of repression/facilitation by the government" (p. 100) greatly affects collective action. Repression is any action taken by a group that raises its contender's cost of collective action, while facilitation lowers it. Repression/facilitation becomes "political" when it is government mandated. Suspending newspapers, forbidding assembly, and arresting political dissenters exemplify political repression.

Chapters 4 and 5 have shown that the political opportunity structure became much more inhospitable for any kind of collective protest from the mid-1920s on, especially after the establishment of the Korean Communist Party in 1925.[19] The colonial government particularly monitored the southern commercialized areas and northwestern region. Eruption of serious tenancy disputes in the former during the 1920s led Japanese authorities (as well as communist leaders) to regard these areas as the "front line of Communist thought," where communist agitation of peasant radicalism would focus.

Also during the 1920s, radical nationalists instigated military incidents, mainly along the northwestern border. A colonial government source reported 2,996 military operations in North P'yŏngan province between 1920 and 1928, involving 14,214 people, but only 1,030 incidents in both North and South Hamgyŏng provinces, involving 3,956 people (Yoo 1974b, p. 269). In 1928, 1,499 police were dispatched to North P'yŏngan, compared with 362 and 623 to South and North Hamgyŏng respectively. Such close Japanese surveillance in the southern commercialized areas and northwestern region must have significantly increased the cost of political collective action. The northeast generally escaped scrutiny until it drew serious attention from Japanese police in the 1930s. In short, sociopolitical and ecological advantages of the northeastern over the southern and northwestern regions made peasant protest more sustainable.

CONCLUSION: HISTORY FROM BELOW

The foregoing explains peasant radicalism of the early 1930s from a sociohistorical perspective. In particular, imperialism so affected rural class structure and state-society relations as to foment a new form of peasant protest. Depression in the late 1920s and early 1930s most seriously struck the owner-cultivator class concentrated in the northeast, which then challenged the local government. That class bore the heavy burden of cash expenditures for taxes and public dues. This new discontent, embodied in complaints against local government and semi-official rural organizations, combined with organizational efforts by educated middle peasants ignited radical peasant protest. Thus the red peasant union protest movement that prevailed in the northeastern region in the early 1930s is best characterized as a state-society conflict led by middle peasants.

Also, evidence suggests that it was not those with nothing to lose who became more radicalized, but their counterparts. Marx thought revolution would require little cost, as desperation drove subordinate groups with only their chains to lose. To the contrary, radical peasant protest in colonial Korea flared when peasants with something to defend and some social strength confronted social transformations that threatened to wrest what they had from them.[20] Furthermore, northeastern advantages of location and terrain made peasant protest more sustainable there than elsewhere. But faced with efficient and repressive colonial police, radical peasant protest faded from 1932 on and almost disappeared by the late 1930s, reviving only with the postwar era.[21] Korean red peasant union activity, lacking Vietnam's jungles and China's Yenan base, could not develop into guerrilla warfare.[22] A highly efficient bureaucracy and police apparatus, combined with fairly well-developed communication and transportation networks, enabled repression of almost every possible protest movement beginning in the late 1930s.[23] As Skocpol (1982, p. 172) points out:

Marginal, inaccessible geographical areas are the most suitable places for the process to begin, but for it to spread and succeed, no doubt exogenous events must intervene to drastically weaken the existing state power. . . . [D]efeats in wars and international military interventions are the most likely ways for existing state power to be disrupted—opening the way either for autonomous peasant revolts, or for appeals by organized revolutionaries to peasant support in the country.

The second phase of revolution did not occur until Japanese defeat at the end of the Second World War. Peasant radicalism then revived in Korea, bringing peasant uprisings in the south and social revolution in the north, as Chapter 9 discusses (see also Cumings 1981b).

The approach I take explains peasant radicalism from the peasant's rather than a leader's point of view. Previous studies on the red peasant union movement have primarily emphasized the role of communist leaders since the December Theses in 1928. For such studies, the structural conditions for peasant radicalism (e.g., exploitation of peasants) were given, and therefore peasants needed only communist organization and correct ideas to turn revolutionary. In explaining the social basis of peasant radicalism in colonial Korea, Lee writes: "[T]he majority of farmers had much to complain about. But the peasants clearly needed leadership to emerge as a revolutionary force. . . . Only when persons who were *not* ordinary peasants provided leadership, were the peasants aroused to action" (1978, pp. 36–37; emphasis added).

Lee's view, interestingly and surprisingly enough, echoes the assertion made by a Japanese author in the 1930s that "tenant farmers were not immersed in these ideas [socialism], and they simply followed the leaders blindly" (quoted in Lee 1978, p. 37). This view, implicitly or explicitly, colors most previous studies on peasant radicalism, whether by South Korean, North Korean, or Japanese scholars. For them, the early 1930s witnessed a Korean *communist* peasant movement, not a *peasants'* peasant movement. That is, Kim Il Sung's following, or the reconstructive efforts of the Korean Communist Party, agitated peasant radicalism. These elitist approaches explain the red peasant union movement from the top down with little attention to its grass-roots social origins. This skewed perspective is hardly surprising in American or South Korean scholarship, but is a bit more disconcerting when used as the basis of supposedly Marxist analysis in North Korean and Japanese scholarship.

A perspective that relates peasant protest to rural socioeconomic structure and how peasants understood their interests, prior to the arrival of any organizers on the scene, must replace this elitist approach.[24] Outside leaders such as radical intellectuals who had studied abroad perhaps did help articulate new interests for peasants or organize unions, but this contribution must be explained from the peasants' perspective. Unless the leaders' ideas make sense to them, the peasants will not rise up in protest. As George Rude's (1980) analysis of French popular protest suggests, and Robert Marks convincingly demonstrates concerning peasant radicalism in South China, peasants are not "passive recipients of outside ideology and organization, but . . . active participants in a relationship in which the ideology and organization of the leaders are as much changed by peasants as vice versa" (Marks 1984, p. xxiv).[25] Indeed, as the foregoing shows, intellectuals' perceptions of peasant interests did not exactly coincide with the peasants' own views. The history of peasants was not made by outsiders, but by peasants themselves carrying forward their own sense of history.

CHAPTER 7

Tenant-Landlord Conflict, 1933-39
Class and Nation

While red peasant union protest movements were a central form of peasant activism in the 1930s, tenant-landlord conflict continued as well, centered in the southern commercialized areas. Unlike the conflicts of the 1920s, which were mainly collective tenant protests against landlords, the tenancy disputes from 1933 to 1939 were more like individual law suits. This chapter examines the roots, nature, and legacy of the 1930s tenant-landlord conflicts.

Two important issues, nation and class, characterize the rural conflict of the colonial period. Peasant protest can be considered national conflict against Japanese colonial rule, yet also class conflict against the landlord class. Most studies stress the former, depicting the disputes as part of an anticolonial and nationalist movement (Asada 1973; Cho Tonggŏl 1979). In my estimation, class figured more prominently. Close study reveals a shift from a landlord-based to a pro-peasant colonial policy in the 1930s because of rural economic deterioration, continued tenant activism, and the Japanese need to mobilize Korean labor and resources for "total war." The disputes of the 1930s signified that Korean tenants were experiencing a growing class consciousness and ability to take advantage of favorable policy change, not simply desperation or ideological motivation. This interpretation accounts for the lack of a mass base for national liberation movements in the colonial period, which is not adequately explained by state repressive power or movement leadership problems such as factionalism in organization and mobilization.

Also, contrary to the conventional view, I argue that continued tenant activism in the 1920s and 1930s facilitated the erosion of dominance by the landlord class. This interpretation helps illuminate postwar peasant radicalism and subsequent land reforms that led to the demise of the Korean landlord class, a crucial precondition for the effective state role in the industrialization of the 1960s and 1970s.

AN OVERVIEW OF TENANT-LANDLORD CONFLICT, 1933-39

The number of tenancy disputes exploded after 1933. Table 7.1 shows 136,175 disputes between tenants and landlords in the seven years from 1933 to 1939, or an annual average of 19,454, a fiftyfold increase over the 1920-32 total of 4,794, and annual average of 369. But tenancy disputes from 1933 to 1939 involved 322,673 tenants, landlords, and agents, a substantial decrease in scale from 15.6 participants per case (1920-32) to 2.37. Also, disputes involved a total of 90,279.8 chŏngbo of land, or 0.66 chŏngbo per dispute, a dramatic decline from the 8.73 chŏngbo of 1920-32.

Most disputes lasted no more than six months. As in the 1920-32 period, primarily either tenancy rights or issues concerning rent ignited disputes, though the proportion addressing tenancy rights or leased land increased to 80.9%, followed by rent (17.4%) and tax/public dues (1.7%). Geographical distribution followed the pattern of the earlier period, with southern commercialized areas again the foci; about 75% of the disputes erupted in six southern provinces (see Table 7.2). But unlike the earlier collective and direct disputes, the majority of 1933-39 disputes were adjudicated by regional tenant committees (26%) or courts (36%) (Chōsen sōtokufu 1940a, pp. 52-87).

For example, when landlord O Chŏngsŏp of Tongbok district of Hwasun county in South Chŏlla province did not respond to tenant Kim Chaehi's demand for rent reduction due to drought in 1935, Kim took the case to court according to the Agricultural Lands Ordinance. After a year-long litigation, Kim prevailed.[1] Most tenancy disputes in the 1930s were similar: relatively brief individual conflicts involving an average of two to three tenants and landlords or agents, centered on tenancy rights and/or rent issues, and often resolved in regional tenant committees or courts.[2]

PAST SCHOLARSHIP ON TENANCY DISPUTES IN THE 1930s

Most studies of tenant-landlord conflict in colonial Korea deal with the years 1920 to 1932. They either assume that tenancy disputes remained unchanged during the entire colonial period (Chu Ponggyu 1981; Hŏ Changman 1963; Kang Hundŏk 1981; Kim Sŏggŭn 1983; Um 1984)

TABLE 7.1
Summary of Tenancy Disputes, 1933–39

---

(1) *Total number:* 136,175

(2) *Participants:*
Tenants: 181,261
Landlords: 125,121
Agents: 16,291
Total: 322,673 (average per dispute: 2.37)

(3) *Land involved:* 90,279.8 chŏngbo
(average per dispute: 0.66 chŏngbo)

(4) *Main issue:*
Tenancy rights or leased land	80.9%
Rent	17.4%
Land tax or public dues	1.7%

(5) *Duration:*
Less than one month	63.8%
One to six months	34.9%
More than six months	1.3%

(6) *Outcome:*
Complete victory by tenant	57.5%
Partial victory by tenant	23.9%
Demand withdrawn	11.7%
Unresolved	7.0%

SOURCE: Chōsen sōtokufu (1940a): (1) pp. 8–9; (2) pp. 26–28; (3) pp. 28–29; (4) pp. 22–24; (5) pp. 34–35; and (6) pp. 36–39.

or simply acknowledge that the Tenant Arbitration Ordinance of 1932 brought change after 1933 (Cho Tonggŏl 1979). The former stance tends to attribute all colonial period disputes to tenants' poverty and exploitation by landlords. Yet even Cho Tonggŏl (1979), who recognizes that disputes changed after 1933, leaves unexplained the mechanism or reason for change. These studies all depict tenancy disputes as anticolonial, nationalist, or socialist movements by the desperate tenant class.

Asada (1973, pp. 209–17) undertakes the only detailed study of tenancy disputes between 1933 and 1939. While he correctly attributes a rapid increase in tenancy disputes since 1933 to the Tenant Arbitra-

TABLE 7.2
Geographical Distribution of Disputes, 1933-39

Province	Number of Disputes
Southern	
South Chŏlla	24,080
North Chŏlla	19,990
South Kyŏngsang	17,141
North Kyŏngsang	15,039
South Ch'ungch'ŏng	11,230
North Ch'ungch'ŏng	13,970
Central	
Kyŏnggi	6,899
Hwanghae	5,787
Kangwŏn	9,312
Northern	
South P'yŏngan	6,955
North P'yŏngan	3,713
South Hamgyŏng	2,017
North Hamgyŏng	42
Total	136,175

SOURCE: Chōsen sōtokufu (1940a, pp. 8-9). This government report also shows the number of disputes at the county level.

tion Ordinance, he discerns no change in their nature. Like most of the writers mentioned above, Asada sees colonial tenancy disputes as uniformly ideological and defensive. However, what follows shows that the 1933-39 tenancy disputes pursued the tenants' concrete economic interests; their intention was to exploit opportunities that the later colonial policy offered in order to protect their rights and restrict landlords' power. Before explaining the altered nature of their disputes, what ensues discusses the relevant socioeconomic and political situation of colonial Korea in the 1930s.

NEW COLONIAL POLICY ON AGRICULTURE AND INDUSTRY

Recovery of Agriculture and Industrial Development

The Korean rural economy, laid low by the depression of the late 1920s and early 1930s, began to pick up by 1934 when agricultural crop

TABLE 7.3
Indices of Agricultural Performance
and Chemical Fertilizer Use, 1920-45

Period	(1) Output	(2) Use of Fertilizer	(3) Labor Productivity	(4) Land Productivity
1920-24	100	100	100	100
1925-29	103	392	99	103
1930-34	111	996	106	111
1935-39	131	2,375	122	129
1940-44	114	1,783	108	114

SOURCE: Hayami et al. (1979). Columns (1), (3), and (4) table K-1a; (2) table K-4b.

prices bounced back to 90% of predepression levels (Suh 1978). Also, as Table 7.3 shows, agricultural output from 1935 to 1939 was 31% above 1920-24 levels, primarily because of augmented chemical fertilizer input. Facilitated by domestic fertilizer production in the 1930s, fertilizer use swelled more than 23-fold between the two periods, and accordingly both labor and land productivity burgeoned by 22% and 29%, respectively (Table 7.3). Such advances indicate that Korean agriculture was beginning to show solid development in the mid-1930s.[3] Although Korean agriculture really took off after the mid-1950s, by the mid-1930s it had achieved labor and land productivity comparable to that of Taiwan and (to a lesser degree) Japan (Ban 1979; Hayami and Ruttan 1979).

Furthermore, the trend toward increasing tenancy eased after 1934, despite rapid population growth, largely through migration of the rural population to Japan and Manchuria as well as to industrial areas. Migration to Japan and Manchuria was already under way in the 1920s, but during the depression it increased rapidly. As Table 7.4 shows, in 1919 less than 30,000 Koreans were living in Japan, but in 1930 almost 300,000 and in 1936 over 600,000 lived there. Korean migration to Manchuria displays a similar pattern. By the end of Japanese rule, about 3.5 million (14%) Koreans were living in Japan or Manchuria.

Both the deteriorating situation of poor peasants and labor demand in Japan and Manchuria facilitated such extensive migration. As Chapter 5 discusses, most of the rural population in the early 1930s suffered subsistence crises. One natural response was to flee to Japan or Manchuria. Stories depict hopeful migrants flooding police stations in port cities

TABLE 7.4
Number of Koreans in Manchuria and Japan, 1919-44

	Manchuria		Japan	
Year	Number	Index	Number	Index
1919	431,198	100.0	26,605	100.0
1922	515,865	119.6	59,851	225.0
1925	531,857	123.3	133,710	502.6
1928	577,052	133.8	243,328	915.0
1930	607,119	140.8	298,091	1,120.4
1936	925,531	214.6	625,678	2,371.7
1940	1,309,053	303.6	1,190,444	4,474.5
1944	1,511,570*	305.6*	1,936,843	7,278.0

*1942.
SOURCES: Gunseibu, Komonbu (Division of Advisers, Department of Defense, Manchukuo), *Manshū kyūsanhi no kenkyū* (A Study of Communist Insurgents in Manchuria), n.p. 1937, pp. 508-9. Tsuboe Senji, *Zai Nihon Chōsenjin jōkyō* (The Condition of the Koreans in Japan), Tokyo, 1965, pp. 9-10. (Both cited in tables 9 and 11 in Lee 1978.)

such as Pusan, seeking permission to enter Japan, most of them landless tenants from southern provinces (Kim Ch'ŏl [1965] 1988; Trewartha and Zelinsky 1955). Furthermore, Japan, especially after the 1931 Manchurian incident, encouraged Korean migration in order to fill its labor needs, especially in the mines.[4] As Mitchell (1967, pp. 77-78) states:

Just before the Manchurian incident of 1931, Japan had approximately 3,000,000 unemployed. The Home Ministry was being pressured to cut off Korean immigration into Japan. The Manchurian Incident so stimulated the economy that within three to four years this situation was beginning to change. From 1933 to 1936 the yearly increase in the demand for labor was double the number of new workers available. By May, 1937, there was a scarcity of labor.

In Manchuria, on the other hand, vast uncultivated areas initially attracted starvation-driven Korean peasants; but after the mid-1930s, industrialization also beckoned migrants.[5]

Also, Japanese policy toward Korean industrialization shifted in the 1930s. Previously the colonial government's main economic concern was agricultural production. When Korea became a colony in 1910, the colonial government foresaw maintaining the country as a simple agricultural colony and market for Japanese manufactured products,

TABLE 7.5
Interprovincial Migration, 1930 and 1940
(thousands)

Province	1930			1940		
	In	Out	Net	In	Out	Net
South Chŏlla	59	91	−32	47	117	−70
North Chŏlla	129	86	+43	48	131	−83
South Kyŏngsang	94	110	−16	85	95	−10
North Kyŏngsang	83	213	−130	59	198	−139
South Ch'ungch'ŏng	108	118	−10	60	163	−103
North Ch'ungch'ŏng	133	128	+5	52	138	−86
Kyŏnggi	180	177	+3	320	124	+196
Hwanghae	96	104	−8	81	116	−35
Kangwŏn	228	102	+126	158	120	+38
South P'yŏngan	90	151	−61	140	108	+32
North P'yŏngan	65	79	−14	63	73	−10
South Hamgyŏng	112	98	+14	160	125	+35
North Hamgyŏng	103	23	+80	259	16	+243

SOURCE: Trewartha and Zelinsky (1955), pp. 18, 20.

including Japanese cotton textiles. In general, only industries that promoted agriculture—such as railroads and rice mills—were allowed to develop, typifying what world-system theorists term a "core-periphery" relationship. But official impediments to Korean industrialization eased after the establishment of Manchukuo in 1932, and even more rapidly and deliberately after the Sino-Japanese War erupted in 1937 (see Woo 1991, chap. 2). While Korean industrialization by 1945 was far from complete, some sectors, such as the heavy and chemical industries, expanded rather rapidly in the 1930s (Eckert 1991). Korea became a "semi-periphery" country within the Japanese empire or the "Northeast Asian political economy" vis-à-vis newly acquired and relatively undeveloped peripheries like Manchuria and North China (Cumings 1984b).

One major impact of industrialization was increased employment opportunities for rural surplus labor. As a result, during the 1930s, northeastern industrial and mining areas (i.e., South and North Hamgyŏng and Kangwŏn provinces) as well as Kyŏnggi province (with the capital) gained population, whereas most southern agricultural areas lost to migration (see Table 7.5). Other population statistics also show that from 1935 to 1939, the urban population increased by 91%, while rural numbers increased a meager 1% (Suh 1978, p. 43). Further, from 1930 to 1940 the percentage of the labor force engaging in agriculture decreased from 78.5% to 72.7% (Kim Ch'ŏl [1965] 1988, p. 137).[6]

Extensive migration of the rural population to foreign countries as well as to urban and industrial areas substantially reduced population pressure on the remaining peasantry and mitigated increasing tenancy. Leased land as a percentage of total cultivated land increased from 50.5% in 1924 to 56.5% in 1932, but thereafter the percentage changed little, from 57.4% in 1934 to 58.0% in 1939 (Chōsen sōtokufu 1940a, p. 109). Also, while from 1927 to 1932 the number of semi-tenants and landless tenants rose 17.7%, from 1934 to 1939 it advanced only 2.9%, less than the natural population increase (Chōsen sōtokufu 1940a, p. 140). While Korean agriculture never suffered a labor shortage (except during the war years), slow rural population growth, combined with increased agricultural productivity, eased rural poverty and brightened peasants' economic prospects. As a result, most per capita indicators of living standards—rice consumption, food availability in calories, and general consumption—steadily increased after the mid-1930s (see Table 4.4). Surveys of the peasant economy in 1933 and 1938 also show that many semi-tenants and even landless tenants enjoyed a surplus income (Chōsen sōtokufu 1940b, 1940c).[7]

In short, demographic shifts and market needs improved the peasants' economic situation after the mid-1930s, but also instrumental were colonial government laws to protect tenant rights and restrict the landlords' ever-growing power.

Rural Unrest and Change in Colonial Policy

As noted previously, early colonial government policy bespoke no radical measures to alter existing land tenure practices, maintaining the traditional landlord system. Significant in terms of landlord-tenant relations was the government's guarantee of ownership for landholders— mostly landlords—but no legal protection for tenants. If tenanted land was sold, the new owner incurred no compulsion to retain existing tenants. Also, no regulations secured tenancy contracts: landlords could cancel tenancy agreements arbitrarily. As Chapter 4 discusses, the depression saw landlords frequently cancel tenancy contracts, and tenants enjoyed no legal recourse. Of course, custom sometimes constrained landlords to both honor a contract, unless the tenant refused to pay rent or mismanaged the land, and reduce rents whenever harvests fell below normal (Chōsen sōtokufu 1930, vol. 1). But if they refused to do so, as in the depression, tenants had no legal grounds for complaint. In effect, then, the economic security of tenants lay outside the realm of law.

The widespread eruption of tenancy disputes in the 1920s, however, significantly affected Japanese colonial agricultural policy. Already well aware of tenancy problems in Japan, the government greatly feared socialist influence in tenancy disputes.[8] After the mid-1920s, it began to probe tenancy relations, abandoning its long-standing policy of nonintervention in disputes. A speech by the director of the Industrial Department of the Government-General at the Industrial Engineers' Conference in May 1930 voiced the government's growing awareness of the need for appropriate legislation to regulate worsening tenant-landlord relations:

> Among the matters requiring careful attention, the most important are the improvement of the prevailing system and customs of tenancy and a wise policy of dealing with disputes between landlords and tenants. Only so can existing barriers be removed from the path of agricultural progress. *We are fortunate in that the tenancy disputes which have arisen in Korea have not assumed the grave proportions which they have reached in Japan.* Nevertheless, the authorities must not neglect to find proper ways of dealing with these difficulties. It is always possible that the situation may grow worse unless we find thorough-going solutions for the tenancy problems and *incorporate these in adequate laws and regulations.* The Government is contemplating such legislation. . . . [Quoted from Lee 1936, p. 178; emphasis added]

In 1927, the colonial government initiated a five-year plan to investigate tenancy customs, establishing the Temporary Committee on Tenancy Custom Survey (Imsi sojak chosa wiwŏnhoe) in the following year. The Committee investigated previous and existing customs with regard to types, rates, and rent; terms of contract; dispute issues; wrongdoings by agents; and more. As a result, two published volumes emerged in 1930, entitled *Chōsen no kosaku kankō* (Tenancy Customs in Korea), each containing more than one thousand pages.[9] Furthermore, the colonial government promulgated the Tenant Arbitration Ordinance (Kosaku chōteirei), 10 December 1932, and passed the Regulations for the Establishment of Owner-Farmers (Zisaku nōchi settei izi zigyō) the following year.[10] Both regulations had already been enacted in Japan in 1924 and 1926, respectively. The arbitration ordinance allowed either landlords or tenants to submit their claims to nonbinding arbitration by local representatives of the county tenancy officers (*kosakukan*).[11] It did not seek to prevent but to settle disputes, and its effectiveness is questionable. Even so, this promulgation indicates that agricultural policy shifted to favor tenants.[12] That is, the colonial government's earlier support of landlordism as a social basis for its rule began to attenuate (Chŏng T'aehŏn 1991; Pak Sŏp 1988).[13]

In April 1934 the colonial government went one step further by passing the Agricultural Lands Ordinance (Nōchirei) regulating tenancy relations, despite strong landlord resistance. It guaranteed a contract of at least three years (seven in the case of perennial crops such as ginseng and mulberry) (Article 7), allowed tenants to propose reduced or remitted rent upon crop failure (Article 16), and renewed the contract unless violated by the tenant (Article 19). It also forbade any agreements that waived tenant rights (Article 6).[14] As discussed previously, high rental rates and arbitrary contract cancellations were the main causes of tenant grievances (see Table 4.1). The new ordinance made permanent the regional tenant-committees which were created in 1933 according to the arbitration ordinance and were empowered directly, or by reference from the competent courts, to hear and arbitrate disputes.[15]

The colonial government spent 55,000 wŏn over eight years preparing this ordinance through a series of surveys and publications on tenancy relations (Yang Kyŏnja 1933). Initially proposed as the Tenancy Law (Sojak pŏb), it met fierce landlord opposition; thus in its final form it restricted landlords less severely than originally intended (Kim Chŏngsil 1934).[16] While the Agricultural Lands Ordinance was not designed to change the land tenure system fundamentally or completely resolve tenants' discontent, it provided legal recourse for complaints and to some extent mitigated the landlords' growing power (Yang Kyŏnja 1933).[17] William R. Langdon, American consul in Seoul, writing on 19 May 1934 to the secretary of state, well described its impact:

The new law has some political significance. Japanese investors, especially in the southern provinces, and the Japanese quasi-government owned organs such as the Oriental Development Company, Chosen Industrial Bank, Bank of Chosen, etc., are among the strongest group of landlords, and the new law would appear to be one of the first measures to set the interests of the mass of the Korean people above those of this group. [See note 17]

Some landlords so disliked the ordinance that they pressed for nationalization of land (Kim San 1934; Ōwa 1982). In Japan similar laws were proposed several times but never passed (Dore 1959). The shift in agricultural policy in favor of tenants largely came from Japan's concern over a deteriorating rural situation and its recognition of the difficulty of "maintaining peace and order among the people unless effective measures to weaken and reduce landlordism were taken" (see also Hong Sŏngch'an 1992; Kim Yongsŏp 1992).[18] Engaged in the Manchuria adventure of 1931 and preparing for another war, Japan undoubtedly feared that increased rural problems would hinder labor and resource mobilization.[19]

Landlords' Response to Social and Policy Change

The Korean landlord class responded to growing rural unrest and unfavorable colonial policy in two major ways, by introducing a modern farm system and by transferring capital to industry.

First, some landlords tried to rationalize their management of tenanted lands by establishing "farms" (*nongjang*) in response to rural unrest (Ch'oi Wŏngyu 1985; Pak Ch'ŏnu 1983). *Nongjang*, then widely used by Japanese landlords, made tenant-landlord relations strictly employee-employer ones based on written contracts, thus reducing grounds for disputes. As Kim Yongsŏp points out in his study of landlord Yi of Naju in South Chŏlla province: "Most landlords in this period were absentee landlords who hired agents [*saŭm*] to manage their land. . . . Yet maltreatment of tenants by agents was a major reason to provoke tenant-landlord conflict. Direct management of farms by landlords could get rid of such sources of conflict" (1992, pp. 167–68).

Farms had an organizational structure similar to modern industrial companies. For instance, according to Hong Sŏngch'an's study of landlord O Kŏn'gi of Tongbok district of Sunch'ŏn county in South Chŏlla province, landlord O's Tonggo farm had three bureaus specializing in agricultural production, marketing, and finance. Each bureau was then further divided into several departments. The farm also hired agricultural technicians to improve land productivity (see Hong Sŏngch'an 1992). No doubt this modern management of farms must have contributed to improved land and labor productivity, as discussed above (see Table 7.3).

Some landlords, instead of establishing a farm, had an agricultural trust company (*sint'ak hoesa*) manage their land. The colonial government, well aware of growing problems of the traditional landlord system, primarily because of rural unrest and agricultural depression, promulgated the Trust Business Ordinance (Chosŏn sint'agŏpnyŏng) in 1931 and established the Korea Trust Company (Chosŏn sint'ak) in the following year (see Kim Yongsŏp 1992, pp. 327–72). The Korea Trust Company established farms to manage trust lands from production to marketing. The Company usually charged 10% of the rent for its management and by 1945 managed 53,000 chŏngbo in 29 farms (Kim Yongsŏp 1992, p. 334). Like most other farms, those established by the Company hired agricultural production technicians and managers, and had a highly specialized organizational structure. The rental rate on these trust farms was generally lower than on other farms.

Landlords also shifted some or all of their capital investment from land to industry in response to the growing rural unrest and unfavorable colonial policy. No comprehensive statistics report how much capital transfer occurred because of rural unrest, but some general statistics and case studies of landlords provide a general picture.

Conventional scholarship on Korean capitalism during the colonial period emphasizes the barriers to landlord investment in industry (Cho Kijun 1973; Suh 1978). Suh (1978) argues that large landlords had little incentive to finance native industries, and landownership was the most profitable investment in colonial Korea. According to his study, the rate of return from landownership outstripped common stocks, at 7.7% versus 6.9% in 1931 and still more, at 8.0% versus 6.5% in 1937 (Suh 1978, p. 85). While barriers to Korean capitalist growth undeniably existed, to claim that landlords had little incentive to invest in industry exaggerates the case: Carter Eckert (1991) avers that such investment data for land and common stocks are misleading since the common stock figures Suh reports do not differentiate specific industries or particular companies. In 1937, for instance, the average dividend rate for commercial enterprises and for the brewing and electrical industries each outperformed the 8% Suh cites for paddy field returns (p. 52). Textile industries yielded profits as high as 19%. As Eckert argues, "many Korean landlords did continue to keep their wealth in the land, but many others ... were also attracted by the prospects of a more diversified investment portfolio" (p. 53).[20]

While Eckert's argument that Korean landlords participated in industrial development in the colonial economy is valid, he considers primarily "pulling" factors—industrial investment incentives—and does not fully take into account "pushing" factors, such as growing rural conflict and subsequent agricultural policy changes. That is, increasing tenancy disputes and unfavorable colonial government policy discouraged further land involvement and pushed landlords to seek more congenial capital investments. Kim Yongsŏp (1972) shows that landlord Kim, on Kanghwa island of Kyŏnggi province, shifted capital investment from land to industry mainly because of growing tenant unrest. He founded a linen and cotton shop in 1928 by selling all his land. Another island

TABLE 7.6
Industrial Investment for Five Landlords

Landlord	Location	Capital Investment in Industry
(1) Kim	Kanghwa island	Linen and cotton company (1928-29)
(2) Hong	Kanghwa island	Investment in a ceramic company (1933) (owned 70% of the shares) Choyang Spinning and Weaving Co. (1936)
(3) Cho	Koksŏng county	Investment in a mining company (1937)
(4) Yi	Posŏng county	Investment in stock and a cotton company (1930)
(5) Mun	Amt'ae island	Honam Bank (1920) Namhae Shipping Co. (1924) Chŏnnam Cotton Co. (1930)

SOURCES: (1) Kim Yongsŏp (1972); (2) Hong Sŏngch'an (1981); (3) Hong Sŏngch'an (1985); (4) Hong Sŏngch'an (1986); and (5) Pak Ch'ŏnu (1983).

landlord, Hong, sold land to start the Choyang spinning and weaving company in 1936. Hong Sŏngch'an (1981, p. 111) explains the main reason for such capital conversion:

Class conflict between landlords and tenants increasingly intensified. . . . Also, the growing influence of socialism [on the conflicts] greatly concerned the colonial government. Promulgation of a series of laws such as the Tenant Arbitration Ordinance . . . and the Agricultural Lands Ordinance shows that the colonial government changed its agricultural policy in favor of peasants. . . . The laws restricted the landlord class. Change in colonial policy made landlord Hong look for a new avenue for investment. In 1936, the landlord converted some land capital into industry. . . . The 1930s was a period of rapid industrialization of colonial Korea. . . . It was a logical decision for landlord Hong to found the Choyang Spinning and Weaving Company when landlordism was constrained by colonial policy and at the same time investment in industry was profitable.

Langdon, American consul in Seoul, agreed that "with the landlord's rights curbed and the tenant's rights extended [by the ordinances], no doubt land will lose some of its attractiveness as an investment, diverting capital and savings to manufacturing and other industrial lines."[21]

Table 7.6 lists five landlords who diverted part or all of their capital from land to industry in response to growing rural unrest and unfavorable colonial policy. Gragert's (1982) study of changes in land tenure in four villages shows a decline in landownership by absentee landlords and an increase by village residents (cultivators) since the mid-1930s. While he provides inadequate explanation for the trend, it could well relate to capital conversion from land to industry. This is not to claim that in the 1930s most landlord capital flowed into industry. Little question obtains that even until the end of the colonial period, most of the capital investment of landlords remained in land. But the 1930s presented significant reallocation of their assets from land to industry. This shift by previously reluctant Korean landlords was a rational response to growing agrarian conflict and unfavorable colonial policy as well as to the attractiveness of industrial investments, but it contributed to their already reduced role in village affairs.

The Nature of Tenant-Landlord Conflict, 1933-39

As socioeconomic and policy changes shifted to favor tenants, the tenancy disputes of the 1930s did not express desperation, poverty, or exploitation. There is also little indication that antagonism primarily represented anticolonial, nationalist sentiments as most previous studies have argued. Table 7.7 presents statistics on tenant-landlord conflicts by nationality. Had disputes signified *national* conflict between Japanese landlords and Korean tenants, one would expect proportionally more frequent disputes between them than ones between Korean landlords and tenants. However, from 1933 to 1936, the former constituted no more than 10% of the total (see Table 7.7), yet Japanese landlords owned almost 20% of the paddy fields. That most Japanese landlords established modern farms to avoid conflict may explain the discrepancy.[22] In short, to argue that tenancy disputes reflected anticolonial, nationalist conflict lacks substantiation.

Rather, disputes reflected the tenants' growing class consciousness and ability to exploit opportunities that favorable economic and political conditions offered. Contemporary publications well recognized this point. For instance, *Kyŏngsŏng ilbo* (*Seoul Daily*) reported on 16 January 1934:

Tenancy disputes in North Ch'ungch'ŏng province are rapidly increasing. Tenants used to take for granted exploitation by landlords, but after the promulgation of the Tenant Arbitration Ordinance of last year, tenants would no longer tolerate the previous exploitation. The recent increase of tenancy disputes is due to tenants' growing consciousness of their own interests.

TABLE 7.7
Tenancy Disputes, by Nationality, 1933-36

	1933	1934	1935	1936	1933-36
Between Japanese	12 (0.6%)	4 (0.1%)	13 (0.1%)	13 (0.1%)	42 (0.1%)
Between Koreans	1,584 (80.2%)	6,360 (84.3%)	22,810 (88.3%)	28,008 (93.4%)	58,762 (90.0%)
Between Koreans and Japanese	379 (19.2%)	1,178 (15.6%)	2,997 (11.6%)	1,948 (6.5%)	6,502 (10.0%)

SOURCE: Asada Kyoji (1973), p. 214.

A government publication also attributed the post-1933 increase to the tenants' growing realization of their need to exploit the legal measures taken by the colonial government (Chōsen sōtokufu 1940a, pp. 6-7). Asada (1973), though he characterizes these disputes as anticolonial and socialist, admits that the legal measures played a key role in provoking disputes. In September 1937, O. Gaylord Marsh, American consul general in Seoul, submitted a similar assessment:

[T]he increasing number of disputes presented to the courts for settlements indicate[s] both the effectiveness of the [tenant arbitration] ordinance and the satisfaction of tenant farmers with the decisions rendered. ... [T]hat of the 9,370 cases presented for arbitration in 1936, the complaints were in 8,984 instances tenants and in only 386 cases landlords ... apparently indicate[s] the satisfaction of tenants with the present arbitration system.[23]

This progressive nature of tenancy disputes in the 1930s is well illustrated by their outcomes.

As Table 7.1 shows, more than 80% of tenancy disputes obtained partial or complete tenant victory, far in excess of earlier times, even the early 1920s (see Chapter 4). Among disputes over leased land or tenancy rights, landlords prevailed in only 10%, retaking leased land or changing tenants. Landlords could no longer easily displace tenants or increase rental rates, previously common practice. As Table 7.8 shows, rental rates dropped from 1933 to 1938, on average in paddy fields from 48.6% to 47.8% and in dry fields from 38.9% to 37.2%.[24] While the reduction was not substantial, the very fact of a decrease is historically

TABLE 7.8
Disputes and Rental Rate Change, 1930s

	Southern*	Central*	Northern*	Total/Ave.
Disputes (1933–39)	56%	35%	9%	100%
Rental rate:				
Paddy (1933)	48.7%	48.1%	49.0%	48.6%
(1938)	47.2%	47.1%	49.1%	47.8%
Dry (1933)	31.1%	33.0%	44.6%	38.9%
(1938)	28.1%	31.4%	43.8%	37.2%

*Southern: North and South Kyŏngsang and Chŏlla provinces. Central: South and North Ch'ungch'ŏng, Kyŏnggi, Kangwŏn, and Hwanghae provinces. Northern: North and South P'yŏngan and Hamgyŏng provinces.
SOURCES: Chōsen sōtokufu (1940a, pp. 8–9; 1940b, p. 20).

important in that the mid-1930s marked the reversal of rural power structure in favor of peasants. It presaged dissolution of the Korean landlord class, which accelerated after liberation and was completed with the postwar land reforms. Still closer scrutiny of the table reveals a positive correlation between disputes and change in rental rate over the period. The southern commercialized areas, where tenancy disputes prevailed in the 1930s, enjoyed the greatest rate reduction, from 48.7 to 47.2% in paddy fields and 31.3 to 28.1% in dry fields. Northern areas, with far fewer disputes, showed a rather slight increase from 49.0 to 49.1% in paddy fields. This finding suggests that tenancy disputes abetted rental rate reduction and thus attenuated landlord power.

That tenancy disputes in the 1933–39 period did not reflect the tenants' desperation but rather a growing ability to address grievances, and that protests eroded landlord power in the countryside, are observations further supported by statistical analysis. Survey results on the peasant economy for tenant households in 1933 and 1938, and statistics on the number of disputes from 1933 to 1939, are available for 204 counties, revealing the relationships of key variables: living standard, degree of exploitation, extent of tenant protest, and change in landlord power. Income balance per tenant (the difference between income and expenses) in 1933 indicates *living standard;* 1933 paddy field rental rate proxies the degree of *exploitation;* 1933–39 dispute number depicts the extent of *tenant protest;* and the 1933–38 change in paddy field rental rates shows

TABLE 7.9
Partial Correlations Matrix ($N = 204$)

	BAL33	DISPUTE	RCHANGE
RATE33	-.06	-.08	-.46***
BAL33		.12**	.11*
DISPUTE			.10*

NOTE: Correlation coefficients are partial ones, controlling for rental type and literacy rate in 1933.
*$p < .10$. **$p < .05$. ***$p < .01$.
BAL33: 1933 income balance per capita (Chōsen sōtokufu 1940b, pp. 94-235).
RATE33: 1933 paddy field rental rates (ibid.).
DISPUTE: Number of tenancy disputes, 1933 to 1939 (Chōsen sōtokufu 1940a, pp. 9-20).
RCHANGE: Change in paddy field rental rates, 1933 to 1938 (Chōsen sōtokufu 1940b, pp. 94-235).

change in *landlord power*. Other than the number of tenancy disputes, from Chōsen sōtokufu (1940a, pp. 9-20), all data are from Chōsen sōtokufu (1940b, pp. 94-235).

The partial correlation coefficients for the four variables, all incorporating control for 1933 type of rent and literacy rate, confirm that poverty or exploitation did not cause tenancy disputes and that disputes helped weaken landlord power. First, as Table 7.9 shows, the partial correlation coefficient for the 1933-39 dispute number (DISPUTE) with 1933 rental rate (RATE33) is -.08 ($p < .15$). In contrast, that for DISPUTE with 1933 income balance (BAL33) is .12 ($p < .05$). The former implies that mere exploitation by landlords did not foment tenant protest; indeed, if anything, it was slightly dissuasive. Conversely, the latter suggests that the less exploited were more likely to mount tenancy disputes. These findings are hardly surprising since relative prosperity probably provided well-to-do tenants with the tactical leverage vis-à-vis their landlords necessary for protest action.[25] Furthermore, a positive correlation emerges between DISPUTE and 1933-38 rental rate reduction (RCHANGE)—$r = .10$ ($p < .10$). This indicates that rate reduction was in part spurred by tenant protest.

These partial correlation coefficients collectively support the proposition that tenancy disputes in the 1930s evinced the tenants' growing consciousness as well as favorable economic and policy changes, not poverty or exploitation. Further, peasant activism enjoyed modest success. To be sure, the Korean landlord class remained quite strong in the late 1930s, but tenants no longer meekly accepted its dominance in local villages, and thus its power began to wane. The fatal stroke fell in the postwar era when most Korean landlords were accused of Japanese collaboration. It is therefore no surprise that postwar peasant radicalism prevailed in areas with a colonial protest history and weak landlord power. Reduced landlord power provided a structural condition conducive to peasant radicalism, and the colonial protest legacy was crucial to the rapid and spontaneous postwar peasant organization and mobilization, as Chapter 9 will show.

CONCLUSION: CLASS AND NATION IN RURAL CONFLICT

Tenancy disputes in the 1930s differed greatly from earlier periods. In both the 1920s and 1930s they centered in southern commercialized areas around issues of rent and tenancy rights; but disputes in the 1930s resembled individual law suits, often being resolved in regional tenant committees or courts. The disputes signified Korean tenants' growing consciousness of their own interests as they exploited new colonial policy opportunities, particularly legal measures to protect tenant rights and reduce landlord power. This specification of the nature of tenancy disputes requires reappraisal of previous works that depict all from 1920 to 1939 monochromatically.

Also, tenancy disputes of the 1930s should be understood primarily as manifestations of class rather than national conflict. Although one cannot deny some nationalist motivation for the disputes, it is hard to substantiate an anticolonial, nationalist character. They instead reflect the tenants' growing class consciousness. Further, that class triumphed over nation as a source of rural conflict in the 1930s has an important implication in explaining the failure of national liberation movements. That is, the lack of a mass base for national liberation movements during the colonial period appears better explained by colonial policy that co-opted peasant concerns than by mere reference to state repression or factionalism/provincialism among movement leaders, factors the conventional scholarship stresses.

Finally, disputes not only enhanced the participants' class consciousness but also eroded the control of landed elites over rural society. The major obstacle to late Chosŏn social and political reform (see Chapter 2), strong landlordism, was reinforced in early colonial years. But tenancy disputes during the 1920s shifted colonial policy from pro-landlord to pro-peasant, undermining landlord power in rural society.

Also, the tenant protest experience was crucial in provoking postwar peasant radicalism (see Chapter 9). Thus tenant-landlord conflict in the 1920s and 1930s provided a crucial legacy for postwar social and political change. But first we need to examine peasant resistance during the last years of Japanese rule.

CHAPTER 8

Japanese Militarism and Everyday Forms of Resistance, 1940-44

While peasant resistance and protest during Japanese colonialism has received extensive study, attention is usually focused on peasant protests of the 1920s and 1930s such as tenancy disputes and red peasant union movements. Peasant resistance during the last years of colonial rule, 1940-44, is rarely explored. One obvious reason is lack of reliable data, except for a few personal stories, on peasant resistance during this period of tight Japanese military control of the Korean economy and society. Korean newspapers and publications other than those that were pro-Japanese were shut down. Overt and collective protest including tenancy disputes became illegal and no written documents cite instances. This dearth of data on peasant resistance during the war years presents a great research challenge.

Nevertheless, a picture of the form and nature of wartime resistance emerges from scattered documents and interviews with peasants who lived through the period.[1] Colonial repression led peasants to devise passive ways to resist: they hid crops from rice collection (*kongch'ul*), changed crops from rice to nonextractable crops such as wheat or barley, and expressed discontent through folk songs or by spreading anti-Japanese rumors. These passive measures, best conceptualized as "everyday forms of resistance" (Scott 1985), were crucial in preserving the peasants' spirit of resistance, which returned to more overt forms in the postwar era. Also, the nation became the main source of conflict, rather than the class conflict typical of the tenancy disputes of the 1920s and 1930s or the state-society conflict of the red peasant union protest movements. Thus examination of wartime peasant resistance not only enriches "repertoires" of peasant contention under Japanese rule, but provides a crucial link between peasant activism in the 1920s and 1930s and postwar radicalism.

JAPANESE MILITARISM AND COLONIAL KOREA

The Japanese launched the Sino-Japanese War in 1937. Four years later the Pacific War erupted, and subsequently Japan declared a national emergency in its colonies as well as in Japan. In March 1938, the Japanese Diet passed the National General Mobilization Law (Kukka ch'ong tongwŏn pŏb) in Japan, providing the military with a "blank check," and then applied the law to its colonies, including Korea (Mitchell 1967, p. 78). The law appropriated all human and material resources to serve the war effort. Also, the colonial government's relatively moderate cultural policy became highly repressive, withdrawing even basic political rights such as freedom of speech, publication, and assembly. As a result, the two main Korean newspapers, *Chosŏn ilbo* (Korea Daily) and *Tonga ilbo* (Far Eastern Daily), were closed on 10 August 1940. As Robinson maintains, "With almost any act defined as a crime against the state, from linguistic scholarship to sabotage, the prisons of the colony overflowed with tens of thousands of political prisoners" (1990, p. 325). A government source indicates that the number of political prisoners increased from 861 in 1941 to 1,142 in 1942 (Yi Chaehwa 1988).

The colonial government also tightened control of the economy, including agriculture. It issued the Rent Control Order (Sojangnyo t'ongje ryŏng) in December 1939 as part of a series of anti-inflationary measures, freezing agricultural rents at current levels and empowering local officials to order rent reductions if necessary. In 1943, the Staple Food Management Law (Singnyang kwanniryŏng] required that all rice be delivered to government warehouses, paid for by the government at officially determined prices, and milled and distributed by government agencies. Peasants exercised little freedom in agricultural production and marketing, and landlords as well were greatly constrained. For instance, Hong Sŏngch'an's study of Tonggo farm in Sunch'ŏn county of South Chŏlla province shows that in 1943, 70.5% of the farm tenants (1,123 households) delivered their rent directly to the government. This portion constituted about 70% of the farm's rent income (1992, pp. 202–3). Japan also attempted to supplement the army's food supply by extracting rice (*kongch'ul*) from Korean peasants using the police. In 1941, a total of 991,000 sŏk of rice were collected to make up for army food shortages. With establishment of the Korean Food Distributing

Company (Chosŏn singnyang yŏngdan) in 1943, rice collection intensified, such that rice collection in 1944 reached 1,384,000 sŏk, or 63.8% of total rice production (Cho Tonggŏl 1979, p. 290; Republic of Korea 1949, p. 38). In short, the colonial economy was under direct government control, and both tenants and landlords were subject to a series of "emergency" measures.[2]

Japanese war mobilization, however, was not confined to material resources. Japan waged "total war," mobilizing both "spiritual and material resources" (Barnhart 1987; Eckert 1996). Governor-General Minami himself explains the importance of "total war" as follows:

With the Great War as a turning point, the essence of modern warfare has consisted in concentrating on the maintenance of national defense by integrating the entire strength of the country. [This] is so-called total war. The main principle of total war is simply to combine these two forces, the spiritual power of the nation and the economic power of the nation. In the end, both the spiritual power of the nation and the integration of materials come down to human factors and material factors. [We] can therefore enhance the effectiveness of general mobilization here by sufficiently bringing the power of government to bear on these two factors with proper, strong and clear authority. [Quoted from Eckert 1996, pp. 15–16]

In fact, the concept of "total war" had already been formulated in the 1930s by Japanese military leaders, and the colonial government later took steps to support the idea. The Rural Revitalization Campaign, begun in 1932, and a series of legal measures to protect tenants (discussed in Chapter 7) were part of this total war preparation to mobilize human resources.

Japanese efforts to mobilize "spiritual resources" were intensified in a policy called *Naisen ittai,* which attempted to obtain ideological hegemony over the Korean people by assimilating them into Japanese culture and identity.[3] Carried out under Governor-General Minami, its goal was

the ultimate eradication of all differences between the citizens of the Japanese homeland and the population of colonial Korea.... [It] would be achieved only when Koreans had been completely stripped of their Korean cultural identity (and indeed of their very racial memory) and had become Japanese both in name and in reality, in body and in soul. Under the slogans of "Japan and Korea as one body" (*Naisen ittai*) and "harmony between Japan and Korea" (*Nissen yūwa*), Minami embarked on a breathtaking program to mobilize Koreans of all walks of life. . . . The forceful assimilation policy of Korea was only a part of the grand plan to bring all of East Asia under the benevolent blanket of Japanese rule. [Robinson 1990, pp. 315-16]

Forced assimilation was carried out by "intensive indoctrination through education and practice in the principles and rites of Japanese Shintōism and the imperial rule" (Eckert 1991, p. 237). Koreans were forced to learn only Japanese in school and assume Japanese names. In Choi Chungmoo's (1993) view, Japan attempted to "colonize consciousness" by imposing its own world view, cultural norms, and values, compelling Koreans to adopt an alien system of thought as their own and thereby disregard or disparage indigenous culture and identity. Thus the assimilation policy represented Japan's effort to establish not only political and economic but ideological dominance in the colony in Gramsci's (1971) sense.

To mobilize human resources effectively, the colonial government began to shut down Korean organizations of all types and create mass organizations to draw all Koreans into the war effort. In 1938, for instance, the government formed the Korean Federation of Youth Organizations and Local Youth Leadership Seminars to bring all students and youth under its control, and the All Korea Writers Federation to direct intellectuals. Similar associations were organized for workers and tenants.[4] In 1940 the colonial government went one step further, organizing the entire colony into 350,000 Neighborhood Patriotic Associations. Each comprised ten households as a basic unit for a variety of government war support programs such as collecting contributions, imposing labor service, maintaining local security, and rationing (Robinson 1990). As the war progressed, Korean youth were conscripted for the Japanese military (*chingbyŏng*) or for labor (*chingyong*) and girls were taken as "comfort ladies" (*chŏngsindae*)—women forced into prostitution to cater to Japanese soldiers (Lie 1992).[5] Many Koreans suffered starvation; the hardships of this period remain fresh and vivid in the minds of millions of Koreans.

As is apparent, the last years of colonialism brooked no outright or collective political/social protest. Tenancy disputes stopped after 1940, and protest movements, when extant, moved underground or to foreign countries. For instance, Korean communists worked with the Chinese Communist Party, and noncommunist resistance forces formed the Korean Restoration Army in 1940, working with the KMT (Kuomintang).[6] Harold B. Quarton, American consul general in Seoul, reported in the "Survey of Current Political Thought and Temper of the Korean People" (15 August 1942): "The measures undertaken by the Government General, the Japanese military authorities and the police in recent years have been so severe that these [Korean nationalist] organizations cannot work to any degree openly in Korea.... The headquarters of Korean nationalist movements in recent years have been in Los Angeles, California, Honolulu, Hawaii, and Shanghai, China.... The branch at Shanghai has naturally cooperated more with the Chinese Nationalist Army than any other branch" (*Records of the Department of State Relating to Internal Affairs of Korea [1940-44]*, reel 1). Although militarist colonial power rendered overt and collective protest almost impossible, Korean peasants chafed under the regime and did not succumb to its assimilation policy. They devised alternative means to express grievance and resistance.

"EVERYDAY FORMS OF RESISTANCE"

James Scott's work, *Weapons of the Weak*, provides an important theoretical framework in understanding Korean peasant resistance during the war years. He argues that most previous studies of peasant protest, including his own (1976), overemphasize the overt, direct, violent, and large-scale rural conflicts such as rebellions, uprisings, and revolutions; but they are rare and marshal only a small portion of peasants. More often peasants employ "everyday forms of resistance," or "weapons of the weak" such as "foot dragging, dissimulation, desertion, false compliance, pilfering, feigned ignorance, slander, arson, sabotage, and so on" (1985, p. xvi). While these kinds of resistance often serve individual survival, they are not trivial. Quoting Marc Bloch, Scott argues that "the patient, silent struggles stubbornly carried on by rural communities over the years would accomplish more than these *flashes in the pan* [the great insurrections]" (1985, p. 28; emphasis added).

According to Scott, everyday resistance is informal, is often covert, needs less coordination, and appears when most subordinate classes such as peasants have little prospect of improving their situation. This seemingly passive form of resistance does not reveal "false consciousness" or "mystification" as some Marxists, such as Antonio Gramsci, would argue, but represents an important dimension of peasant protest. Modifying Gramsci's (1971) concept of "hegemony," Scott argues that even when the ruling class controls economic and political realms, it never dominates ideologically. He says "neither capitalism nor feudalism has been successful in achieving the internalization of the dominant ideology by subordinate classes" (1985, p. 320). Hence, subordinate classes may submit to overt political domination by the ruling class, but remain defiant in the ideological realm, as illustrated by "everyday forms of resistance."[7]

Scott's view well captures peasant resistance in Korea during the war years. Faced with the militarist colonial regime, Korean peasants resorted to passive ways of resistance such as hiding rice, refusing to harvest crops or deliver meat, changing crops from rice to wheat and barley in order to avoid rice collection, hiding from conscription, voicing folk songs of discontent, or spreading rumors against Japanese war efforts. Resistance most commonly entailed hiding rice from collection. A woman (b. 1933) from Kangwŏn province, whose father leased clan land, recalls her family's ploy:

> Usually my father dug soil to hide rice from collection, and during the night he took needed rice from there. I remember I often went to get it since I was small enough. In my family, I was the only child (the eldest) who knew where rice was hidden, for my parents were afraid the other younger children might tell the police who even offered candy for information. In addition, when cash was needed, my father carried rice in a fertilizer container to sell on the market. In order to avoid meeting police, he usually left home in the very early morning, before dawn. I thought similar tactics of survival and resistance were widespread in my village, but nobody would tell of them even to close neighbors.[8]

Additional popular caches included a "natural fertilizer [*t'oibi*] container in the field," "room cabinets [*changnong*]," "under the floor [*maru*]," and "bunches of rice straw [*pyŏtjip*]."[9] Also, while hiding rice was mostly a noncollective strategy of survival and resistance, some evidence implies cooperation among villagers. In 1944, 70 peasant households in a village of Haenam county of South Chŏlla province successfully hid half of the total crop from rice collection (Kim Sangjo 1981). No precise statistics exist, but my own interviews with a dozen former peasants who lived through the war years clearly suggest that these forms of resistance were widespread.

The American counsel general's 1942 report on the "Survey of Current Political Thought and Temper of the Korean People" agrees:

> [D]uring the last two years the seditionary movements among the Korean population have been most in evidence in the agricultural and mountainous regions. . . . [We find] lack of cooperation of the Korean agriculturalists in the rice program. . . . [T]he Korean people generally have failed to respect the Japanese orders regarding food and commodity controls and

seem to offer *passive resistance* to these measures. This has brought about considerable disorganization, and efforts of the police, who make food collections, are especially abhorrent to the native population. The orders are merely not respected and supplies are hidden. The police have to go out to get supplies, especially in winter . . . [but] did such a poor job in the winter of 1941-42. [Emphasis added] [10]

The report claims that hiding crops was the peasants' "normal tendency" and cites similar resistance with meat:

The farmers refused to deliver meat because . . . the meat price fixed by the police was . . . cheaper than what the farmer could get for his live animal. Naturally there were few deliveries of meat to the cities during February and March, and a virtual "meat famine" prevailed.

The report concludes that "as the war progresses the Korean people are more opposed to their Japanese taskmasters" and that "the spirit [of resistance] is there." In fact, the Japanese themselves lamented the "increasing tendency among Korean peasants to hide crops and change them into nonextractable ones, and troubles with food collection officials" (Pak Kyŏngsik 1986, p. 511).

Crop conversion was another important everyday strategy of survival and resistance. For instance, peasants in Pong'an village in Kyŏnggi province shifted from rice to barley and wheat to avoid rice collection (Kim Yonggi 1980) and peasants in a village in South Kyŏngsang province changed dry fields into paddy fields to thwart Japanese orders to cultivate cotton.[11] Table 8.1 shows that from the 1930-36 period to the war years, the cultivated area devoted to rice decreased 16%, whereas that for barley and wheat increased 13%. The shift occurred despite increased rice productivity (by 14%) and decreased barley and wheat productivity (by 13%), and strong encouragement of rice cultivation by the colonial government (see Table 8.1). While fertilizer and labor shortages were perhaps responsible for reduced total agricultural production, the changes in cultivated areas suggest that peasants were avoiding rice collection, though no direct evidence confirms this.

Also, resistance to the labor draft was widespread. As mentioned above, the Japanese drafted peasants and other youth to supplement the labor shortage in industrial areas or Japan, and resistance was common. A former tenant (born in 1918) of Naju county of South Chŏlla province explained his experience as follows:

During the Pacific War, I was drafted and sent somewhere in Hamgyŏng province as a mine worker. But I fled to Ch'ŏngjin as a free worker, then to

TABLE 8.1
Cultivated Areas and Productivity (Average), 1930–44
(index in parentheses)

Period	Cultivated Areas (chŏngbo)		
	Rice	Barley and Wheat	Other Crops
1930–36	1,226,462 (100)*	1,013,194 (100)	268,137 (100)
1940–44	1,034,797 (84)	1,152,416 (113)	287,324 (107)

Period	Productivity (sŏk per chŏngbo)		
	Rice	Barley and Wheat	Other Crops
1930–36	11.68 (100)*	8.47 (100)	5.38 (100)
1940–44	13.26 (114)	7.33 (87)	4.32 (80)

*Average for 1933–36.
SOURCE: Republic of Korea (1949), p. 28.

Tanch'ŏn, and finally to Manchuria which had a labor shortage. I worked in a Japanese factory where I was treated pretty well before coming back home in April 1945.[12]

A mining company in Hokkaido lost 35.6% of its workers when they chose to "flee" between October 1939 and October 1942 (Pak Kyŏngsik 1988). A government source similarly indicates that between 1941 and 1943 more than one-third of those drafted for forced labor in Japan fled (Yi Chaehwa 1988, p. 435). Peasants also left Korea for Manchuria to avoid labor and military conscription.

Peasants also showed their discontent with the colonial regime through folk songs (*minyo*). Long an important expression of rural popular culture, folk songs conveyed Korean resistance to foreign incursion even before the Japanese accession in 1910. For instance, the Ŭibyŏng (Righteous Army) sang "Ansimga" from "Yongdam yusa" (Teachings of Yongdam) of Tonghak, which "defies and insults the Japanese as 'kae kat'ŭn waenom (dog-like Japs),' or 'kae kat'ŭn waejŏk nom (dog-like Japanese thieves)'" (Nahm 1975, p. 190).

The importance of folk songs as everyday cultural resistance was even greater during the war. As discussed above, Japan suspended Korean language instruction in schools and strictly forbade the use of Korean in public. It promoted Shintoism and Japanese martial songs and other "patriotic" songs to facilitate "spiritual" war mobilization. In contrast,

Korean songs with any hint of nationalism were outlawed. As a result, Korean writers and poets retreated to "the domain of pure poetry ... remote from politics, philosophy, and the problems of society" (Lee 1965, p. 106). Folk songs thus were an important medium to express peasant cultural resistance to Japanese hegemony. As one popular folk song of the time pleads:

Dear peasants working in paddy fields,
Please weed out the Japs from the fields
so that our crops can grow.
Dear ladies working in the dry fields,
Please weed out the Japs from the fields
so that our crops can grow.
Or the Japs will run to destroy our crops.
[Translated from Kim Sangjo 1981, pp. 355–56]

Another adjures:

Dear peasants, when you place your feet on the fields
please do it firmly.
Or the Japs will come to destroy our crops.
[Translated from Kim Sangjo 1981, p. 356]

And another:

Our good farm lands are taken away for railroads,
Our beautiful maidens become prostitutes.
[Quoted from Nahm 1975, p. 201]

Though peasants may have endured colonial political and economic dominance, they resisted in the ideological realm. Nahm's study of colonial period songs and poems reaches the conclusion: "the Korean people were far from being satisfied or happy with Japanese rule and they told and retold countless numbers of stories about the trials and tribulations of the subjugated and oppressed people" (1975, p. 227).

Korean peasants also attributed natural disasters such as drought and flooding to the Japanese war efforts. For instance, peasants in Chŏng'ŭp county of North Chŏlla province spread rumors that "the current drought is caused by the Sino-Japanese war since souls of soldiers killed in the war wander away in the air to change wind direction." Among peasants in Kyŏngju county of South Kyŏngsang province there was a rumor that "unless the war stops now, this year's crop will be less than half of the average" (Miyata 1988, p. 416). Similar rumors were widespread in other areas such as Yŏnggwang county of South Chŏlla,

Miryang county of South Kyŏngsang province, and Kaesŏng county of Hwanghae province (see Miyata 1988). Attributing natural disaster to war is of course connected with the tradition of rural popular culture that human loss or sacrifice of the innocent will lead to natural disaster. Also, peasants spread rumors like "Japan will lose the war soon," "Japan is no match to the U.S.," or "The current war has nothing to do with Korean welfare" (Miyata 1988; also my interview on June 1993). In fact, the colonial government was concerned that the growing power of such rumors (*yuŏn piŏ*) would hinder its war mobilization. As in folk songs, spreading rumors was an effective everyday means of expressing anti-Japanese sentiments when no such sentiments were allowed in print or in public speech.

Thus, as the war progressed the focus of conflict and resistance shifted from class to nation. Tenancy disputes of the 1930s were in essence class conflicts, but during the war years peasant resistance became increasingly anticolonial. Also, the fact that the Korean elite and middle class actively collaborated with Japanese war efforts further provoked despair and resentment among the peasants. As Robinson (1990, p. 320) explains:

Class conflict would have been severe enough at the end of Japanese rule, but resentments rooted in class antagonisms were heightened by this issue of collaboration and the cultural betrayal it implied. Entrepreneurs who profited in the Japanese system, landlords, and Korean policemen were obvious targets of resentment. . . . The political and cultural apostasy of such opinion leaders was psychologically damaging, particularly at a time when there seemed so little hope for a resurgence of Korean nationalism. Ultimately, this issue of collaboration caused deep wounds in Korean society that would continue to fester long after liberation.

Since landlords were a major contingent of the Korean elite who collaborated in Japanese war mobilization, peasant consciousness and resistance assumed an added dimension. Postwar peasant radicalism shows that confrontation with landlords went beyond the class antagonism of the 1920s and 1930s to include national issues. Eckert (1991, p. 251) points out:

[I]t is clear from the great spontaneous outburst of nationalist feeling and activity at the time of Liberation that the terrible trial of war and Naisen Ittai, far from destroying popular nationalist sentiment, had in fact inflamed it. In the first flush of freedom in August 1945, when Koreans all over the country were ripping down Japanese war posters and flags and smashing the windows of Japanese shops and homes, one of the first objects singled out for retribution was the local Shintō shrine, the key symbol of the hated Naisen Ittai policy. Soon thereafter the focus of anger shifted to those Koreans who had served or collaborated with the colonial regime and its policies.

This passage clearly shows the Korean peasants' increasing national consciousness, a clue to understanding postwar peasant radicalism, discussed in the next chapter.

In summary, the "passive" forms of peasant resistance mentioned above went largely unrecorded in written documents, but appear to have been widespread in the countryside. While less collective, overt, and violent than earlier forms of protest, wartime recalcitrance nonetheless sustained the spirit of resistance and impeded colonial food collection: the police simply had great difficulty finding hidden crops.[13] Passive forms of Korean peasant resistance during the war years, rather than reflecting false consciousness, were the most plausible and perhaps effective forms, given economic and political dominance by the militarist colonial power.

CONCLUSION: THE COLONIAL LEGACY
OF PEASANT PROTEST

Korean peasants resisted colonialism until it collapsed. While more passive and covert resistance figured during the war years, it kept their national consciousness and spirit of resistance alive. In Taylor's usage, the war years were a period of "abeyance . . . a holding process by which movements sustain themselves in nonreceptive political environments and provide continuity from one stage of mobilization to another" (1989, p. 761). The "latent" national and political consciousness under the militarist regime, raised through superficially passive forms of resistance, became "manifest" as political action in the liberated period. Had such consciousness not formed through colonial experience in protest and resistance, rapid and spontaneous peasant organization and mobilization in the postwar era would not have been possible. Also, the constant challenge of landlords by tenants in the 1920s and 1930s (see Chapters 4 and 7) paved the way for dissolution of the landlord class, and the 1930s red peasant union movements produced many key leaders active in the postwar era. In short, the colonial legacy of peasant activism greatly illuminates peasant radicalism and the demise of the landlord class in liberated Korea, which the next chapter explores.

CHAPTER 9

Historical Origins of Peasant Radicalism in Liberated Korea

Defeat in World War II halted Japan's 36-year-old colonial rule in Korea, unleashing Koreans' hopes and opportunities of achieving independence and building a new Korea. Within weeks, like most other postcolonial societies (see Lai et al. [1991] for Taiwan), liberated Korea fostered numerous social and political organizations intent upon forming a new social and political order. Peasants enthusiastically participated. They organized peasant unions (*nongmin chohap*) and were active in people's committees (*inmin wiwŏnhoe*), which proposed popular plans such as land reform and stripping collaborators of authority positions. In the North these organizations provided a popular basis for the new regime (Kang 1988). In the South they often functioned as de facto governments before American occupation forces arrived. As Cumings points out, these people's committees and peasant unions "marked a period of rural participation unmatched in Korean history before or since" (1981b, p. 267).

But American arrival (in the South) changed local politics. The American military government in Korea suppressed these organizations, accusing them of Soviet-backed North Korean manipulation. It restored government officials active under the Japanese, ignored such pressing demands from peasants as land reform, and reestablished the hated rice collection program. Korean peasants regarded such measures as unjust and illegitimate and thus rebelled, their actions culminating in the 1946 uprisings. The uprisings swept the South, engaged peasants, workers, and students en masse, and greatly colored subsequent social and political changes.

How could peasants form and mobilize protest organizations and subsequent uprisings? Were the 1946 uprisings "revolutionary" attempts or

Historical Origins of Peasant Radicalism in Liberated Korea 145

"traditional rebellions?" Were peasant organization and mobilization activities "manipulated" by outsiders or indigenous and "spontaneous"? Were they truly "organized" actions or simply "anomic" expressions? What explains regional variation in peasant radicalism? This chapter addresses these issues from a historical perspective that relates bases of postwar peasant radicalism to colonial experience in resistance and protest, first describing postwar Korean peasant political participation.

HOPES AND FRUSTRATIONS: DECOLONIZATION AND PEASANTS IN POLITICS

We have seen that peasant political participation through protest and resistance was not foreign to Korea's past.[1] But the scale of such participation in the liberated era and its impact on Korean society and politics were surely unprecedented. According to one report, by November 1945, less than three months after liberation, peasant unions appeared in 188 counties, 1,745 districts, and 25,288 villages with a total membership of 3,322,937 (Pak Hyesuk 1987, p. 382). Although perhaps exaggerated, such figures suggest that an average of about one person per peasant household joined the unions. Yet no national organization sponsored this union growth; peasant unions were localized, and their organizational strength and radicalism varied greatly. In fact, the national convention of peasant unions (*chŏnguk nongmin chohap yŏnmaeng kyŏlsŏng taehoe*) was held in Seoul on 8–10 December 1945, only after most peasant unions had already organized. Representatives of peasant unions at the convention depicted most as localized and spontaneous (see Kim Namsik 1974, vol. 2, pp. 128–209). Some unions were radical and attempted to dispossess Japanese and Korean landlords immediately, while others were moderate and worked to reform tenancy relations, rents, and so on (Meade 1951, p. 207). Some union members even beat and jailed landlords, former policemen, and government collaborators with the Japanese. Many unions also organized rice collection, storage, and distribution during the harvest. As Cumings indicates, "[B]y the end of 1945, peasant unions were probably stronger in terms of sheer numbers than any other organizational form in Korea" (1981b, p. 77).

Also, peasants became active in people's committees, a major political organization in liberated Korea. Immediately after liberation, nationalist and communist leaders led by Yŏ Unhyŏng organized the Committee for the Preparation of Korean Independence (Chosŏn kŏn'guk chunbi wiwŏnhoe) to preserve "peace and order" and "prepare for independence" (Cumings 1981b, chap. 3). In September, the committee was transformed into the Korean People's Republic (Chosŏn inmin konghwaguk), with people's committees (*inmin wiwŏnhoe*), or PCs, an important suborganization that dominated local politics in many parts of the country in the fall of 1945. The class composition of people's committees was eclectic (not only peasants joined but also workers and even a few landlords), but peasants predominated (An Chongch'ŏl 1990, pp. 98–99).

People's committees and peasant unions worked together, often sharing members or even offices. Most committee leaders were indigenous, with colonial period social and political experience such as in the March First independence movement, peasant protest movements, student/youth movements, and the Sin'ganhoe (An Chongch'ŏl 1990, pp. 102–5; Chŏng Haegu 1988, pp. 37–44). The fall of 1945 saw people's committees organized in every county but seven. Yet just like the unions, the committees varied greatly in organizational strength. According to Cumings (1981b), among the 123 counties considered here, 7 had no people's committee (PC), 55 had a nongoverning people's committee (NGPC), and 61 had a governing people's committee (GPC).[2] In counties without committees or with a nongoverning one, former government officials and landed elites still were powerful in local politics. For instance, in Chŏng'ŭp of North Chŏlla province and Miryang of South Kyŏngsang province it was the very strength of "landed elements" that prevented the emergence of strong GPCs (see Cumings 1981b, chap. 9, for details on committees).

In sharp contrast, in counties governed by a PC, the committee functioned as a de facto government collecting taxes and maintaining social order. For instance, a South Chŏlla province peasant union representative reported to the opening convention of the National League of Peasant Unions (Chŏn'guk nongmin chohap ch'ong yŏnmaeng; or Chŏnnong) on 8 December 1945, in Seoul, that province peasants refused the orders of district officials and obeyed only the PCs (Kim Namsik 1974, vol. 2, pp. 158–59). He also claimed that peasants controlled most police stations. An American military government official in the province agreed that "all governmental agencies became powerless," and that PCs "preserved the peace and collected necessary taxes," preventing "looting, bloodshed, and rioting" (Meade 1951, pp. 56–71). Some committees even "took a census," "assembled other vital statistics," and had armed defense units, posing a "threat to military government" (U.S. Army 1948/1988, 3:250). These portraits of local politics in liberated Korea closely approximate Charles Tilly's conception of a "revolutionary situation": "previously acquiescent members of that population find themselves confronted with strictly incompatible demands from the government and form an alternative body claiming control over . . . or . . . to *be* the government . . . , [which they] obey" (1978, p. 192).

But U.S. arrival altered local politics. Upon occupying the South in September, the American military government began to suppress these political groups, alleging Soviet-backed North Korean manipulation. It assumed that PCs had close "ties with the communists," possibly with Russians, and thus "seriously impeded political unity" (U.S. Army 1948/1988, 3:235). It declared all political organizations dissolved, including PCs. Although timing and extent of PC suppression varied by locality, some members were fired from government positions and even arrested. On 15 November 1945 in Namwŏn county of North Chŏlla province, five PC leaders were arrested, and in March 1946 the county executive of Haenam county in South Chŏlla province, a PC member, was fired by the military government. In South Kyŏngsang province, which featured "strong" and "efficient" PCs, the military government accused PCs of having a "communist background," relieved four *kunsus* [county executives] and 160 police as well as numerous other minor officials, and arrested "about three-hundred" members (U.S. Army 1948/1988, 3:250). Such suppression provoked a strong reaction from PC members: in Namwŏn, three persons were lost to police fire as over 14,000 demonstrated against the arrest of their leaders. Yet such protests were just a foretaste of coming uprisings.

While suppressing popular organizations such as PCs, the military government kept the Japanese governing framework and even restored officials who had served under the Japanese. Japanese economic agencies such as the Oriental Development Company, Chosen Food Distributing Company, Korean Import Materials Control Corporation, and Chosen Petroleum Distributing Company were revived as, respectively, the New Korea Company, Korean Commodity Company, Materials Control Corporation, and Petroleum Distributing Agency (U.S. Army 1948/1988, 3:142-43). Also, about 85% of the notorious Korean policemen in the Japanese force were retained, including those who fled from the North charged with collaboration. As Henderson points out, they had "records of brutality in arresting and torturing their fellow countrymen" (1968, p. 85), and continued to abuse their power, thanks to the Americans. A July 1946 report by Lieutenant Colonel Rankin Roberts and Captain Richard Robinson of the American military government told of widespread police abuse of power, beatings, and torture, and recommended that high-ranking police who had served under the Japanese be removed (U.S. Army 1948/1988, 3:320-25). In August,

Colonel William Maglin warned against police unpopularity, advising that they should not be "autocratic, intolerant, abusive, and repressive" and that "too much torture was still being practiced by the police" (U.S. Army 1948/1988, 3:326). The June 1946 survey on police by the Department of Public Relations (Kongbobu) shows that the main complaints against them were (1) retainment of police who served under the Japanese (18%), (2) unkindness (16%), and (3) misuse of power (13%) (*Chosŏn inminbo*, 6 July 1946).

Korean peasants, of course, regarded restoration of the colonial system and reappointment of collaborators to key positions as unjust and illegitimate. An American military government official described the general feeling at the time: "The liberators had become the oppressors, and a common popular mold was [that] the only difference between the former overlord and the present was in skin pigmentation" (Meade 1951, p. 62). By the fall of 1946, just before the October uprisings, the South alone saw 81 police stations and 23 government agencies raided.

Furthermore, the military government ignored peasant demands for land reform, adjuring delay until a new Korean government could be established. The military government insisted that land reform was a "basic question" to be settled by the Koreans themselves (Kang Jeong-koo 1988, p. 343). Instead, the military government established the New Korea Company (Sinhan kongsa; NKC) to appropriate lands formerly owned by the Japanese, and restricted rent to no more than one-third of the crops. The NKC owned 13.4% of the cultivated land in the South, and over 25% of the peasant population worked it (Yi Hyesuk 1988, p. 243).

This system disappointed many peasants who expected immediate redistribution of previously Japanese-held land. Further, the NKC angered tenants by attempting to exact rent for the second crop on double-cropped land; traditionally, even under the Japanese, rent was paid only for the main crop (*Chosŏn inminbo*, 30 May and 8 June 1946). Such second charges often elicited strong protest, as on Haŭi island in August 1946 (Meade 1951, pp. 230–32). The Central Committee of the People's Committee attributed creation of the NKC to "ignorance of the Americans of the Korean situation," and Chŏnnong urged "free distribution of land formerly owned by Japanese to poor peasants and returning migrants" (*Chosŏn inminbo*, 16 March 1946).

Again, the military government's Ordinance 9 restricted rent to no more than one-third of the crops. Although it ostensibly controlled landlord exploitation, this restriction amounted to a recognition of current practices in many parts of the country and also legitimized the existence of landlordism, signaling no immediate free land distribution (Chang Sanghwan 1985; Kang Jeong-koo 1988). Also, the regulation had no effective enforcement mechanism, and accordingly was violated by landlords in areas where their power remained strong, inciting disputes. In 1946, for instance, North Kyŏngsang province alone sponsored 1,552 tenancy disputes (Chŏng Haegu 1988, p. 81). Particularly when rice collection commenced, the tenants' living situation was little improved from the colonial period. A peasant in Kangwŏn province summarized the situation: "Since we went through the terrible years under the Japs, we have been trying to be patient with the current situation. . . . But how long should we stand this poverty?" (*Hansŏng ilbo*, 24 June 1946).

Then, in the spring of 1946, news of land reform in the North hit the South.[3] *Haebang ilbo* of 12 and 19 March reported free land distribution, and *Tongnip sinbo* of 6 and 7 August vividly described the "joy and satisfaction of North Korean peasants" with land reform. News of North Korean land reform deepened peasant discontent and escalated complaints against landlords and government policies in the South. Chŏnnong expressed peasant sentiments by urging that: (1) "land be distributed to peasants," (2) "transfer of landownership be prohibited," (3) "Japanese and national traitors' land be confiscated," and (4) "landlords' land exceeding five chŏngbo be confiscated and if they want to cultivate land themselves, the same amount of land as peasants be allowed to them" (*Chosŏn inminbo*, 16 March 1946). Yet the military government ignored such pressing popular demands, and aroused still more anger by reestablishing the hated Japanese rice collection program.

Upon arrival, the military government established a free market system for rice. Yet without the proper administrative structure regulating the market, "an orgy of speculation, hoarding, and over-consumption" ensued (Cumings 1981b, p. 204). In early 1946, the military government abandoned the unsuccessful policy and reinstated the old "rice rationing" and "rice collection" programs to "insure against wide scale starvation, malnutrition, disease and civil unrest." This ordinance (no. 45) required "all farmers and rice-owners to surrender to the proper local officials all excess rice" (U.S. Army 1948/1988, 4:51).

But peasants vividly recalled war-era collection and suspected the goals and intentions of the military government. A Pusan newspaper article relayed the popular sentiment in the words of one peasant: "Though the war has ended, they continue to collect rice. I believe that the U.S. military government is adopting the policies of Japanese imperialism" (quoted from U.S. Army 1948/1988, 4:53). Many peasants believed that rice should be collected from rich landlords and decried collection quotas and fixed rice prices. In a letter to the military government, Chŏnnong urged that "rice be thoroughly collected from landlords and rich merchants and imbalanced prices of rice compared to commodities be corrected" (*Haebang ilbo*, 20 March 1946). An editorial in *Chosŏn inminbo* (26 March 1946) argued that "fixed rice prices without controlling money circulation and inflation would reduce substantially peasants' purchasing power and thus foment discontent." The price index had already increased by more than four times within a year after liberation.

Police involvement in rice collection further exacerbated peasant discontent. Initially, when assigned rice was not turned in or rice collection officials were impeded, police were dispatched. But police often went "by themselves and collected grain on their own initiative with no idea of the quotas assigned" (U.S. Army 1948/1988, 3:316–20); in the case of poor peasants without sufficient rice, police made "their collection through seizure of cattle or other property, selling these and purchasing rice with the proceeds" (p. 365). Police not rarely beat and jailed peasants who refused to deliver rice or could not meet the quota. Peasants complained that rice was exacted "much in the same [way] as under the Japanese," but now the "treatment received was much worse." Many believed their quota unfair and that collection was controlled and manipulated by reactionary landlords and collaborators with police support. They often refused to yield rice to collection officials and police: in 1946 only 12.6% of the scheduled rice was collected (Hwang Nam-chun 1987).

The massive influx of Korean immigrants from Japan and Manchuria worsened the situation. As was discussed in Chapter 7, when Japanese rule ended, about 3.5 million, or 14%, of Koreans lived in the two countries. Upon liberation, they began to return to their home villages en masse. According to the American military government's G-2 report, as of 16 October 1945, the number of returnees from Japan amounted to 73,364. The pace of repatriation accelerated thereafter with 1,108,967 returnees from Japan and Manchuria as well as North Korea two months later. Almost 2 million Koreans were in Japan at the end of colonial rule, but only some 233,000 remained by the spring of 1946 (Trewartha and Zelinsky 1955, p. 25; see also Table 7.4). Yet returnees found "no job, no place to live, difficulty feeding themselves; the gifts they received were starvation and unemployment" (*Hansŏng ilbo*, 21 April, 24 June 1946).

Disappointed, some returned to Japan. As Trewartha and Zelinsky summarize, a "countermovement set in shortly afterward when it became apparent that Japan's employment market was superior to South Korea's; . . . 509,000 Koreans were reported in Japan in October, 1947" (1955, p. 25; see also Mitchell 1967, chap. 8). David Conde likewise concludes: "Many families had returned to Korea highly enthusiastic at the prospect of rebuilding their homeland, only to find that Japanese or Japanese collaborators remained in key positions" and "no jobs, houses or furniture were available" (*Far Eastern Survey*, 26 February 1947). *Tongnip sinbo* alleges that as of 27 August 1946, five thousand returnees secretly had gone back to Japan; 2,122 were arrested in Japanese ports and forced back to Korea. Returning migrants became a politically explosive social issue in liberated Korea.

Further, many returnees had been exposed to radical movements and leftist ideology, experiencing "social mobilization" in Karl Deutsch's parlance. As Cumings (1981b, pp. 276–77) argues:

[P]ronounced population growth in and up-rooting of peasant societies were central factors in loosening the peasants from their ties to tradition and "making them available" for social and political mobilization. The Korean peasants who were sent from their native homes to Japan, Manchuria, and northern Korea, from agrarian to industrial circumstances, returned to Korea no longer peasants and yet not quite workers. . . . [S]uch extensive population shifts were probably responsible for stimulating political consciousness in Koreans of the liberated period.

Indeed, Korean laborers in Japan frequently engaged in labor disputes; in 1939, for instance, 32 disputes with Japanese management erupted involving 4,140 Korean laborers; the number increased to 787 involving 49,532 Koreans by 1942 (Mitchell 1967, pp. 79–81). These political experiences of migrants figured in the uprisings, as is shown below.

Koreans in general and peasants in particular had much to complain about: reestablishment of the old Japanese system, delay in social (land) reform, continued abuse of police power, rice collection, rice rationing, returnee problems, and so on. Peasant discontent and grievances were already expressed in disputes with landlords, opposition to rice collection, raids on government agencies, and protest against suppression of peasant unions and PCs. But they exploded into the major uprisings of twentieth-century Korea in the fall of 1946.

THE 1946 UPRISINGS

In addition to peasant protests against landlords, police, and government officials, frequent food demonstrations disrupted the spring and summer of 1946. In February and March, for instance, 120 workers in the Songha Electric Company, 150 in the T'aeyang Garment Company, 50 in the Aeji Printing Company, and 50 in the Kyŏngsŏng Electric Company mounted food demonstrations (*Haebang ilbo*, 31 March 1946; *Chosŏn inminbo*, 28-29 March 1946). In March, about 2,000 people gathered at Seoul's city hall to protest food policy, seeking increased rice rations (*Hansŏng ilbo*, 31 March 1946). In April, several thousand also launched food protests in Seoul, shouting "Rice, Give Us Rice" (*Hansŏng ilbo*, 3 April 1946). Then, on 23 September, some 8,000 railroad workers in Pusan went on strike, demanding rice ration increases, higher wages, and housing and rice for jobless workers and returnees. Workers in other cities and industries such as printers, electrical workers, postal employees, and even students followed suit. An estimated 251,000 workers, most mobilized under Chŏnp'yŏng (National Council of Korean Labor Unions) auspices, participated in the strikes (Cumings 1981b, pp. 352-54).

The strikes escalated into uprisings after 1 October, when about 300 railroad workers in Taegu, a major central South Korean city, struck for increased rice rations.[4] The police killed a striker, and the following morning a crowd estimated at more than 1,000 marched through the city carrying the slain body and raided the city police station, capturing 50 policemen. By 6 October, 38 Taegu policemen had been killed; martial law ensued and American tanks patrolled the streets.

The sparks from Taegu set fires elsewhere, particularly in the countryside. In Yŏngch'ŏn county, near Taegu, an estimated 10,000 protesters attacked the police station, killing the county executive and many other officials and policemen who had served under the Japanese and yet were retained by the Americans. They also killed some 20 "reactionaries and evil landlords" (Cumings 1981b, p. 358). As discussed above, most Koreans deemed these former officials and collaborative landlords unjust and illegitimate. Accordingly, the major targets of attack were big landlords, police stations, local government offices, and rice collection agencies such as the New Korea Company. About 5,000 protesters seized county government control at Ŭisŏng; another 2,000 raided the Waegwan police station, killing the police chief, and wrecked the homes of 50 police and county officials. Also, 400 Hwanjung protesters overran the NKC warehouse, burning all records of rice and grain collection. The protesters were mainly local peasants, most of them affiliated with peasant unions and PCs. The Ŭisŏng police chief reported that of the nine Ŭisŏng protest leaders, five belonged to the local PC, two to the People's Party branch, one to the county peasant union, and one was an unaffiliated school teacher (Cumings 1981b, p. 358). They often wielded sticks, farm implements, and clubs as well as rifles and pistols taken from raided police stations (U.S. Army 1948/1988, 3:347–64).

Rural peasants were responsible for transforming the initially urban Taegu strike into major uprisings that swept the countryside in North Kyŏngsang province, then South Kyŏngsang, South and North Ch'ungch'ŏng, Kyŏnggi, and South and North Chŏlla provinces.[5] By the end of 1946, some 40 South Korean counties, or about 30%, had witnessed peasant uprisings. They appeared localized, with little indication of national organization behind them, except perhaps in the early stages of the Taegu protests (Chŏng Haegu 1988; Cumings 1981b). Major demands and issues stressed local problems, such as "the authority of colonial police, brutal grain collection policies, hoarding of grain by landlords and rich peasants, and the systematic suppression of the local people's committee structure" (Cumings 1981b, p. 367). Chŏng Haegu's analysis of demands in North Kyŏngsang confirms this: 38% targeted police and government officials who had served under the Japanese, and 36% the autonomous administration of PCs (1988, p. 148). Estimates suggest that 2.3 million (mostly peasants) staged the 1946 uprisings, with 1,000 protesters and 200 policemen killed, and another 30,000 protesters arrested. The uprisings were the largest and most significant protest movement by Korean peasants since the Tonghak peasant wars of 1894, and clearly showed the urgent need for social and political reform, especially land reform.

What explains such massive and violent mobilization of Korean peasants into uprisings? How were their discontent and grievances organized and mobilized into political protest movements? Were the uprisings organized actions or pathological phenomena? Were they simply engineered by communists or spontaneous and conscious political movements? What explains regional variation in radicalism? Before addressing these questions, the following section briefly discusses previous accounts of the 1946 uprisings.

PREVIOUS VIEWS OF THE 1946 UPRISINGS

Both the American and South Korean governments cited communist agitation as the source of the uprisings. The American investigation led by Major General Brown immediately after the events in Taegu identified sixteen causes, the top three being "grain policy," "insufficient distribution of food," and "methods employed by police in enforcing collection of grain" (U.S. Army 1948/1988, 3:365).[6] Yet it also insisted on the role of communists in instigating and directing the riots: "[P]lans had been carefully drawn up and only an opportunity was needed.... [R]efugees, farmers, miners, and others who were employed under the Japanese, but were now without employment, proved a fertile field for agitations." The report concluded that "the riots were Communist-inspired and directed, . . . directly fostered from North Korea, . . . [and] in no sense spontaneous" (U.S. Army 1948/1988, 3:365–71).

General Hodge similarly said the riots were caused by "those who do not reside in the South" and "the majority of people [workers, peasants, and students] were manipulated by the criminals." He also acknowledged serious food problems, but demurred: "food problems were widespread all over the world after the war.... [T]he Korean situation was not among the worst" (*Hansŏng ilbo*, 15 October 1946). The Korean national police chief Cho Pyŏngok also accused North Korean–backed communists of staging "nation-wide opposition to the military government," adding that it is "more than a riot, it is a rebellion, planned and carried out on national scale" by communists (U.S. Army 1948/1988, 3:374). The investigation by the Joint Korean-American Conference in suit accused Pak Hŏnyŏng, a South Korean communist leader, of attempting through the riots the "complete overthrow of the present government and police in favor of a radical regime" (U.S. Army 1948/1988, 3:371).

Again, these accounts of the uprisings acknowledged failure of government policies, such as grain collection and food distribution, and abuse of police power, but accused North Korean or Pak Hŏnyŏng-led communists of agitating the jobless and frustrated mass. Although some evidence suggests that the Taegu strikes on 1 October were mobilized by Chŏnp'yŏng, these investigations focus only on Taegu in early October, not on the underlying causes of the uprisings that subsequently engulfed the countryside.

Criticizing such official renditions, Gregory Henderson attributes the 1946 uprisings to the "abnormality of mass society" characterized by "anomie, chaos, unemployment, crime," and so on. Using Kornhauser's (1959) "mass society theory," Henderson depicts postwar Korea as a "mass society" with "displaced masses lacking all other forms of group life or integration." He writes that "the rushed urbanization, industrialization, and mobilization of 1937–45, plus the economic collapse, population dislocations, and lack of leadership during the first year of Liberation" combined to create a mass society and subsequent mass radicalism in postwar Korea (1968, pp. 141–47). Just as mass society theorists (Arendt 1951; Kornhauser 1959) and collective behavior theorists (Smelser 1963) understand social protest and movement, Henderson views the 1946 uprisings as "anomic violence" and "mob behavior." Although his account differs from government versions in rejecting communist inspiration, it echoes their interpretation of the uprisings as "abnormal," "pathological," and "anomic" behaviors of the "rootless" mass.

Bruce Cumings's (1981b) seminal work on the origins of the Korean war rejects both Henderson's and government explanations of the uprisings. Primarily drawing on declassified documents of the American armed forces in postwar Korea, he argues that the uprisings were not communist-agitated riots, but conscious and spontaneous efforts of local residents. Any possible North Korean influence was indirect "through the demonstration effect ... of thoroughgoing land reform and labor reform laws." Cumings claims that demands for "land and labor laws such as those in North Korea [were made] not because they were being ordered ... by leaders in the North, but because the reforms in North Korea struck responsive chords in the South" (1981b, p. 374). He emphasizes the organization and mobilization of protesters by local and spontaneous groups such as "local people's committees, *nongmin chohap, nodong chohap,* and other PC-affiliated organizations."

He also rejects Henderson's characterization of liberated Korea as a mass society and of the uprisings as anomic or pathological.[7] Instead, he argues, "far from being pathological anomalies, [they were] the predictable and logical culmination of more than a year of unheeded Korean demands for meaningful reforms, labor unions, peasant unions, and self-governing organs of power" (Cumings 1981b, p. 374). In short, for Cumings, the uprisings were not the result of communist agitation of a rootless, anomic mass, but conscious, spontaneous efforts of local residents affiliated with grass-roots organizations to redress the injustice and illegitimacy of reactionary elites and collaborators who retained power with American sanction.

Unlike other studies that seek the causes of postwar peasant radicalism, Cumings explains why radicalism varied by region. In particular, his effort to show the local and indigenous character of peasant radicalism identifies seven socioeconomic conditions conducive to peasant radicalism in 1945 and 1946 (1981b, pp. 348-49):

(1) a pattern of population loss in the 1930s or early 1940s, followed by a sharp gain after liberation; (2) land conditions in which peasants were not primarily tenants but possessed some independence and leverage within an eroded or weak landlord structure of power; (3) a long interregnum between Japanese and American rule; (4) either relative difficulty

in communications and transportation, or possession of those facilities by the [people's] committee; (5) a history of peasant radicalism; (6) a relatively differentiated occupational structure; and (7) a political complexion where, over a substantial period of time, neither Right nor Left were completely dominant, or where a dominant Left followed moderated policies.

Cumings supports his arguments with either county-level or province-level data (chap. 8) or with a "thick description" of instances (chap. 9). Although his analysis needs the theoretical and methodological honing presented below, it remains the most significant work on postwar Korean peasant radicalism.

More recently, Chŏng Haegu's (1988) analysis of the 1946 uprisings in North Kyŏngsang province points out, like Cumings, the importance of protest experience during the colonial period. Yet he avers that Cumings (1981b) overstresses both the peasants' role and the uprisings' spontaneous character. He argues further that demands went beyond local problems, becoming revolutionary (Chŏng Haegu 1988, pp. 10–12). In this sense Song (1989) agrees with Chŏng Haegu in characterizing the uprisings as an "incomplete revolution."

Despite their attempts to critically refine Cumings's explanation, these studies are descriptive and provide no rigorous test of his argument. Although what follows echoes Cumings's understanding of the 1946 uprisings not as anomic riots but as conscious efforts to redress injustice, theoretical and methodological flaws are corrected by a historical perspective that relates postwar radicalism to colonial experiences in the various forms of peasant protest the previous chapters discussed. Attention is directed less to why uprisings flared—earlier discussion in this chapter as well as other works (e.g., Chŏng Haegu 1988; Cumings 1981b) have identified the causes—and more to how some peasants could organize a strong protest organization (such as a governing people's committee; GPC) and engage in the 1946 uprisings, others organize but not participate, some not organize yet rise up, and still others do nothing. First, however, the theoretical and methodological problems in Cumings's (1981b) work will be discussed.

THEORETICAL AND METHODOLOGICAL PROBLEMS IN
THE ORIGINS OF THE KOREAN WAR

Cumings's (1981b) analysis of peasant radicalism in postwar Korea presents five methodological and theoretical problems.[8]

First, his "peasant radicalism" index suffers some conceptual and measurement flaws. Cumings assesses "2 units for a non-governing PC,

3 for a red peasant union in the 1930s, 6 for a GPC, 8 for evidence of rebellion in the autumn uprisings in 1946, and 10 for counties judged particularly rebellious" (1981b, p. 453). Besides its arbitrary and subjective scale for particular political activities (e.g., why 6 units for a GPC and 8 for occurrence of rebellion?), the existence of a red peasant union in the 1930s and a PC in 1945 should be conceptually and empirically separated from uprisings in 1946 rather than combined in one index, since how these variables interrelate is a major research issue.

Second, Cumings's claims about the impact on postwar radicalism of the peasants' social mobilization through migration require qualification. Deutsch calls social mobilization a "process in which major clusters of old social, economic, and psychological commitments are eroded or broken and people become available for new patterns of socialization and behavior. . . . [It involves] change of residence, of occupation, of social setting, of face-to-face associates, of institutions." In countries where the mass of the population stands largely outside the framework of political activity, social mobilization "brings with it an expansion of the politically relevant strata of the population" (quoted in Cumings 1981b, pp. 61–62). Koreans who migrated to Japan and Manchuria during the colonial period, Cumings alleges, experienced such mobilization. Although social mobilization indeed affected the uprisings, its contribution is complex, as shown below, primarily because many Korean peasants were already active in, *not* outside of, politics during the colonial period. The relative effect of social mobilization and colonial protest experiences on postwar radicalism must be specified.

Third, while Cumings attends to the impact of colonial protest experience on postwar radicalism, he considers only the red peasant union movement of the 1930s and leaves out the tenant protests of the 1920s and 1930s. This omission is serious, since the latter rather than the former prevailed in the South, as the previous chapters have shown. The relative contribution of these historical variables to postwar radicalism must also be assessed. Furthermore, Cumings's statistical analysis of the impact of colonial protest on postwar radicalism simply correlates the existence of the 1930s red peasant unions with the strength of postwar PCs (see pp. 287–89). Their impacts on uprisings should be examined.

Fourth, his claim that peasant radicalism prevailed where "over a substantial period of time, neither Right nor Left were completely dominant" (1981b, p. 349) has not been statistically tested. According to Cumings's definition, areas with GPCs featured such a "balance of power": if the Left ruled, PCs were quickly suppressed, while if landlords or the Right ran a committee, it quickly disappeared or merged with the conservative Korean Democratic Party. Yet his index of "peasant radicalism" contains information on PCs rather than examining the effect of their strength on uprisings.

Finally, Cumings's statistical analysis is based on simple correlations without control for other related variables. This risks spurious correlations, an example of which arises between social mobilization (measured by population change) and peasant radicalism. When other variables, such as degree of commercialization, are controlled, the significant correlation coefficient disappears. Multivariate analysis is essential to assess the precise effects of the variables Cumings considers on peasant radicalism or uprisings.

HISTORICAL ORIGINS OF THE 1946 UPRISINGS

The subsequent analysis aims primarily at tracing the historical bases of postwar peasant radicalism back to colonial experiences in protest and resistance. As previous chapters discuss, Korean peasants participated in tenancy disputes in the 1920s and 1930s, in red peasant union movements in the 1930s, and even during the war years in "everyday forms of resistance" against the colonial regime. To be sure, other studies (e.g., Chŏng Haegu 1988; Cumings 1981b) have well indicated the importance of such historical experiences in provoking postwar peasant radicalism. Yet they usually (1) simply present cases describing how leaders in postwar peasant unions and PCs were active in colonial period social and political movements (Chŏng Haegu 1988), or (2) aver that colonial experiences in protest and resistance raised "national and class consciousness," omitting any empirical verification (Kang 1988), or (3) offer sketchy correlations between the existence of 1930s red peasant unions and postwar PC strength, with some supporting examples (Cumings 1981a). This "historical experience" thesis thus begs a rigorous empirical test with sound theoretical arguments. Accordingly, what follows first briefly discusses the theoretical bases for hypothesizing an effect on postwar radicalism traceable to the Korean peasants' experience in colonial period protest and resistance. An empirical test is then described and discussed.

Experience, Consciousness, and Collective Action

In his study on the "making of the English working class," E. P. Thompson (1966), a British social historian, shows that past political experience influences future class action by developing class consciousness. According to Thompson, class or class consciousness does not exist prior to class collective action; rather, in the process of "struggling," the subordinate group discovers itself as a "class" and comes to know this discovery as "class-consciousness" (1978, p. 149). For him, class consciousness is not structurally determined by class position, as structural Marxists (e.g., Althusser) argue, or to be raised by the elite, as Leninists claim, but historically and collectively constructed through political experience such as participation in protest.[9]

Korean peasants in the first half of the twentieth century, like English workers in the late eighteenth and early nineteenth centuries, had developed class, political, and national consciousness through various forms of protest and resistance, in the former case as colonial subjects: Korean tenants engaged in "class" conflict with their landlords in the 1920s and 1930s (Chapters 4 and 7), the red peasant union protest movements in the 1930s evinced "state-society" conflict (Chapters 5 and 6), and during the war years peasants resisted colonial power in "passive" ways (Chapter 8). These various forms of political experience developed "class," "political," and "national" consciousness, respectively. Postwar organization and mobilization, as seen above, were undoubtedly affected by these experiences.[10] That the 1946 uprisings embodied combined class, political, and national conflict and struggle was no coincidence.

Yet enhanced consciousness did not automatically instigate uprisings. As recent sociological theories of social movement, especially resource mobilization theory, and previous chapters stress, even enhanced consciousness, if not effectively organized and mobilized, does not necessarily spur collective action (Gamson 1975; McCarthy and Zald 1977; Tilly 1978). In fact, peasants affiliated with local unions and PCs were the uprisings' main participants, suggesting the crucial role of those organizations. Conversely, without historically raised consciousness, such rapid and massive organization and mobilization would have been much more difficult. In sum, neither consciousness nor organization *alone* suffices for collective action, rather their combination.

While past political experience can promote future collective action by providing an important resource (i.e., enhanced consciousness), its contribution is complex. A subordinate group that perceives an unjust and oppressive situation, but feels powerless to effect change, lacks the crucial motivation for collective action. Members must share a strong sense of efficacy: "People who ordinarily consider themselves helpless come to believe that they have some capacity to alter their lot" (Piven and Cloward 1977, p. 4). As Scott's analysis of peasant rebellions in Southeast Asia during the 1930s (1976, pp. 226–27) points out:

The tangible and painful memories of repression must have a chilling effect on peasants who contemplate even minor acts of resistance. It may well be that the experience of defeat for one generation of peasants precludes another rebellion until a new generation has replaced it.... [T]he memory of repression is one of the principal explanations for the absence of resistance and revolt.

In contrast, a successful outcome not only raises protesters' consciousness but can enhance their sense of protest efficacy. As McAdam's study of American civil rights movements during the 1950s and 1960s reveals, "the successful outcome of earlier association-sponsored cases over time contributed to a growing sense of political efficacy within the black community that in turn stimulated further growth in the association" (1982, p. 111). That is, those with an increased sense of efficacy are most readily recruited to social movements. But again, while consciousness often develops into a sense of efficacy, the two are conceptually distinct: consciousness may alternatively breed resignation. Such a conceptual separation helps explain why in postwar Korea, a GPC, a main protest organization, prevailed in areas that had carried out successful tenant protests in the 1930s, as shown below.

Furthermore, a successful protest can change the political opportunity structure in favor of future action. As the previous chapter showed, successful tenant protests attenuated landlord power, which in turn helped PCs achieve a governing position. On the other hand, failed disputes left landlord power intact in local villages, presumably preventing such popular organizations from obtaining a postwar governing role. In short, successful protest can facilitate future organization by both developing a strong sense of political efficacy and creating a favorable political opportunity structure.

In summary, Korean peasant experience in protest and resistance during the colonial period most probably (1) raised class, political, and national consciousness, which, when mobilized, provided uprisings with a crucial resource, and (2) when successful, promoted a sense of protest efficacy and created a favorable political opportunity structure that facilitated protest organization, in turn increasing the likelihood of collective action.

Research Design and Measurement

Statistical analysis of county-level data collected by the Japanese colonial government (Chōsen sōtokufu) and American military intelligence (primarily compiled by Cumings 1981b) tests the "historical experience" thesis discussed above. The county (*kun*) in Korea historically has been an important administrative unit and even today remains an "economic, sociocultural, and political unit" (Kim T'aeil 1990, p. 63). Also, the red peasant unions of the 1930s and the postwar peasant unions and PCs were organized at the county level. Further, the county is a much more homogeneous unit (with an average 1945 population of 138,000 per county, excluding Seoul, the capital) than the nation-state, a unit that comparative studies of rebellions and revolutions frequently use (Russet 1964; Boswell and Dixon 1990; Walton and Ragin 1990), thus mitigating a common problem with aggregate data: spurious ecological correlation. Analysis portrays 123 counties, omitting those few without relevant data, and excludes cities, since rural uprisings are the issue (the lists in Appendix 4 include counties).

Dependent Variable. The dependent variable, *peasant uprising,* is measured by whether a county had a 1946 uprising. For reasons specified above, this simple measure is preferred to Cumings's peasant radicalism index. That index is decomposed here: a red peasant union movement is an independent variable, a PC an intervening variable. The number "1" signifies a 1946 uprising, "0" none, since no other precise county-level information such as the number of casualties is available. Of the 123 counties, 40 participated in the 1946 uprisings.

Independent Variables. Two indicators represent the degree of *colonial experience in protest:* (1) the number of tenancy disputes from 1933 to 1939 that the Japanese colonial government recorded (Chōsen sōtokufu 1940a) and (2) a "radicalism index" of red peasant unions in the 1930s, as Chapter 5 specifies.[11] These reflect two distinct dimensions, as their low correlation coefficient illustrates ($r = -.01$, n.s.). Because of its nonlinear relationship with the dependent variable, the tenancy dispute measure is converted into a logarithmic scale.[12]

The amount of paddy field rental rate reduction from 1933 to 1938 assesses the level of *success in past protest* (Chōsen sōtokufu 1940b). As Chapter 7 discusses, since rent reduction was a major dispute demand, and the disputes played a leading role in such reduction, a greater reduction of the rental rate should indicate a more successful tenant protest.[13] Since no complete information exists to assess the success of red peasant union protest, that aspect is omitted from the analysis.

Intervening Variable. Because the *people's committee* was the main protest organization mobilizing peasants for the 1946 uprisings, its strength is introduced as a variable affecting the impact of experience in dispute and red peasant union protest on uprising, and mediating the effect of dispute success on uprising.[14] As discussed above, counties fall into three categories: those with no PC ($N = 7$), those with an NGPC ($N = 55$), and those with a GPC ($N = 61$). Only in counties with a GPC could the committee function as a protest organization. Also, no significant difference obtains between the first two types in terms of other variables included in the analysis. For these reasons, the first two categories are collapsed, separating them from the third one.[15] I assign "1" for a county with a GPC, and "0" otherwise. For the data, see Cumings (1981b, appendix D).

Control Variables. Population change, a measure of social mobilization, is introduced as a control variable, since Cumings (1981b) claims its positive effect on the 1946 uprisings. Cumings's measure (i.e., 1944–46 population change) is revised here: population change in the 1930–40 period is subtracted from that in the postwar era (1944–46). Population change seems a good measure of social mobilization since the nearly 20% increase in population found within one year after liberation is well above a natural increase. See Cumings (1981b, appendix D) for the data.

Tenancy rate is controlled, because some argue that a tenancy system provokes revolutionary peasant movements (Paige 1975; Stinchcombe 1961; Zagoria 1974). According to Paige (1975), the sharecropper or tenant possesses characteristics conducive to class conflict that are similar to those of the working class: weak ties to the land, occupational homogeneity, and work group interdependence. In contrast, Alavi (1965), Wolf (1969), and Hofheinz (1977) suggest that the existence of a tenancy system indicates a strong landed power that might hinder organization and mobilization of the tenant class in forming a protest movement (see Chapter 1). The extent of the tenancy system is measured by the percentage of arable land leased in both paddy and dry fields. Cumings (1981b, appendix D) supplies tenancy rate data.

Since incursion of market relations into peasant villages is often considered responsible for peasant uprisings (Hobsbawm 1959; Migdal 1974; Scott 1976; Wolf 1969), *commercialization* of agriculture is included in the analysis. I measure the spread of capitalist market forces in Korean agriculture by the percentage of total arable land used as paddy fields, where the main commercial crop in colonial Korea, rice, was grown (from 1931 to 1940, 37.2% of rice production was exported to

TABLE 9.1
Means and Standard Deviations of Variables
(N = 123)

Variable	Mean	S.D.
DISPUTE (number of tenancy disputes, 1933–39)	864	714
RCHANGE (paddy field rental change, 1933–38)	1.7%	4.2%
POPCHG (relative population change, 1930s–40s)	15.5%	18.8%
TENANCY (tenancy rate, 1945)	68.5%	9.6%
PADDY (percentage of paddy fields, 1945)	59.3%	11.5%
LITERACY (literacy rate, 1938)	30.9%	10.8%
RUNION (index of 1930s red union movement)	.37	.72
Number of counties with a GPC	61	
Number of counties with uprisings	40	

Japan); most subsistence crops such as beans and wheat were cultivated in dry fields (Suh 1978). Again, data come from Cumings (1981b, appendix D).

Modernization theorists argue that a rising rate of *literacy* promotes political participation by breaking down traditional world views (Levy 1966), whereas Scott (1976) and Wolf (1969) claim that peasants with "entrenched precapitalist values" become rebellious. Chirot and Ragin (1975) further argue that neither rising literacy nor commercialization, but their combined effect, fosters rebellion: only where market forces are strong but peasants remain traditional is rural unrest high. The literacy rate is measured by the percentage of peasant household members who could read Korean. Since no literacy rate data are available for 1945, Japanese colonial government data for 1938 are used (Chōsen sōtokufu 1940b); I assume no significant change from 1938 to 1945.

The dichotomous nature of the dependent variable (uprising versus no uprising) violates the assumptions of ordinary least-squares regression, thus requiring that I use logistic regression analysis (Hanushek and Jackson 1977). Table 9.1 presents means and standard deviations for the variables.

Analysis Results

Table 9.2 presents the results of logit regression of the 1946 uprisings. The first model shows the logistic regression coefficients of uprising on the "structural variables" (i.e., population change, tenancy rate, per-

TABLE 9.2
Logit Coefficients Describing Predictors' Effects on Uprising
($N = 123$ counties)

	Model 1		Model 2		Model 3		Model 4	
Constant	3.668	(1.667)	.409	(2.271)	.620	(2.302)	5.610	(5.159)
DISPUTE (log)			1.387*	(.822)	1.338	(.847)	-.443	(1.347)
RCHANGE			.088*	(.055)	.062	(.057)	.054	(.060)
RUNION			.425	(.302)	.377	(.311)	.107	(.751)
POPCHG	.013	(.013)	.016	(.015)	.019	(.015)	.079***	(.030)
TENANCY	-.097***	(.032)	-.101***	(.035)	-.102***	(.036)	-.123***	(.040)
PADDY	.042*	(.023)	.030	(.026)	.023	(.027)	.019	(.072)
LITERACY	-.020	(.021)	-.023	(.022)	-.023	(.023)	-.038	(.136)
GPC					.831*	(.490)	-7.847	(4.833)
DISPUTE (log)*GPC							3.718**	(1.727)
RUNION*GPC							.472	(.846)
POPCHG*GPC							-.093***	(.034)
PADDY*LITERACY							.001	(.002)
Model chi-square	24.3***		32.4***		35.3***		49.4***	

NOTE: S.E. in parentheses.
*$p < .10$. **$p < .05$. ***$p < .01$ —all one-tailed.

centage of paddy fields, and literacy rate) without the two earlier experience measures (i.e., dispute number and the red union index) and dispute success measure. This step is needed to see whether experience and success exert effects independent of underlying conditions identified in theories of peasant protest and rebellion. Model 1 in Table 9.2 shows that tenancy rate has a highly negative effect on uprising, being statistically significant at $\alpha = .01$, and the effect of percentage of paddy fields is positive and significant at $\alpha = .10$. These findings alone seem to support the middle peasant thesis and commercialization theory: the existence of a strong landed class hindered mobilization of peasants for uprising, whereas commercialization promoted it.

Model 2 introduces three major independent variables into Model 1: dispute number, the red union index, and change in rental rate. This model shows effects of the two earlier experience measures and success measure on uprising, controlling for population change, tenancy rate, percentage of paddy fields, and literacy rate. Both of the experience measures, dispute number and the red union index, have weak positive effects on uprising; the former impact is significant at $\alpha = .10$, the latter at $\alpha = .15$. The dispute success measure, change in rental rate, also has a positive effect on uprising, being statistically significant at $\alpha = .10$. Further, model chi-square significantly improves after adding these experience and success measures; the difference in model chi-square is 8.1 ($df = 3$) and statistically significant at $\alpha = .05$. The tenancy rate effect on uprising remains highly negative in Model 2, but the commercialization effect becomes statistically nonsignificant.

To see whether the strength of a protest organization measured by the presence of a GPC mediates effects of the number and success of tenancy disputes on uprising, this factor is introduced into the second model. It was expected that the success effect would be directly mediated through the GPC, but not the dispute number or red union effect. If the relationship between dispute success and uprising were entirely mediated through the existence of a GPC, the success measure logit coefficient would reduce to nearly zero after introducing the GPC as an additional predictor variable into the second model. Also, the relationship between dispute success and the existence of a GPC should be significant, and the logit regression coefficient of GPC on uprising significantly positive. Model 3 in Table 9.2 presents the results.

Only the success effect is well mediated through the existence of a GPC. First, logit coefficients of both the dispute number and success become statistically nonsignificant at $\alpha = .10$ after introducing the organization variable (the radicalism effect nonsignificant at $\alpha = .20$). GPC,

TABLE 9.3
Logit Coefficients Describing Predictors' Effects
on Governing People's Committees
(N = 123 counties)

Constant	−3.810	(2.085)
DISPUTE (log)	.986	(.665)
RCHANGE	.157***	(.052)
RUNION	.295	(.291)
POPCHG	−.011	(.012)
TENANCY	−.023	(.029)
PADDY	.044*	(.023)
LITERACY	−.008	(.020)
Model chi-square	19.5***	

NOTE: S.E. in parentheses.
*$p < .10$. **$p < .05$. ***$p < .01$ — all one-tailed.

as expected, also shows a significant positive effect on uprising. As Table 9.3 shows, however, only the success variable's effect on GPC is positively significant ($p < .01$); that of dispute number or the red union index is not statistically significant at $\alpha = .10$. These findings suggest that only the success effect on uprising is mediated through the organization of a GPC, and the dispute-number effect (to a lesser extent the red union effect) is accounted for (not mediated) by GPC.[16] In other words, successful 1930s tenant protests helped PCs obtain a postwar governing position, which in turn increased the chance of a 1946 uprising.

Why is the dispute-number (or red union index) effect on uprising not directly mediated through the existence of a GPC? The theoretical reasoning given above holds that although protest experience raised peasant consciousness, such consciousness alone did not foment an uprising. Its contribution turned upon effective organization and mobilization. Thus an interaction effect of dispute number and the red union index with existence of a GPC should obtain; only when class and political consciousness raised through tenant protests and a red peasant union movement in the 1930s was mobilized by a GPC would it promote an uprising.

Model 4 in Table 9.2 presents the results of logistic regression of uprisings with interaction terms. The equation comprises four interaction terms: dispute number*GPC, red union index*GPC, population change*GPC, and percentage of paddy field*literacy rate.[17] First, the nonadditive model (as presented in Model 4) offers better model specification than the additive one (Model 3); the difference in model chi-square is statistically significant at $\alpha = .01$ ($\chi^2 = 14.1$, $df = 4$). Second, if we examine individual interaction terms (Model 4), of the two protest experience measures, dispute number has a statistically significant positive interaction effect with GPC on uprising (coefficient of 3.72, $p < .05$), but not the red union index. Population change also has a statistically significant interaction effect with GPC on uprising, though it is negative (coefficient of $-.093$, $p < .01$). No interaction effect obtains between percentage of paddy fields and literacy rate on uprising.

These results support the view that at least the tenancy dispute experience of the 1930s contributed to 1946 uprisings when mobilized by a protest organization, a GPC; red peasant union movement experience does not show the same result. But such an insignificant effect of red peasant union activity is not surprising, given that it, as discussed above, prevailed in the North. It is also perhaps related to the fact that red peasant union movements suffered severe colonial government repression; this chilly memory may have impeded postwar peasant organization and mobilization (see Scott 1976, pp. 226–27).

Contrary to Cumings's argument, however, population change exerts no significant effect on uprising (Table 9.2) or PC strength (Table 9.3). Yet it has a strong negative interaction effect with GPC on uprising (Model 4 in Table 9.2): the negative interaction indicates that the effect of population change is weaker for counties with a GPC than for those without. Specifically, examination of the POPCHG coefficients for separate subsamples of counties with and without a GPC shows that the effect of population change is positive and significant for counties without a GPC, but is negative and nonsignificant for counties with a GPC (this can also be seen by deviating the interaction coefficient from the POPCHG coefficient in Model 4 in Table 9.2). Why is this so?

A basic assumption of social mobilization theory is that social mobilization can influence the political behavior of people *"who live in areas in which the mass of population are largely excluded from political participation,"* by bringing with it "an expansion of the politically relevant strata of the population" (Deutsch 1961, p. 499; emphasis added). In fact, peasants in counties with a GPC in 1945 had been much more active in politics in the 1930s than those in counties without a GPC. For instance, counties with a GPC averaged 960 tenancy disputes per county from 1933 to 1939, whereas counties without one averaged 770 disputes; the difference is statistically significant ($t = 1.48$, $p < .10$). Similarly the difference in the radicalism index of red peasant union movement of the 1930s between counties with and without a GPC is statistically significant at $\alpha = .10$ ($t = 1.43$). It thus seems plausible that in counties without a GPC where peasants had relatively little colonial period political experience, returning migrants who had experienced "social mobilization" provided a "politically relevant" stratum for the uprisings. In this sense, a significant effect of social mobilization (measured by relative population change) only in counties without a GPC (Model 4 in Table 9.2 shows a logistic regression coefficient of .079 [$p < .01$] for counties without a GPC [i.e., GPC = 0]) makes sense.[18]

Also, the insignificant effect of population change on PC strength suggests that one should not overemphasize the role of returning migrants in postwar politics. Although there is some evidence that the influx of returning persons provided new recruits, statistical analysis shows that it did not help PCs obtain a governing position. Cumings, combining PC strength with the occurrence of uprising to create an index of peasant radicalism, cannot separate the effect of population change on each. This also recommends my dependent variable measure over Cumings's.

Other features of the findings relate to previous studies. First, tenancy rate consistently exerts a highly negative effect on uprising, statistically significant in both additive and nonadditive models (see Table 9.2). This contradicts the class conflict model prediction that a tenancy system is more likely to provoke revolutionary movements (Paige 1975; Stinchcombe 1961), and instead supports the middle peasant thesis (Alavi 1965; Wolf 1969—see Chapter 1). Given that in Korea the tenancy rate was high in areas with big landlords who controlled a substantial amount of land, a high rate probably indicates a strong landed class. One can suppose that in such areas the landed class could hinder the organization and mobilization of peasants for uprisings (Cumings 1981b).

Yet the persistence of a highly negative effect of tenancy rate on uprising cannot merely be attributed to strong landed power. For, if so, it should have wielded a similarly significant negative effect on PC strength. That is, existence of a strong landed class should have hindered PCs from obtaining a governing position; although negative, its effect is not statistically significant (see Table 9.3). The highly negative effect of tenancy rate on uprising but not on PC strength suggests that the effect on uprising may simply indicate regional differences between Kyŏngsang and Chŏlla provinces. Tenancy was historically much higher in the latter than in the former, and because the 1946 uprisings started in Taegu (North Kyŏngsang), they spread much more rapidly in North Kyŏngsang areas than in Chŏlla (to South Chŏlla in late October

TABLE 9.4
Comparison between Kyŏngsang and Chŏlla Provinces

Province	Uprising Started	Tenancy Rate	Percent of Counties with Uprisings
North Kyŏngsang ($N = 22$)	Early October	57.9%	82%
South Kyŏngsang ($N = 17$)	Mid-October	61.8	35
South Chŏlla ($N = 20$)	Late October	72.2	30
North Chŏlla ($N = 13$)	Mid-December	81.1	15
Average for the South	($N = 123$)	68.5	33

NOTE: N indicates number of counties analyzed.

and North Chŏlla only in mid-December), especially when we confine analysis to 1946.

To examine this possibility of a "differential spread effect," I compare the extent of uprising participation and tenancy rate among Kyŏngsang and Chŏlla (both North and South) provinces. As Table 9.4 shows, as uprisings spread from North Kyŏngsang in early October to South Kyŏngsang in mid-October, to South Chŏlla in late October, and finally to North Chŏlla province in mid-December, participation substantially declined (from 82% to 35% to 30% to 15%). The decreasing uprising participation perhaps then coincidentally joined with an increasing tenancy rate to produce a highly negative correlation between the two (see Table 9.4). Although we cannot determine precisely whether the persistently strong negative effect of tenancy rate on uprising is due to the existence of a strong landed class or simply reflects a differential spread effect, the findings presented above suggest that perhaps both factors are valid.

Finally, we see no significant effect of commercialization or literacy rate on uprising, nor any interaction effect between the two (see Table 9.2). This result is not unexpected, since penetration of market forces into the villages was not a major issue in the 1946 peasant uprisings. If the uprisings had been a response to market forces that undermined peasant interests, we would expect a significant commercialization effect. They were instead political protests against the military government, the local government officials who had also served during Japanese rule, and the collaborative local elites such as landlords.

That the commercialization measure had no direct significant effect on uprising, however, should not be interpreted as invalidating the commercialization thesis altogether. Commercialization had a significant positive effect on uprising in Model 1 before introducing protest experience measures (see Table 9.2) and also a significant effect on the strength of PCs (Table 9.3), and thus had an indirect effect on uprising through a GPC. How do we explain this?

First, the disappearance of a significant commercialization effect on uprising in the second model in Table 9.2 seems due to its high correlation with tenancy dispute number ($r = .37$). Although no causal claim can be made about the effect of commercialization on tenancy disputes, since the former was a postwar measure and the latter a prewar one, if we assume that the percentage of paddy fields reflects the extent of commercialization in the prewar period, especially the 1930s (which I think is quite true), we can state that commercialization was related to tenant activism. In fact, as discussed in Chapters 4 and 7, commercialization was highly responsible for the tenancy disputes of the 1920s and 1930s. Accordingly, the tenancy dispute number perhaps mediates the commercialization effect.

Also, the indirect effect of commercialization on uprising through a GPC suggests that its effect on peasant activism is more complex than argued in previous theories of peasant protest and rebellion, most of which target the disruptive (Scott 1976; Wolf 1969) or opportunistic (Popkin 1979) effect of commercialization on the peasant economy. Yet in Korean uprisings, as shown above, market forces were not a major issue. Nevertheless, they may have influenced uprisings by altering the rural occupational structure, especially after they became a major factor in the rural economy and society (in Korea, market mechanisms were in full force in the 1920s and 1930s). In other words, perhaps commercialization increased differentiation among peasants in such a way as to "break their ties to tradition and to longstanding work patterns and make them available for new forms of activity, including political participation" (Cumings 1981b, p. 347). In fact, Cumings's (1981b) analysis of 15 counties with relevant data shows a significant positive relationship between PC strength and a more differentiated occupational distribution. That is, PCs were strong in counties with "a low percentage in agriculture and high percentage in skilled and unskilled occupations, students and professionals, and school graduates" (p. 348). Also, of the 14 counties (which excludes Puk Cheju, with no data available), the

7 with high occupational differentiation showed more commercialization than the 7 with low differentiation (64% of land in paddy fields versus 52%). This suggests that commercialization contributed to uprisings by producing a differentiated occupational structure that facilitated the emergence of strong political organizations like GPCs in postwar Korea.

CONCLUSIONS

First, peasant radicalism in liberated Korea did not materialize overnight or without presage. It was not simply a result of agitation by communists as official accounts alleged, or by returnees from Japan and Manchuria with radical ideas as Cumings argues. Nor did Japanese defeat in the Second World War simply provoke radicalism. Instead, it emerged from peasants' long development of both consciousness and a sense of efficacy through participation in colonial protest and resistance, particularly tenancy disputes. While destruction of colonial power no doubt provided structural conditions for the uprisings (e.g., Skocpol 1979), that Korean peasants could have been mobilized into uprisings in the same way *without* such political experience is doubtful. These experienced peasants provided a most important resource for the uprisings: a potentially mobilizible body of participants. On the other hand, where peasants had little political experience, migrants who returned to home villages after experiencing social mobilization abroad were another potential source of recruits.

Yet experience in red peasant union movements during the 1930s does not appear to have had the same effect. While one cannot deny the role of some key leaders of colonial-period red union movements in postwar activism, at the aggregate level red union experience did not prove as crucial a resource as tenancy dispute experience. This insignificance seems to result primarily from the fact that the movements prevailed in the North. Although beyond the scope of this chapter, it is highly plausible that experience in red peasant union movements had a greater effect on postwar radicalism in the North, and some studies indeed substantiate this theory (Lee 1978). But chilling memories of repression of red peasant union activity by the Japanese colonial government could also have impeded postwar organization and mobilization of peasants.

Such varying effects of different colonial protest experiences compel the rethinking of studies that link postwar peasant activism to colonial protest experiences without specifying the *kind* of experience. As mentioned above, most research has linked postwar activism to red union experience, using case studies (An Chongch'ŏl 1990; Chŏng Haegu

1988; Cumings 1981b), without considering tenant protest experience or mounting any rigorous empirical test. The statistical analysis of colonial and postwar peasant activism advanced here clearly shows that dispute experience was more crucial to the occurrence of the 1946 uprisings.

Second, the significant effect of the GPC on uprisings belies Henderson's (1968) characterization of the uprisings as pathological, anomic phenomena. It instead supports Cumings's (1981b) argument that most participants were not a "rootless mass" but affiliated with local organizations such as PCs: the contribution of peasant protest experience to uprisings turned upon the mobilization of local PCs. That is, where PCs obtained a governing position in 1945, uprisings in 1946 were more likely. Findings also show that success of tenant protest in the 1930s helped postwar PCs gain a governing position, and only in such counties did PCs function as a protest organization able to mobilize members for uprisings. This discredits official government accusations of Soviet-backed North Korean agitation.

Third, we need to understand peasant radicalism as depending not only on the characteristics and situation of the peasantry but just as much on those of the upper class (see Chapter 1). Even if peasants feel exploited and are highly politicized, a powerful landlord class can prevent peasant consciousness from translating into actual protest. Findings show that a peasant uprising was more likely to flare in areas with weak landlord power (measured by a low tenancy rate). The mighty power of the Korean landlord class began to wane after the mid-1930s, as Chapter 7 discusses. When colonialism ended, many landlords, once powerful rural elites, were tainted as collaborators with the Japanese and lost legitimacy in their villages. The general weakening power of the landlord class was conducive to peasant uprisings. But where landlords managed to retain power, peasant radicalism was weak and developed slowly.

Fourth, while the foregoing analysis focuses on uprisings in the countryside, the role of workers, students, and intellectuals should not be discounted. They not only started the uprisings in October 1946, but often provided PC leadership in rural areas. That peasants' protest *experience* (either tenancy disputes or red peasant union movements) had no significant effect on the existence of a GPC but needed to be mobilized for uprising by the PC suggests that a substantial part of PC leadership presumably came from other than the peasantry, as holds for most other peasant uprisings and revolutions (Migdal 1974; Wolf 1969). Unfortunately, lack of relevant data precluded including such leadership information in the analysis, but some indirect evidence seems to support the contention.

As shown above, the significant effect of the commercialization measure can be interpreted as indicating that market forces associated with the growth of cities and trade affect the social organization of traditional agricultural communities so as to cut peasants' traditional ties to the rural landed elite and render them available for political mobilization (Paige 1975). In other words, increased commercialization throughout the colonial period produced a more differentiated occupational structure that included workers, students, and intellectuals who would play a key role in protest organization.

Finally, the structuralist approach to peasant politics (e.g., Skocpol 1979) needs to be reconsidered. Analysis here clearly shows that the uprisings did not just "come" as Skocpol would argue, but were "made" through human initiative. Although such radicalism might well not have erupted in Korea without Japanese defeat, equally or more likely would it not have appeared without peasant action. This recommends a research approach that combines structuralist with voluntarist views of peasant protest, as Chapter 1 elaborates.

Conclusion

Toward Reform and Revolution

Korean peasant activism in the first half of the twentieth century has greatly influenced society and politics in the second. In the North, postwar peasant activism provided a crucial basis for social revolution by way of sweeping land reform: the exploitative rural class structure, including the tenancy system, was completely abolished and land was freely given to actual cultivators (Cumings 1981b; Kang 1988; Lee 1976). The 1946 land reform confiscated 95% of the land under tenancy without compensation; in consequence, 70% of all farm households benefited from land redistribution. While land reform gave only "permanent ownership" of land to peasants, rather than "private ownership," the major principle underlying the reform was "land to the tiller," and farm collectivization did not begin until after the Korean War (Lee 1976). The reform also eliminated the "private agricultural labor market" and nationalized "commodity and credit markets" that had functioned to reinforce capitalist and exploitative relations in agricultural production (Kang 1988).

Although Soviet forces contributed to North Korean land reform by eliminating the possibility of any counterrevolutionary campaign by an alliance of Korean landlords and former colonial forces, there is no evidence that they intervened directly in the initiation and formulation of the land reform (Kang 1988, p. 386). Contrary to Lee Chong-sik's claim that "peasants with retarded consciousness [were] skeptical of the land reform" and did not initiate it, in fact "loathed it" (1963, pp. 68–69), popular response was favorable. According to Washburn's observation, "meetings were held at which Korean peasants . . . expressed their warm thanks to the Provisional People's Committee for enacting the law. . . . [T]he PPC received 30,000 letters of thanks in the first month after the law had been enacted" (1947, p. 156). Within two years after the reform, peasant membership in the Korean Workers' Party tripled, from 105,000 in July 1946 to 374,000 in March 1948—an indication of peasant approval of the reform (Ha 1971, p. 147). Stories of "joy and satisfaction of North Korean peasants with land reform" filled South Korean newspapers—both radical and conservative—and struck a responsive chord in the South, further deepening peasant discontent with delayed reform there.

To be sure, trained cadres were dispatched from the central government into each village to carry out land reform, but peasants (especially those with little or no land) were the major mobilizing force. As in China, "poor peasants were relied on, middle peasants were cultivated, rich peasants were isolated, and landlord control was broken" (Cumings 1981b, p. 412). In fact, fearing this, many rich peasants and landlords fled south even before the land reform began in the North. According to Washburn, "after these landowners had gone, the landless peasants in a number of places seized the discarded fields and divided them among themselves" (1947, p. 156). Kang Jeong-Koo makes a similar point: "ad hoc revolutionary land reform preceded in civil society and the de facto state merely finalized and finished [it]" (1988, p. 514). As Powelson and Stock (1987) stress, peasants joined in land reform's popular support as active "reform-makers," achieving it "by leverage"; and the reform law of 1946 served only to "legalize the existing situation in the name of the PPC" (Washburn 1947, p. 156). In short, postwar North Korea inaugurated "what most Koreans and many Western observers thought would be the inevitable result of the end of Japanese rule—a thoroughgoing revolution," and peasant colonial and postwar activism provided its social basis (Cumings 1981b, p. 382).

In the South, in contrast, social revolution aborted (Cumings 1981b; Song 1989). Landlord power remained stronger, and American occupational forces reestablished the colonial system by restoring to key positions Koreans who had collaborated with the Japanese. Popular protests and demonstrations against such injustice and illegitimacy, culminating in the 1946 uprisings, were crushed by reactionary forces under the auspices of the American military government. Undoubtedly the "chilly memory" of such repression has strongly contributed to peasants' subsequent political conservatism. Nevertheless, peasant radicalism in postwar South Korea achieved "liberal" land reform—liberal in the sense that land was redistributed to cultivators without eliminating capitalist relations in agricultural production, unlike "revolutionary" land reform in the North (Kang 1988). The American military government and

Korean government could no longer ignore the pressing demand for land reform, and landlord resistance failed to prevent its enactment. When colonial rule was over, big landlords, 3% of the rural population, controlled 60% of the land, while a remaining 80% of the rural population were landless tenants or semi-tenants with little land. But by 1957, after land reform, 88% of the rural population were full owner-cultivators. The ancient tenancy system was simply replaced by owner cultivation.

Although land reform in the South was less complete than in the North, and "never enriched the peasantry" or "overflowed the state tax coffers," it still created far more equitable income and land distribution, redirected capital away from land speculation to manufacturing, uprooted a class that had not proved itself progressive, and brought political stability in the countryside, thus clearing the way for strong centralized state power in the postreform era (Amsden 1989). In short, land reform provided the structural preconditions for rapid and successful industrialization and economic growth after the 1960s.

While postwar peasant radicalism was largely responsible for reform in the South and somewhat for revolution in the North, it did not materialize without precursors or simply as a result of Japanese defeat in the Second World War. Nor did peasant radicalism erupt merely because of social mobilization in the form of agitation created by Koreans forced to leave for Japan and Manchuria during the colonial period who now returned to their home villages after liberation with new radical ideas such as socialism. Nor was it the "anomic" or "pathological" expression of a "rootless mass," or a Russian-backed North Korean communist plot. Peasant radicalism in liberated Korea had much deeper historical origins: Peasant activity in politics through the various forms of colonial-era protest and resistance provided the basis of postwar radicalism. In particular, the tenant protests of the 1920s and 1930s, the red peasant union protest movements of the 1930s, and the "everyday forms of resistance" in the war years represent distinctive types of peasant protest and resistance during the colonial period; these experiences raised class, political, and national consciousness, respectively, among the participants, a crucial resource for postwar radicalism. When successful, such experiences instilled a sense of protest efficacy and changed the political opportunity structure in favor of future action—that is, postwar radicalism.

Although Japanese defeat undoubtedly provided a structural precondition for such postwar activism, the removal of Japanese oppression did not automatically lead to peasant radicalism. On the contrary, landlords, though tainted by their collaboration with the Japanese, still exercised strong influence over local politics in many parts of the country. Without enhanced consciousness and a sense of efficacy through colonial experience in protest and resistance, rapid grass-roots postwar political movements would not have been possible. Postwar radicalism primarily built upon such colonial experiences; statistical analysis shows that the tenant protest experience of the 1930s figured more prominently in the South. In other words, reform and revolution, contrary to the structuralist argument (e.g., Skocpol 1979), did not just *come;* they were *made* by peasant action based on a historical process that raised consciousness through protest and resistance.

In explaining various forms and motives of colonial-era peasant protest and resistance, the approach adopted in the foregoing chapters rejects the currently dominant "pauperization-revolution" thesis. That thesis claims that Japanese colonialism produced structural conditions conducive to revolution: exploitation and pauperization of the peasantry and subsequent polarization of rural class structure into big, parasitic landlords and poor, landless tenants. By oversimplifying the effects of colonial rule and rural class structure, this view exaggerates the potential for revolution. It also sees diverse forms of peasant protest and resistance as minor variations on either nationalist or communist movements. Leadership problems or colonial repression purportedly prevented the success of protest movements.

The perspective adopted in this book considers the logic and rationality of peasant protest and resistance by looking at the actual socioeconomic situation of peasants. Especially observed are the varying effects of colonialism and commercialization on different rural class strata, resulting in different forms and motives of protest and resistance. Contrary to the conventional view, colonialism and agricultural commercialization in the early years did not polarize, but greatly diversified, rural class structure. This realization better explains the reformist nature of tenant protest movements of the early 1920s. For instance, the economic boom of the late 1910s, along with a moderate colonial policy after the March First independence movement of 1919, provided structurally favorable conditions for tenancy disputes, in which relatively well-to-do tenants and semi-tenants sought to improve their terms of trade with landlords. Such efforts engendered offensive, well-organized, reformist, and successful tenant protests. Demands were hardly revolutionary. They were rooted in concrete economic issues such as rent reduction and secure tenancy tenure. Reformist demands did not proceed from "false consciousness" or "conservative character," but from the tenants' perception of how best to defend and promote their socioeconomic interests.

During the depression years, however, landlords usurped leverage in local villages. As rural society became more polarized and impoverished, tenant disputes grew much more defensive, often as a matter of survival. Small landlords especially tried to supplement reduced income by resuming cultivation or by changing tenants. Faced with the threat or the actuality of eviction from leased land by these landlords, tenants tried to defend their subsistence rights through disputes. They, like Scott's (1976) peasant, frequently used the right to subsist and the benevolent role of the landlord to justify their protest. But they usually were unsuccessful, and thus either left their villages for Japan or Manchuria, or accepted unfavorable terms such as higher rent. Scott's moral economy model that depicts defensive struggles of poor peasants suffering subsistence crises aptly describes depression-era tenant-landlord conflicts.

Despite frequent defeat, tenant protest movements of the 1920s and early 1930s greatly altered state policy. Unlike the conventional view of the colonial state, which assumes perpetual support of the landed class at the expense of the rural subordinate class, the colonial policy of the 1930s changed in favor of the tenant class. Concerned with growing rural unrest and a deteriorating rural economy and society, the colonial state promulgated a series of tenant regulations to check the escalating power of the landlord class. In particular, the Tenant Arbitration Ordinance of 1932 and the Agricultural Lands Ordinance of 1934 increased state involvement in rural affairs at the expense of landlord influence in local villages. A rapid increase in successful tenancy disputes reflects this policy shift and the tenants' efforts to exploit the opportunities it offered. Although one cannot deny some possible nationalist motivation behind these disputes, they mainly reflect a growing class consciousness among tenants.

This interpretation of tenancy disputes echoes Popkin's articulation of peasant protest movements as rational "forward-looking efforts." Also, that class triumphed over nation as a source of rural conflict in the 1930s has an important sociological implication in explaining the failure of colonial-era national liberation movements. To be sure, colonial state repression and factionalism/provincialism among movement leaders, as the conventional scholarship stresses, may have been crucial; but the lack of a mass base for the movements seems better explained by a colonial policy that co-opted peasant concerns.

Finally, a series of government regulations and subsequent increases in tenant protest induced some Korean landlords to divert capital from land to industry. Such conversions further reduced their role in village affairs and thus facilitated the demise of Korean landlord power. Thus

Conclusion: Toward Reform and Revolution   179

colonial-era agrarian class conflict in the form of tenancy disputes offers a historical basis for the destruction of the once powerful Korean landed aristocracy—a destruction completed with postwar land reforms.

In addition to class friction between tenants and landlords, the 1930s witnessed the red peasant union movement, a new form of peasant protest, herein conceptualized as "state-society" conflict. Unlike tenancy disputes, red peasant union protest movements prevailed in the northeast peninsular region and directly confronted local governments to contest tax increases or interference in village affairs. They grew increasingly radical and often violent. Contrary to class-conflict model predictions, however, this radicalism predominated not where high tenancy rates prevailed, but in areas with a high percentage of owner-cultivators, primarily because small owner-cultivators were most seriously affected by the depression and also had tactical leverage to engage in radical protest. Also, the remote, mountainous areas of the Northeast offered the kind of terrain favorable to radical protest, fitting well Eric Wolf's (1969) "middle peasants" model. But faced with efficient and repressive colonial police, radical red peasant activity began to fade in 1932 and had almost disappeared by the late 1930s. Lacking Vietnam's jungles or China's Yenan base, it could not develop into guerrilla warfare. Nevertheless, many red peasant union leaders came to play a major role in the grass-roots organization and mobilization of the peasants in the postwar era.

During the war years, militarist colonial rule prohibited direct and collective protest. To mobilize both "spiritual" and "material" resources for the "total war" they sought, the Japanese tightened control of Korean society with repressive policies and pursued Korean assimilation into Japanese culture and thought. Faced with this fascist colonial regime, Korean peasants resorted to "passive" yet quite effective forms of resistance such as hiding crops from government collection, changing from rice to nonextractable crops, expressing their discontent through folk songs, and spreading anti-Japanese rumors. These forms of protest, following Scott (1985), are best conceptualized as "everyday forms of resistance." Although such resistance did not end colonial rule, it impeded Japanese war mobilization efforts and contributed to the spirit of resistance manifested in postwar activism.

These diverse forms and motives of colonial-era peasant protest and resistance show that their conventional interpretation as mainly nationalist or communist movements is an oversimplification. Class, nation, and the state constituted the main sources of domination and conflict, and the relative importance of each element varied among the different forms of peasant activism. The foregoing chapters show that the tenancy disputes of the 1920s and 1930s were largely instances of class conflict, whereas the red peasant union movements of the 1930s were closer to state-society conflicts. Yet in the wartime "passive" resistance what figured most prominently was the concept of nation as a source of conflict, and the 1946 uprisings revealed the combined character of the three elements. One must recognize the multiple sources of domination and conflict in Korean rural society. Also, the divergence in motives and interests behind peasant protest and resistance further suggests that debating whether peasants were moral or rational, whether the nature of protests was defensive or offensive, or whether the character of protests was revolutionary or reformist is not appropriate. Again, peasant protests were diverse and complex in nature, varying with different rural strata and historical conditions, and thus requiring the integrated view advocated in Chapter 1.

Finally, the sociohistorical perspective herein proposed relates peasant protest to rural socioeconomic structure and the peasants' own perception of social change. This sharply contrasts with the conventional emphasis on the ideological nature of peasant protest, focused on the revolutionary elite or the politics of revolution. This conventional, essentially elitist view traces peasant protest to national or communist influence, ignoring the role of common people in making their own history. While these leaders presumably provided organizational skills or helped articulate peasant interests through nationalism or communism, this contribution must be explained from the peasants' perspective. Unless the ideas of leaders make sense to peasants on their own terms, peasants will not rise up in protest. Accordingly, Korea from the 1920s to the 1940s witnessed not so much a Korean nationalist or communist peasant movement as a Korean *peasants'* peasant movement.

APPENDIX 1

Main Activities of Red Peasant Unions*

South Chŏlla
(1) Kwangyang: tenancy disputes (Apr 1924), night schools, nonong yŏnhaphoe, ch'ŏngnyŏnhoe, nodonghoe.
(1) Sunch'ŏn: tenancy disputes (Sep 1923, Feb 1925), nongmin chohap undong (Oct 1931), night schools, nononghoe, nongminhoe, ch'ŏngnyŏnhoe.
(1) Kangjin: related to Kwangju student protests (Jan 1930).
(1) Haenam: tenancy disputes in Haman nongjang (Apr 1934).
(1) Kwangju: tenancy disputes (May 1923, May 1924), nodong chohap—communist movements (May 1936), sojagin yŏnhaphoe.
(1) Naju: nongmin chohap undong (Dec 1926), night schools, nononghoe, and ch'ŏngnyŏnhoe.
(1) Changsŏng: nongmin chohap undong (Feb 1928), night schools, nodong chohap, ch'ŏngnyŏnhoe.
(2) Yŏsu: nongminhoe—protest against railroad construction (July 1929), night schools, nondonghoe, ch'ŏngnyŏnhoe.
(1) Muan: tenancy disputes (islands).
(2) Cheju island: nongmin chohap—communist movements (Dec 1934, Jan 1935, Feb 1937), night schools, 13 prosecuted (Apr 1937).

North Chŏlla
(1) Okku: tenancy disputes (Nov 1926, Dec 1927), nongmin chohap undong (Mar 1928), sojak chohap, ch'ŏngnyŏnhoe.
(1) Chongŭp: night schools, nodong chohap, ch'ŏngnyŏnhoe.
(1) Puan: tenancy disputes (Dec 1934), communist movements by nodong chohap (Apr 1934).

*The main sources for information are *Chosŏn ilbo* and *Chosŏn ilbo hang'il kisa saegin, 1920-40* [Index of Reports on Anti-Japanese Activities in the *Korean Daily*] (1986), supplemented by Japanese court documents such as *Shisō ihō*, *Shisō geppō*, "Chŏngp'yŏng nōmin kumiai kenkyo gaikyō" (1931), "Chŏngp'yŏng nōmin kumiai jiken hanketsu" (1933), "Tanch'ŏn nōmin kumiai kyōgikai jiken" (1933), and "Sekishoku Yŏnghŭng nōmin kumiaiin bōdō jiken" (1934). The number in parentheses before each county is a radicalism scale of the corresponding red peasant union: (1) mere existence of a red peasant union; (2) evidence of protest; (3) protest with violence; (4) particularly rebellious unions. Where information on red peasant unions was not available, other activities in that county such as tenancy disputes or previous organizations are listed instead for reference.

182 Appendix 1. Main Activities of Red Peasant Unions

South Kyŏngsang
(3) Yangsan: tenancy disputes (Apr 1931), nongmin chohap—300 members attacked the police office March 1932, 200 arrested, 1 killed.
(1) Kimhae: tenancy disputes (Oct 1925), mongmin chohap—communist movements (Jan 1937–Feb 1938), night schools.
(2) Haman: tenancy disputes (Oct 1925), nongmin chohap—tenancy disputes (Aug 1931), suri chohap, water tax, assn. fee (Jan 1930–May 1935).
(1) Ŭiryŏng: tenancy disputes (July 1931), nongmin undong (Dec 1931)—both led by nongmin chohap.
(1) Chinju: tenancy disputes (Dec 1923), night schools, nongmin undong led by the union (Feb 1933).
(1) Ch'angwŏn: nongmin undong led by the union (May 1933), ch'ŏngnyŏnhoe.
(1) Kosŏng: suri chohap; water tax, assn. fee (Dec 1924), ch'ŏngnyŏnhoe.
(2) Ulsan: tenancy disputes (Dec 1923), suri chohap; water tax, assn. fee (July 1930, Mar 1931), nodong undong (Jan 1930).
(1) Samch'ŏnp'o: nongmin undong (Sept 1931–Feb 1933), tenancy disputes (July 1931).
(1) T'ongnyŏng: nongmin chohap, nongmin undong (Oct 1931).

North Kyŏngsang
(1) Ponghwa: ch'ŏngnyŏnhoe, ch'ŏngnyŏn tongmaeng.
(1) Yŏngju: Yŏngju nongmin chohap nongmin undong (Apr 1929).
(1) Kŭmch'ŏn: Kŭmch'ŏn secret society, communist movements (Jan 1928).
(1) Andong: tenancy disputes, ch'ongnyŏnhoe.
(1) Waegwan: night schools, underground movements (Apr 1927).
(1) Ŭisŏng: student movements.
(1) Kyŏngju: nongmin chohap: communist movements (June, Aug 1935, May 1936).
(1) Yech'ŏn: tenancy disputes (Mar 1926), nongmin undong (Sep 1936).

South Ch'ungch'ŏng
None.

North Ch'ungch'ŏng
(2) Yŏngdong: tenancy disputes (Dec 1926), nongmin chohap—30 arrested (Mar 1932).

Kyŏnggi
(1) Suwŏn: nodong chohap, ch'ŏngnyŏn tongmaeng, Suwŏn nongmin high school related to communist movements (Oct 1935).
(1) P'yŏngt'aek: nodong ch'ŏngnyŏnhoe.
(2) Yangp'yŏng: nongmin chohap protest against forest tax—6 prosecuted (Dec 1931).

Hwanghae
(1) Chaeryŏng: tenancy disputes (1924), ch'ŏngnyŏnhoe—related to communist movements (Dec 1926).

Kangwŏn
(3) Yang'yang: 300 members of nongmin chohap arrested and 35 prosecuted (Dec 1932); related to night schools and underground movement.

(3) Samch'ŏk: 30 members of nongmin chohap arrested and 14 prosecuted (Dec 1931), attacked a district office (kŭndŏk myŏn) in protest of local tax (Puyŏk).

(3) Kangnŭng: tenancy disputes (June 1927); 15 members of nongmin chohap prosecuted (Mar 1933); sannim chohap, ch'ŏngnyŏnhoe.

(3) Uljin: the first red peasant union in Kangwŏn; raising peasant consciousness by night schools and publishing newsletter; more than 100 union members arrested and 15 prosecuted.

(2) Kosŏng: torch protest on the arrest of union members (Nov 1931).

South P'yŏngan
(1) Anju: Kidok ch'ŏngnyŏnhoe, nongminsa, suri chohap.
(2) Kangsŏ: suri chohap: water tax, assn. fees (Dec 1925, Jan 1926, May 1927).
(1) Yonggang: no specifics.
(1) Kaech'ŏn: nongmin chohap; related to communist movements (June 1935).

North P'yŏngan
(3) Yongch'ŏn: tenancy disputes and protest against suri chohap (Jan 1925, Jan 1929, Apr 1930); 200 union members arrested and 20 prosecuted.

(1) Sinŭiju: tenancy disputes (Dec 1927), nodong chohap; related to communist movements (Oct 1931)/sobi chohap; mulsan changnyŏ undong (Feb 1923).

South Hamgyŏng
(4) Chŏngp'yŏng: protest against police interference with night schools and raid on union office: 1 member killed and 150 arrested (July 1930).

(4) Hongwŏn: attacked county office, house of county executive, and the rich, protest against interference in night schools and tax increase: 1 member wounded and 500 arrested (Dec 1930).

(3) Kowŏn: tenancy disputes with Oriental Development Co. [ODC] (Nov 1930), nongmin undong by nongmin chohap (Sep 1931), involving 2,000 peasants, suri chohap—water tax, assn. fee, etc.

(4) Yŏnghŭng: attacked the rich and district office, protest against police interference in night schools, also demand for reform in tenancy system: 3 killed, more than 300 arrested (Oct 1931).

(3) Hamhŭng: tenancy disputes with ODC (Feb 1926), nongmin undong by the union (Jan 1928); suri chohap—water tax, assn. fee (Nov 1927).

184 *Appendix 1. Main Activities of Red Peasant Unions*

(4) Tanch'ŏn: attacked county, district, and police offices, protest against forest policy: 16 killed, 26 wounded, and 400 arrested; lasted 7 months (July 1930).
(3) Pukch'ŏng: 17 prosecuted and 2 Japanese policemen accused of killing 2 members by torture (July 1933), nodong chohap.
(3) Munch'ŏn: protest against interference in night schools; 61 prosecuted (Nov 1931–May 1939); published *chumŏk* (fist); financed the union with communal work; organized 14 branches.
(3) Hamju: 350 night schools closed by the police 1931–33; protest against the closure: 46 prosecuted.
(1) Kapsan: night schools; nodong chohap; ch'ŏngnyŏn tongmaeng.
(2) Iwŏn: nongmin undong led by the union (Nov 1930–Feb 1931): 20 arrested (Feb 1932).
(3) Tŏgwŏn: ch'ŏngnyŏn yŏnmaeng; 20 night schools; protest, with 7 prosecuted (Nov 1933).
(1) Wŏnsan: workers' strikes.
(3) Anbyŏn: 20 arrested (Nov 1934); suri chohap; ch'ŏngnyŏn yŏnmaeng.
(1) P'ungsan: tenancy disputes (May 1924); related to communist movements (Nov 1934).

North Hamgyŏng
(4) Myŏngch'ŏn: tax protest (Feb 1935): 213 arrested, 42 prosecuted; the last red peasant union.
(1) Kilju: ch'ŏngnyŏn tongmaeng—related to communist movement (Nov 1928).
(4) Sŏngjin: organized more than 2,000 peasants; 14 branches in 7 districts; night schools and publications; after dissolving Sin'ganhoe; demands for destruction of debt documents and rent reduction; protest against interference in night schools; 300 arrested (2 die in prison) (Apr 1931–Apr 1939).
(1) Ŏdaejin: fertilizer industry; strikes (Oct 1931).
(2) Onsŏng: night schools; underground movement (Aug 1931); suri chohap—water tax, assn. fee (Nov 1927).
(1) Hoeryŏng: nodong undong led by nodong chohap (Nov 1931).
(3) Kyŏngsŏng: student movement (May 1932): 22 prosecuted.

APPENDIX 2

Peasant Radicalism Index in Relation to Number of Red Peasant Unions and Socioeconomic, Demographic, and Religious Variables

Province	Radicalism Index	Number of Red Unions
(1) South Chŏlla	12	10
(2) North Chŏlla	3	3
(3) South Kyŏngsang	14	10
(4) North Kyŏngsang	8	8
(5) South Ch'ungch'ŏng	0	0
(6) North Ch'ungch'ŏng	2	1
(7) Kyŏnggi	4	3
(8) Hwanghae	1	1
(9) Kangwŏn	14	5
(10) South P'yŏngan	5	4
(11) North P'yŏngan	4	2
(12) South Hamgyŏng	42	15
(13) North Hamgyŏng	16	7
Average	9.6	5.3

	(1) Peasant Households in Spring Poverty (%)	(2) Wage Laborers (%)	(3) Tenants (%)	(4) Owner-cultivators (%)
(1)	56.4	47.0	53.2	18.9
(2)	62.2	48.1	73.8	4.4
(3)	46.5	39.7	53.7	13.4
(4)	42.1	29.7	48.2	17.3
(5)	69.7	50.7	67.7	7.2
(6)	57.5	38.2	62.0	10.7
(7)	54.3	41.7	67.7	6.2
(8)	46.5	27.6	58.1	13.5
(9)	45.9	32.8	39.8	20.7
(10)	36.6	24.4	45.6	18.8

Appendix 2. Peasant Radicalism Index

	(1) Peasant Households in Spring Poverty (%)	(2) Wage Laborers (%)	(3) Tenants (%)	(4) Owner-cultivators (%)
(11)	28.6	22.3	49.8	18.7
(12)	38.1	33.2	26.1	32.0
(13)	20.5	24.5	16.7	52.1
Average	46.5	35.4	51.0	18.0

	(5) Returnees from Manchuria (No.)	(6) Students in Japan (No.)	(7) Tenancy Disputes (No.)	(8) Participants in Ten. Disputes (No.)
(1)	6	276	451	5,303
(2)	13	94	1,667	5,081
(3)	52	307	464	5,135
(4)	79	210	87	5,523
(5)	9	93	692	4,553
(6)	4	57	69	678
(7)	38	247	204	3,340
(8)	24	98	43	3,633
(9)	31	46	12	594
(10)	165	234	3	102
(11)	583	161	13	4,307
(12)	612	176	1	9
(13)	189	88	—	—
Average	139	161	285	2,943

	(9) Labor Disputes (No.)	(10) Participants in Lab. Disputes (No.)	(11) Clan Villages (No.)	(12) Mutual Aid Associations (%)
(1)	23	2,352	238	35
(2)	48	6,407	92	17
(3)	54	6,437	135	65
(4)	39	3,189	246	75
(5)	35	2,484	131	20
(6)	8	482	134	70
(7)	181	11,661	235	38
(8)	20	2,435	143	51
(9)	27	1,706	79	81
(10)	72	6,683	112	63
(11)	25	1,525	48	72
(12)	81	7,750	63	81
(13)	38	3,347	29	90
Average	50	4,343	130	58

Appendix 2. Peasant Radicalism Index

	(13) Population Change (%)	(14) Population Density	(15) Literacy Rate (%)	(16) Christians (No.)	(17) Ch'ŏndogyo (No.)
(1)	6.5	167.9	20.91	16,070	10,618
(2)	3.5	176.3	22.28	22,920	6,277
(3)	-3.5	173.6	19.59	20,220	48,428
(4)	7.2	127.3	17.83	37,516	46,150
(5)	13.1	170.7	22.61	10,623	2,562
(6)	3.4	121.4	19.58	9,857	2,331
(7)	.4	168.4	32.47	46,027	10,975
(8)	1.2	91.1	25.38	36,444	1,098
(9)	12.5	56.6	20.41	15,297	746
(10)	10.6	89.2	31.18	51,344	3,903
(11)	4.8	54.9	27.13	56,316	1,302
(12)	9.8	49.4	24.16	13,944	2,800
(13)	11.9	36.6	27.37	8,683	4,671
Average	6.3	114.1	23.92	26,559	10,914

SOURCES: See Table 5.2.

APPENDIX 3

Leadership Characteristics in Selected Red Peasant Unions

(1) Chŏngp'yŏng Peasant Union, South Hamgyŏng Province
   67 prosecuted 14 June 1931
   41 convicted 14 December 1933
   Average age: 25.8
   Occupation: peasant (33), reporter (2), teacher (3), clerk (1), unemployed (2)
   Education: at least ordinary school (11), unknown (30)
   Origin: Chŏngp'yŏng county (41)
   Foreign experience: Yi Tongsŏn, Hwang Sŏnghwan, Chu Tugi (Japan); Han Pongjŏk (Japan and Manchuria)

(2) Munch'ŏn Peasant Union, South Hamgyŏng Province
   (a) 32 prosecuted 26 June 1933
      8 convicted 11 March 1935
      Average age: 27.8
      Occupation: unemployed (5), worker (2), fisherman (1)
      Education: at least ordinary school (5), unknown (3)
      Origin: Munch'ŏn county (2), unknown (2), other county (4)
      Foreign experience: Im Minho (Manchuria), Ko Kyŏngin (Japan), Han Tonghyŏk (Russia)
   (b) 33 prosecuted 2 November 1934
      11 convicted 22 April 1935
      Average age: 24.4
      Occupation: peasant (11)
      Education: at least ordinary school (11)
      Origin: Munch'ŏn county (11)
      Foreign experience: none

(3) Uljin Peasant Union, Kangwŏn Province
   50 prosecuted 29 November 1934
   14 convicted 12 July 1935
   Average age: 28.8
   Occupation: peasant (12), rice miller (1), worker (1)

Origin: Uljin county (14)
Education: at least ordinary school or classic education (14)
Foreign experience: Yi Ujŏng, Yun Tuhyŏn, Chu Chinhwang,
  Chŏn Yŏngkyŏng (Manchuria)

(4) Yŏnghŭng Peasant Union, South Hamgyŏng Province
  (a) 217 prosecuted 20 April 1932-23 August 1933
      20 convicted 12 July 1934
      Average age: 26
      Occupation: peasant (16), teacher (1), worker (1), unemployed (2)
      Education: at least ordinary school or classic education (13),
        unknown (7)
      Origin: Yŏnghŭng county (13), unknown (7)
      Foreign experience: Ch'ae Such'ŏl, Kim Kilgu (Japan);
        Kim Kyŏnghwan (Manchuria)
  (b) 39 prosecuted 27 July 1934
      15 convicted 10 June 1935
      Average age: 26
      Occupation: peasant (13), worker (2)
      Education: at least ordinary school (2), unknown (13)
      Origin: Yŏnghŭng county (13), unknown (1), other county (1)
      Foreign experience: Kim Hŏnsik (Japan)

(5) Pukch'ŏng Peasant Union, South Hamgyŏng Province
    93 prosecuted 17 December 1933
    21 convicted 28 January 1935
    Average age: 24.3
    Occupation: peasant (12), teacher (3), student (3), unemployed (3)
    Education: at least ordinary school (8), unknown (13)
    Origin: Pukch'ŏng county (20), unknown (1)
    Foreign experience: Chu Chinyŏng (Manchuria)

(6) Kangnŭng Peasant Union, Kangwŏn Province
    100 prosecuted 10 May 1934
    15 convicted 17 July 1935
    Average age: 28.1
    Occupation: peasant (5), worker (5), teacher (1), reporter (2),
      unemployed (2)
    Education: at least ordinary school (7), unknown (8)
    Origin: Kangnŭng county (5), unknown (10)
    Foreign experience: Yi Chinil, Chŏng Tongwŏn, O P'ildŭk, O Yunpong,
      Yi Yunkwang (China); Hong kwangjung (Manchuria); Yi Kangmyŏng
      (Japan and China)

190 *Appendix 3. Leadership Characteristics*

(7) Yangp'yŏng Peasant Union, Kyŏnggi Province
    6 convicted 8 August 1935
    Average age: 25.3
    Occupation: peasant (1), reporter (2), rice miller (1), district official (1), unemployed (1)
    Education: at least ordinary school (6)
    Origin: Yangp'yŏng county (4), other county (2)
    Foreign experience: Sim Sŭngmun (Japan)

(8) Myŏngch'ŏn Peasant Union, North Hamgyŏng Province
    578 prosecuted February 1936
    Age: younger than 21 (132), 21–25 (312), 26–30 (113), 31–35 (20), older than 35 (1)
    Occupation: peasant (534), worker (10), fisherman (24), unemployed (10)
    Education: at least ordinary school (94), classic education (328), uneducated (43), self-educated (113)

(9) Kyŏngsŏng Peasant Union, North Hamgyŏng Province
    72 prosecuted 16 June 1934
    23 convicted 16 June 1936
    Average age: 28.6
    Occupation: peasant (16), merchant (2), worker (3), clerk (1), unemployed (1)
    Education: at least ordinary school (3), classic education (1), unknown (19)
    Origin: Kyŏngsŏng county (23)
    Foreign experience: Kim Kyunam (Manchuria), Chŏng Ch'angsŏp (Japan)

(10) Tanch'ŏn Peasant Union, South Hamgyŏng Province
    71 convicted 6 October 1933
    Average age: 27.4
    Occupation: peasant (64), reporter (3), worker (1), unemployed (3)
    Education: at least ordinary school (6), classic education (1), unknown (64)
    Origin: Tanch'ŏn county (71)
    Foreign experience: Kim Chaegyu (Russia); Kang Tuik, Kim P'yŏng (Manchuria)

SOURCES: (1) *Shisō geppō* 3(10): 13–24; (2) *Shisō ihō* 3 (1935): 10–47; (3) *Shisō ihō* 4 (1935): 9–20; (4) *Shisō geppō* 4(5): 14–44 and *Shisō ihō* 4 (1935): 22–54; (5) *Shisō ihō* 2 (1935): 46–57; (6) *Shisō ihō* 4 (1935): 20–32; (7) *Shisō ihō* 4 (1935): 54–96; (8) Kim Chŏngsuk (1958): 29; (9) *Shisō ihō* 5 (1935): 163–77; (10) *Shisō geppō* 3(8): 11–35.

APPENDIX 4

List of Counties Analyzed
(N=123)*

North Chŏlla
Chin'an, Kŭmsan, Muju, Changsu, Imsil, Namwŏn, Sunch'ang, Chŏng'ŭp, Koch'ang, Puan, Kimje, Okku, Iksan.

South Chŏlla
Kwangsan, Tamyang, Koksŏng, Kurye, Kwangyang, Yŏsu, Sunch'ŏn, Kohŭng, Posŏng, Hwasun, Changhŭng, Kangjin, Haenam, Yong'am, Muan, Naju, Hamp'yŏng, Changsŏng, Wando, Chindo.

North Kyŏngsang
Talsŏng, Kunwi, Ŭisŏng, Andong, Ch'ŏngsong, Yŏngyang, Yŏngdok, Yŏng'il, Kyŏngju, Yŏngch'ŏn, Kyŏngsan, Ch'ŏngdo, Koryŏng, Sŏngju, Ch'ilgok, Kŭmch'ŏn, Sŏnsan, Sangju, Mun'gyŏng, Yech'ŏn, Yŏngju, Ponghwa.

South Kyŏngsang
Ŭiryŏng, Haman, Ch'angnyŏng, Miryang, Yangsan, Ulsan, Tongnae, Kimhae, T'ongyŏng, Kosŏng, Sach'ŏn, Namhae, Hadong, Sanch'ŏng, Hamyang, Kŏch'ang, Hyŏpch'ŏn.

Kyŏnggi
Koyang, Yangju, P'och'ŏn, Kap'yŏng, Yangp'yŏng, Yŏju, Ich'ŏn, Yong'in, Ansŏng, P'yŏngt'aek, Suwŏn, Sihŭng, Puch'ŏn, Kimp'o, Kanghwa, P'aju, Changdan, Kaep'ung.

North Ch'ungch'ŏng
Ch'ŏngju, Poŭn, Okch'ŏn, Yŏngdong, Chinch'ŏn, Koesan, Ŭmsŏng, Ch'ungju, Chech'ŏn, Tanyang.

*Province in italics.

Appendix 4. List of Counties Analyzed

South Ch'ungch'ŏng
Taedŏk, Yŏn'gi, Kongju, Nonsan, Puyŏ, Sŏch'ŏn, Poryŏng, Ch'ŏngyang, Hongsong, Yesan, Sŏsan, Tangjin, Asan, Ch'ŏnan.

Kangwŏn
Kangnŭng, Samch'ŏk, Uljin, Chŏngsŏn, P'yŏngch'ang, Yŏngwŏl, Wŏnju, Hoengsŏng, Hongch'ŏn.

Notes

INTRODUCTION

1. For discussion of comparative national income distribution data, see Mason et al. (1980, chap. 12).

2. Some argue that land reform failed economically because new smallholders could not supply critical materials, such as commercial fertilizers and improved seeds, formerly provided by landlords (Cho 1964; Rhee 1980). Although land reform caused temporary dislocations in agricultural production, high productivity ensued once peasants were provided with capital, fertilizer, and other supplies (see Ban et al. 1980 and Lee 1979).

3. Perry (1980) and Marks (1984) practice such a sociohistorical approach.

CH. 1. EXPLAINING PEASANT PROTEST

1. The moral economy versus political economy debate is discussed in articles published in a special issue of the *Journal of Asian Studies* (1983), vol. 42 (4). For a review of the debate in the Japanese context, see Bowen (1988). Cumings (1981a) and Roeder (1984) deal with the same issue.

2. Paige's *Agrarian Revolution,* for instance, does not present a general theory of peasant protest, but a typology.

3. This macro-micro issue is not new in sociology (see Weber 1968), and has recently reemerged with vigor. For a variety of debates, see Alexander et al. (1987), Elster (1985), and Taylor (1988).

CH. 2. SOCIAL CHANGE AND LAND TENURE
IN TRADITIONAL KOREA

1. For the origins of private ownership in Korea, see Palais (1982–83), who traces its existence back to the late Sylla dynasty (tenth century).

2. The Chosŏn dynasty society comprised three main status groups: the *yangban,* the commoners, and the lowborn. The first inherited upper status and

prestige from their forebears, usually land and wealth and the opportunities for education and public office. Commoners were free men with virtually no privileges and all the burdens of taxation; the vast majority were peasants, who either owned small plots of land, tenant-farmed the land of others, or worked as agricultural laborers. The lowborn consisted mostly of slaves, but also entertainers, shamans, and outcast groups. See Palais (1975, pp. 6-9).

3. Sudō Yoshiyuki (1937) estimates the figure at 1.5 million out of a total population of 4 to 5 million in the mid-fifteenth century. While this may be plausible, it is unsubstantiated. Shikata Hiroshi's (1937) well-known study of the Taegu population registers reports that slaves constituted about 37% of the population in 1690. Sommerville's (1974) study of the Ulsan district shows a slave population of 26.5% in 1729.

4. For a compelling critique of this demographic explanation of the rise of Western capitalism, see Brenner (1976). Brenner sees the relative class strength of peasants and landlords as a key variable in explaining the rise of the West. Studies on the rise of the West are too voluminous to be cited here, but for a concise review, see Lachmann (1989).

5. Michell calculates this by multiplying the number of households by 7.95, "based on the assumption that, on the average, the number of households were underestimated by 50 percent, and about 23 percent of the members of recorded households escaped the hojŏk [register]" (1981, p. 74).

6. Citing evidence from *T'aejong sillok, Sejong sillok,* and *Mongmin simsŏ,* Hŏ Chongho estimates that in early Chosŏn the average landowner cultivated about 5 kyŏl, but by the reign of King Sejong, only about 1-2 kyŏl, and then less than 50 pu by the eighteenth century (1965, pp. 70-71). Also, for the complex nature of measuring kyŏl, see Appendix 1, "Yi Dynasty Measurements," in Susan Shin (1973).

7. In addition to population pressure, the custom of dividing the inherited patrimony among legitimate sons was perhaps responsible for decreased average landholding size.

8. For instance, the landlord Yun family in Haenam county of South Chŏlla province owned 483 slaves in 1760, but merely 24 in 1888. See Ch'oi Wŏngyu (1985).

9. For a discussion on the similar development in Tokugawa Japan, see Smith (1959), especially pp. 87-107.

10. Traditionally, merchants held lower status than peasants.

11. I thank Professor Kimura Mitsuhiko for providing me with the original data to construct Figures 2.1 and 2.2.

12. Note that such integration was slow and gradual. Carter Eckert properly observes, "Korea's economy was not transformed overnight. The country's main ports were wedged open and developed by Japan and the other powers only slowly and in piecemeal fashion. . . . It was also not until the 1890s that manufacturing in Japan began to replace agriculture in relative importance and

increased the need both for export markets and for rice to feed a growing industrial work force" (1991, pp. 9–10).

13. Philip Huang's study of modern China's peasant economy well points out that "commercialization is not always driven by capitalist enterprise. . . . [It] could as well be driven mainly by population pressure, by peasants marketing for survival more than capitalist profit" (1991, p. 629; also see Huang 1985 and 1990). For a critique of Huang's view of China's peasant economy, see Myers (1991).

14. The commercialization index increased to 97.4% for the landlord class and to 71.7% for semi-tenants by 1936 (Chang Siwŏn 1980, p. 115).

15. Between 1898 and 1910, Mokp'o export volume increased more than fivefold. See Kim Yongsŏp (1992, p. 144).

16. For a full summary of the debates, see *Yŏksa kwahak* 1964(4) and 1965(6).

17. For similar critiques of theories of capitalism (e.g., Immanuel Wallerstein's [1979] world-system theory) that deem it a market relation rather than mode of production, see Brenner (1977) and Wolf (1982, chap. 10).

18. The landlord Hong family in Kanghwa island of Kyŏnggi province provides a good example of capital and land accumulation through usury. The family loaned at an average annual 51% interest, with a range of 20.4% to 72% from 1888 to 1894. Interest income amounted to 16,808 ryang in 1889 and more than tripled by 1894. Such usury reaped more than rent. For instance, in 1893 the price of one durak of land was 162 *ryang*. Its rental brought 29 *ryang*. But loaning the same amount of money to buy one durak of land yielded 77 *ryang* as interest. See Hong Sŏngch'an (1981) for a detailed analysis. The landlord Cho family in Koksŏng county and landlord Yi family in Posŏng county of South Chŏlla also exploited usury as the main means of augmenting wealth. See Hong Sŏngch'an (1985, 1986).

19. For instance, Kim Am'u in Koksŏng county, who leased land from the landlord Cho, had to supplement his income by working as a horse driver (Hong Sŏngch'an 1985, p. 139).

20. For a theoretical discussion on "economics of survival," see Chayanov in Thorner et al. (1986), Huang (1985), and Scott (1976).

21. Changing state interests may also have abetted the rising tenancy rate. Previous policy exempted slaves as well as *yangban* from military service and taxation, burdens mainly imposed upon commoners. Ample evidence shows that commoners sometimes relinquished their status to become slaves in order to avoid conscription and taxation. But shrinking numbers of army conscripts and declining tax revenue, especially after the Japanese invasion in 1592–98, led the state to permit the lowborn to become commoners in return for military service or grain contribution. A mid-fifteenth-century census numbered state-owned slaves outside the capital at over 352,000, but this decreased to 27,297 in 1755. Shikata Hiroshi's (1937) study shows a decline in the proportion of slaves in Taegu from 37.1% in 1690 to a mere 1.5% in 1858. Sommerville's

(1974) study of the Ulsan population reports the same trend; in 1729, slaves constituted 26.5% of the population, but only 0.5% in 1810. Title sales as an important state revenue source apparently continued until the end of the dynasty, substantially decreasing unfree labor. Most of these freed slaves remained with their master, but now in a tenant-landlord relation. Even before obtaining commoner status, some slaves (*oigŏ nobi*) who lived outside the master's house and cultivated his land functioned almost as tenants (Ch'oi Wŏngyu 1985).

22. According to a Japanese survey, under the most common forms of Korean rent payment (1) the landlord paid the land tax and the tenant provided seeds with the ratio of rent set at 50% or (2) the same conditions held but the landlord also provided seeds. For a more detailed discussion of local variation in tenancy customs, see Shin (1978).

CH. 3. COLONIALISM AND KOREAN AGRICULTURE

1. See "The British Rule in India" (1853) and "Inaugural Address of the Working Men's International Association" (1864), pp. 653-58 and 512-19, respectively, in *The Marx-Engels Reader,* edited by Robert Tucker (1978).

2. An official document reports that 0.5% of landowners were involved in a dispute of any kind (see Gragert 1982).

3. While royal lands were confiscated and transferred to the colonial government, the Japanese came to own overall no more than 5% of Korean lands.

4. Examples include (1) fallow land such as in the Ŭiju and Yongch'ŏn districts, bordering on the Yalu and Kojin rivers, respectively; (2) land frequently subject to natural disasters such as villages in Chaeryŏng, Sinch'ŏn and Anak counties; and (3) island land such as on Amt'ae and Songga. These parcels garnered substantial lifetime tenure in exchange for tenants' capital and labor investment to make them arable. See Chōsen sōtokufu (1930), vol. 1, pp. 707-78; Hŏ Chongho (1965), pp. 158-204; and Yi Yŏnghun (1988), pp. 95-125 for concrete examples of *tojigwŏn* practices.

5. Evidence shows that the Japanese also studied cadastral land surveys conducted in Egypt and India (see Kajimura 1989).

6. Given that per capita Korean rice consumption in 1912-15 was 0.64 sŏk (see Suh 1978, table 40), this seems plausible.

7. This index requires cautious use since it is based on cases reported in *Han'guk chung'ang nonghoebo* and *Chosŏn nonghoebo* rather than nationwide statistics.

8. The commercialization index for 1937 seems more reliable than the one for 1910, since it is based on 2,973 rural households (105 landlords, 546 owner-cultivators, 738 semi-tenants, and 1,584 landless tenants) surveyed by the colonial government (see In Chŏngsik 1949, table 4).

9. However, the colonial government's deep involvement in agricultural production, both through incentives and coercion, should not be overlooked.

10. Use of chemical fertilizer increased substantially after the late 1920s, to 97,000 metric tons in 1928 and 232,400 in 1932 (see Keidel 1981, table V-13).
11. After 1932, the colonial government dropped this distinction.
12. For instance, landlord Cho in Koksŏng county lent money at an annual rate above 30%, which funded the expansion of his holdings from 37.7 chŏngbo in 1915 to 61.0 in 1921 (Hong Sŏngch'an 1985).
13. For statistics showing income balances for different rural classes in different regions, see Chōsen sōtokufu 1929, pp. 35-37.
14. In 1915 only 223,100 persons were employed in industry; in 1941; 1,071,700 (Keidel 1981, p. 27).
15. For a list of local term variations, see Chōsen sōtokufu 1930, vol. 2, pp. 41-45. For a detailed discussion of the history and main features of *koji*, see Yun Sujong (1990).

CH. 4. TENANT-LANDLORD CONFLICT, 1920-32

1. Tenancy was completely abolished in North Korea with the 1946 land reform. In South Korea, tenancy became negligible after the 1950 land reform; in 1957, for instance, 88.1% of the rural population were full owner-cultivators. For discussions of the recent growth in South Korean tenancy rates, see Chang Sanghwan (1988), pp. 146-75, and Burmeister (1990), pp. 713-14.
2. Tenancy disputes flared until 1939. Yet after 1932, with the Tenant Arbitration Ordinance, direct and collective disputation of tenants against landlords became illegal; disputes required court mediation, unlike earlier disputes. Analysis in this chapter treats only disputes from 1920 to 1932. Chapter 7 considers tenant-landlord conflict from 1933 to 1939.
3. Most precolonial peasant protests, such as the 1862 peasant uprisings and the 1894 Tonghak peasant wars, addressed corruption of local government officials (see Han Wugŭn 1971; Han'guk yŏksa hakhoe 1991-92; Kim Chinbong 1970; Lew 1990; Pak Kwangsu 1969; Sin Yongha 1985; Song Ch'ansŏp et al. 1988).
4. Note that the data used here for the number of disputes were collected by the colonial government Bureau of Police Affairs until 1924, and thereafter by the Bureau of the Increase in Production. The former probably included only incidents that drew police attention, whereas the latter included almost every incident (see Lee 1978, table 13 footnote). Therefore, the apparent increase in disputes after the late 1920s could be partly an artifact of data collection. However, changes in the nature of disputes over time certainly arose, as is shown below, and almost every colonial government publication dealing with tenancy problems used the data presented here.
5. This effort brought both a series of surveys on tenancy customs and tenancy legislation. See Chapter 7 for details.
6. The decrease in average scale does not preclude large-scale, organized dis-

putes during the depression years. As shown below, during these years small-scale, defensive disputes simply dominated.

7. Of course, Marx ([1852]1981) himself portrays peasants as a "sack of potatoes." But other Marxists, such as Frantz Fanon and Mao Zedong, stress the importance of the poor peasantry in a communist revolution. See Chapter 1.

8. Pak Myŏnggyu (1987) argues for the importance of middle peasants in colonial-period peasant movements, but he leaves unspecified their role in tenancy disputes.

9. The colonial government divided each rural stratum further into four subgroups. For instance, landless tenants were subdivided into upper, middle, lower, and tiny tenants. See Table 3.2.

10. The periodization in this section is somewhat arbitrary. I chose a 1926–27 cutoff because (1) promulgation of the Peace Preservation Law (Ch'ian yujibŏp) in 1925 restricted any involvement of outside organizations in tenancy disputes, (2) establishment of the Association for Systematic Agriculture (Kyet'ong nonghoe) in 1926 sought to strengthen colonial government control over rural society, and (3) around 1927 the Korean rural economy began to feel the impact of agricultural depression. These developments increasingly impeded tenant organization and mobilization. See Shin (1990).

11. Note that Gragert's data were selected not on the basis of representative value, but because of the existence of a long time series (1880s–1945). Despite this potential weakness, however, the study is probably the best empirical analysis available on modern Korean land tenure changes.

12. Ralph Gleason (1956), using the United Nations formula, calculates the average daily per capita calorie requirement to be 2,030 for Taiwan. As Table 4.4 shows, Korean colonial-period consumption fluctuated around 2,000 calories. Such an intake seems adequate, given that the South Korean average in 1973 was 2,198.9 (Lee 1979, p. 46).

13. From 1910 to 1925, the Korean population increased 23.7%, from 15,380,926 to 19,020,030. Also, the percentage in the 0–14 age span increased from 38.1% to 39.7% and the percentage of females from 47.7% to 48.9%. See Ishi (1972), table 3.6.

14. Enrollment in primary schools increased from 20,000 in 1910, to 90,000 in 1920, and 901,000 in 1937 (Ho 1984, p. 353; see also Tsurumi 1984).

15. See Palais (1975), especially pp. 61–67.

16. The importance of semi-tenants in disputes is illustrated by the high partial correlation coefficient of "number of participants" with "proportion of semi-tenants" for 13 provinces, controlling for rural population ($r = .30$, $p < .20$).

17. From 1920 to 1926, 26% of the disputes occurred in South Ch'ungch'ŏng province, but participants constituted only 5% of the total disputants (see Table 4.5).

18. For a discussion of the usefulness of this theory in explaining peasant collective action in an authoritarian polity such as tenancy disputes in colonial Korea, see Shin (1990).

19. Waswo (1977, p. 129) suggests this idea.

20. This government survey of tenancy customs reports such resumption of cultivation as a "recent trend."

21. For a concrete example, see footnote 47 in Hong Sŏngch'an (1985).

22. For very telling stories of evicted tenants, see "Sojaggwŏn" (Tenancy Rights) in *Nongmin* (Peasants) 1930, 4(1): 63–68; and "Sojagin ŭi ttal" (Daughter of a Tenant) in *Nongmin* 1930, 4(2): 49–54, and 4(3): 49–54.

23. In 1921 the annual percentage of transferred tenancy rights ranged from 7% (South P'yŏngan province) to 30–40% (South Kyŏngsang province). See Lee (1936), p. 165.

CH. 5. THE RED PEASANT UNION MOVEMENT, 1930-39, PART I

1. The term "red peasant union" was used by Japanese authorities to indicate the communist (red) influence on the movement.

2. One Japanese source estimates these figures at 9 branches with 12,000 members (*Shisō geppō* 4[5], 14–44).

3. Democratization movements with strong anti-American nationalist overtones in the 1980s increased interest in anticolonial, national liberation movements during the colonial period. For the rise of anti-Americanism in 1980s Korean democratization movements, see Shin (1995).

4. This new usage embodies a significant disinclination of young scholars to use the term coined by Japanese authorities. However, it is not clear what is meant by "revolutionary." For instance, Chi Sugŏl includes in the category of "revolutionary peasant union movements": "(1) movements led by a red or leftist peasant union, (2) attempts to transform a legal peasant union to a revolutionary one, and (3) preparation movements to build a complete red peasant union" (1993, p. 17). Yi Chunsik (1993) also seems to equate "revolutionary" with "illegal" or "underground." I invoke the conventional term, "red peasant union movement," since I do not agree with their definition of "revolutionary"; also, as I show in the next chapter, peasant protest being considered here was not always "revolutionary."

5. Ch'ŏndogyo, or Tonghak, is a Korean native religion with elements of Confucianism, Buddhism, Taoism, and traditional Korean shamanism. The peasant wars of 1894 are considered Tonghak rebellions.

6. Occasionally a close connection appears between active tenancy disputes in the 1920s and the organization of red peasant unions. For instance, Okku in North Chŏlla province; Ponghwa, Yŏngju, and Andong in North Kyŏngsang province; Yongch'ŏn in North P'yŏng'an province; and Kowŏn and Tanch'ŏn in South Hamgyŏng province show both activities. This is more than balanced, however, by areas of active tenancy disputes that organized no red peasant unions. Pongsan of Hwanghae province; Talsŏng of North Kyŏngsang province; and Amt'ae, Chaŭn, and Haŭi islands of South Chŏlla province are examples. Furthermore, where the most active red peasant unions developed (South and

North Hamgyŏng provinces), few tenancy disputes disrupted the 1920s. See Appendix 1 for details.

7. Bruce Cumings (1981b) argues for a significant effect of returnees from Japan and Manchuria on peasant radicalism in liberated Korea, as Chapter 9 discusses.

8. For general discussions of the role of intellectuals in protest movements, see Gella (1976), Gramsci (1971), Mohan (1987), Pinard and Hamilton (1989), Schumpeter ([1942]1950), and Zald and McCarthy (1987).

9. Studies on the 1919 nationalist movement are voluminous. See Baldwin (1969), Ku (1985), and Han'guk yŏksa yŏn'guhoe (1989). Regarding Korean nationalism, see Gardner (1979), Lee (1964), Robinson (1988), and Wells (1990).

10. Most cultural nationalists came from the landlord class whose interests conflicted with those of the peasantry. For the nature of a representative cultural nationalist, Kim Sŏngsu, see Eckert (1991).

11. Sorensen's (1992) comparative analysis of Korean peasant literature (*nongmin munhak*) of the 1930s with that of the 1970s well points out that in the former (e.g., Yi Kwang-su's "Soil") the tone is "intellectual," written from "the point of view of the urbanite." In contrast, the latter (e.g., Pak Kyŏng-ni's "Earth") expresses "the point of view of the peasants themselves."

12. To separate radical nationalists from communists in the Third World is often difficult since the former are attracted to communism as an ideology of national liberation. Mitchell's portrayal of colonial-era Korean communists in Japan as "ardent nationalists first and communists second" illustrates this inseparability (1967, p. 61). See also Robinson (1988).

13. Moderate cultural nationalists also began peasant mobilization in the mid-1920s with modest success. Of particular importance were peasant movements of the Chosŏn nongminsa led by Ch'ŏndogyo (Tonghak), focused on peasants' education and enlightenment and opposed to direct landlord or state confrontation. This enlightenment movement prevailed in the northwestern region, the P'yŏngan provinces where Ch'ŏndogyo was strong. By February 1928, Chosŏn nongminsa had 158 branches with 16,579 members. See Chi Sugŏl (1985), Cho Tonggŏl (1979, pp. 169–83), and Yoo (1974b, pp. 246–61).

14. For detailed discussions on the December Theses, see Kim Chunyŏp and Kim Ch'angsun (1973, vol. 3, chap. 15) in Korean and Suh (1970, part III) in English.

15. This article was published in August 1928 in an exile journal called *Hyŏn'gyedan* (The Present Step), in Japan. On the author, see Pae Sŏngch'an (1987, pp. 406–26).

16. The debate between Marxists and populists on the class nature of social revolution was heated in prerevolutionary Russia. Russian populists such as Daniel'son and Vorontsov did not consider the (industrial) proletariat the sole revolutionary social class, but only one of the exploited elements that eventually

would carry out a socialist revolution. In contrast, the Marxists, led by Lenin, firmly endorsed the proletariat's leading role in the Russian Revolution while recognizing the agrarian nature of Russian society and thus the importance of the peasantry. Korean radicals adopted the Leninist view. For a discussion of the Marxist-populist debate in Russia, see Kingstone-Mann (1985, pp. 27–73).

17. The journal was published in Beijing, China. For the author, see Pae Sŏngch'an (1987, pp. 389–98) and Kim Chunyŏp and Kim Ch'angsun (1973, vol. 3, pp. 207–9).

18. Korean radicals believed that the Korean revolution must be a bourgeois revolution, but since the bourgeoisie was too weak to lead, the proletariat must take charge. No debate arose such as the one between the *kōzaha* (Seminar faction) and the *rōnoha* (Farmer Labor faction) in Japan during the 1920s. The former espoused a two-stage bourgeoisie-proletariat revolution, whereas the latter endorsed only a proletariat revolution (see Hoston 1986). Most Korean radicals believed that the Korean revolution must be an anticolonial, national liberation movement in addition to a bourgeois revolution (see Kim Yongsŏp 1992, pp. 445–53).

CH. 6. THE RED PEASANT UNION MOVEMENT, 1930–39, PART II

1. See numerous reports and analyses of peasant misery in such magazines as *Kaebyŏk* and *Nongmin*.

2. Japan saw the same process during the depression years. See Waswo (1977).

3. Note that agricultural prices fell more sharply than prices of manufactured goods. For instance, in 1930 the former were only one-third of 1919 prices, the latter two-thirds (Suh 1978, p. 169).

4. While small owners bore a heavy tax burden, colonial government policy gave tenants and tenancy problems higher priority. This was because the Japanese, already well aware of tenancy problems in Japan, were very much concerned with the alleged influence of socialist thought on tenancy disputes. See Chapter 7 for detailed discussion on the change in the colonial government's agricultural policy in the 1930s.

5. Haman, Kosŏng, and Ulsan peasant unions (South Kyŏngsang province); Changsŏng union (South Chŏlla province); Kangsŏ union (South P'yŏngan province); Kowŏn, Hamhŭng, and Anbyŏn unions (South Hamgyŏng province); and Onsŏng union (North Hamgyŏng province) protested irrigation fees (*suri chohapbi*). Yangp'yŏng union (Kyŏnggi province); Kangnŭng union (Kangwŏn province); and Tanch'ŏn union (South Hamgyŏng province) resisted forest fees (*sallim chohapbi*). Appendix 1 provides information sources. For detailed analysis of the Tanch'ŏn case, see Yi Chunsik (1984).

6. Discussion here of the background of union leaders relies mainly on Japanese court documents such as *Shisō ihō* (Thought Report Series) and *Shisō geppō* (Monthly Thought Report).

7. For 30 of the 41 convicted leaders, educational background is not known. However, since they read radical materials, they must have had some modest education (see Appendix 3).

8. American missionaries, perceiving such a thirst for education, established numerous elementary and secondary schools as a mission strategy (see Tsurumi 1984).

9. For a detailed list of these publications, see pp. 27-28 in the Japanese court document, "Chŏngp'yŏng nōmin kumiai kenkyo gaikyō" (1931). The Chosŏn nongminsa also extensively used night schools to educate peasants, but with much more moderate materials. See Cho Tonggŏl (1979, pp. 200-227).

10. A list of all the red peasant union night schools and reading circles would be too extensive to include here. For detailed information, see *Shisō ihō* and *Shisō geppō*.

11. Another 1.88%, probably Japanese, could read and write only Japanese.

12. A 1933 survey by the Agricultural Association records that owner-cultivators, on the average, spent 11.9 wŏn for education, and semi-tenants and landless tenants spent 3.4 wŏn and 0.5 wŏn respectively (In Chŏngsik 1939, pp. 135-36).

13. While Japanese authorities rarely mentioned the class background of convicted union leaders, a few examples cite a poor peasant profile (*pinnong*), for instance, for Chu Tŏghŭm, Cho Chonghan, and Hwang Chŏngjun in the Munch'ŏn peasant union (*Shisō ihō* 3: 36-41). However, available records do not reveal whether they were landless.

14. Wagner (1977) argues that the early discriminatory preference for southern candidates in civil examinations disappeared by the end of the Yi dynasty. For instance, among 1,913 successful higher civil service examination candidates from 1392 to 1499, only 7 are known to have resided in the north. But in the late nineteenth century, especially the last 30 years of the examinations, the percentage grew to 22.8%, approximately equal to their proportion in the total population. Among the northerners, however, about 70% came from P'yŏngan provinces. The Hamgyŏng provinces remained outside the center of Korean politics.

15. Historically, Korea had many different types of *kye*. For a historical review of these, see Kim P'ildong (1990). Also, on the character of contemporary *kye*, see Janelli and Yim (1988-89).

16. For an interesting discussion of the persistence of such communal solidarity in contemporary Korea, see Chang (1991). According to Chang, market development did not lead to "individualistic" or "utilitarian" orientations as in the West, but to "personalistic" or "collectivist" attitudes and ethics.

17. Also, note that the village *kye* was often used as a social network in the initial organization and mobilization of peasants by union leaders (*Shisō ihō* 1935 [4]: 54-96).

18. While the Kabo reforms of 1894 officially abolished the status system, the influence of former *yangban* on local affairs was tenacious during the colonial period, and is so even today. See Brandt (1971, pp. 88-91).

19. For instance, the Sin'ganhoe held national conventions only twice, once for its establishment and then for its dissolution.
20. For a theoretical discussion on middle-class radicalism, see Calhoun (1988).
21. Between March 1931 and July 1932 alone, police raided 31 red peasant unions, arresting 950 union members.
22. The sole exception was the guerrilla struggle in Manchuria led by Kim Il Sung against the Japanese during the 1930s. But this also diminished to insignificance during the Pacific War years.
23. For discussions on the role of repressive state power in rebellion and revolution, see Tilly et al. (1975) and Skocpol (1979).
24. Both Scott's (1985) "history according to losers" and Wolf's (1982) "people without history" emphasize the importance of looking at history from the common people's point of view.
25. For a discussion on Rude's vision of "history from below," see Krantz (1985).

CH. 7. TENANT-LANDLORD CONFLICT, 1933-39

1. See Hong Sŏngch'an (1992, pp. 127-29) for details.
2. This does not preclude large-scale, collective protest. According to a police document, for instance, on 24 October 1938, 121 tenants in Anak county of North Kyŏngsang province demanded rent reduction. But the proportion of such relatively large-scale, collective disputes fell far short of 1%. For examples of collective disputes in 1938, see Chōsen sōtokufu (1938, pp. 100-102).
3. For a definition of "development" in contrast to "intensification" and "involution," see Chapter 3.
4. For a detailed discussion of the history and current situation of Koreans in Japan, see Kang and Kim (1989), and for a telling story of Koreans in the Japanese mines, see Hane (1982, pp. 235-42).
5. In 1930, for instance, 90% of Korean migrants in Manchuria pursued agriculture, but by 1940 only 69% (Kim Ch'ŏl [1965]1988, p. 124).
6. Mitchell notes that colonial policy even *discouraged* Korean migration to Japan: "[T]he government-general was luring workers to the north of Korea by granting reduced railway fares. Officials in Pusan interviewed laborers going to Japan and encouraged those without prior commitments to remain in Korea" (1967, p. 79).
7. The colonial agricultural department investigated the peasant economy of both semi-tenant and landless tenant households with regard to the number of family members, education, age, household income, expenses, rental rate, amount of owned and leased land, and so forth. The 1933 survey probed 1,919 semi-tenant households and 1,778 tenant households, with a follow-up five years later. Semi-tenants averaged a surplus income of 16.32 yen per household in 1933 and 49.11 yen in 1938 (Chōsen sōtokufu 1940c, pp. 23-24), and landless

tenants of 9.07 yen and 28.29 yen (Chōsen sōtokufu 1940b, pp. 24-25). But survey data are for "middle" tenants and semi-tenants, thus probably slightly overstating general tenant and semi-tenant living standards and suggesting cautious interpretation.

8. For discussions of the prevalence of tenancy disputes in prewar Japan, see Dore (1959, N.B. Part I), Waswo (1977), and Smethurst (1986). To illustrate, from 1920 to 1931, 24,321 tenancy disputes occurred involving 304,981 landlords and 1,225,553 tenants (Waswo 1977, p. 100).

9. Investigation of tenancy disputes predated this major project. For instance, in 1923 the South Chŏlla provincial government surveyed tenancy customs in the province. Similar surveys by other provincial governments ensued. Also, the colonial government's Department of Agriculture (Nōrinkyoku) published the results of numerous surveys on causes and consequences of tenancy disputes, cited extensively in Chapter 4 and used again here. Clearly the colonial government followed the same survey methods as those used in Japan. For instance, it too classified rural households into landlords (A), landlords (B), owners, semi-tenants, landless tenants, and wage laborers.

10. For the full text of the ordinance, see Cho Tonggŏl (1979, pp. 249-53).

11. In 1933, 150 county tenant committees existed in Korea.

12. See also a letter sent to the U.S. Secretary of State by O. Gaylord Marsh, American consul general in Seoul, entitled "Tenant Arbitration Cases in Korea" (September 1937) in *Records of the Department of State Relating to Internal Affairs of Korea (1930-39)*, reel 2.

13. For a contrasting view, see Chi Sugŏl (1984).

14. For the full text of the law, see Cho Tonggŏl (1979, pp. 153-57). For an English translation, see *Records of the Department of State Relating to Internal Affairs of Korea (1930-39)*, reel 2.

15. In 1934, Korea had 234 county tenant committees (basically one per county) with the county executive as chair and four other members (Chōsen sōtokufu 1940a, pp. 52-87).

16. For example, the original Tenancy Law guaranteed a minimum contract of five years and allowed transfer of the tenancy right to a third person.

17. An American consul in Seoul even predicted this law would destroy "the ancient incubus of landlordism." See a letter sent to the U.S. Department of the State by Wm. R. Langdon, American consul in Korea, entitled "Tenant Farmer Legislation—Chosen Agricultural Lands Ordinance" (19 May 1934) in *Records of the Department of State Relating to Internal Affairs of Korea (1930-39)*, reel 2.

18. Ibid.

19. In 1932 the Japanese also launched Nōson sinkō undō (Rural Revitalization Campaign) emphasizing "mental awakening" and "self-reliance." See *Annual Report on the Administration of Chōsen* (1934-35, pp. 216-22) and Han Tohyŏn (1986).

20. In addition, Japanese control of around 90% of the total paid-in industrial capital of Korea by the end of the colonial period is often cited to show

the underdevelopment of Korean capitalists. But the statistics include only corporations and subscribed capital, though many Korean establishments were unincorporated, and exclude joint Japanese-Korean companies, thus underestimating Korean industrial investment (Eckert 1991). For a fine study of Korean capitalists Kim Sŏngsu and Yŏnsu of the Kyŏngsŏng Spinning and Weaving Company, see Eckert (1991). McNamara (1990) also examines the colonial origins of four selected Korean entrepreneurs, Min Tae-sik and his brother Kyu-sik of the Hanil/Tongil Bank, Pak Hŭng-sik of Hwasin, and Kim Yŏnsu of Kyŏngsŏng Spinning. In addition, Woo (1991) shows that colonial industrialization was integral to rapid and successful economic growth after the 1960s.

21. See Langdon, "Tenant Farmer Legislation—Chosen Agricultural Lands Ordinance" (19 May 1934).

22. My interviews with colonial period tenants and semi-tenants in the summer of 1993 suggest that little differentiated Korean from Japanese landlords. For instance, a former tenant (born in 1918) in Naju county of South Chŏlla province claims, "there was not much difference between Korean and Japanese landlords, except that tenants had to present gifts like chicken in order to keep leased land of the former. Also, relations with Japanese landlords were in general more formal" (June 1993 interview).

23. See "Tenant Arbitration Cases in Chosen" (September 9 1937) in *Records of the Department of State Relating to Internal Affairs of Korea (1930-39)*, reel 2.

24. A case study of landlord Yi in Posŏng county in South Chŏlla province shows that rent was lower in the late 1930s than in depression years (Hong Sŏngch'an 1986, pp. 186-87). Also, rates for the landlord Cho family in Koksŏng county of South Chŏlla province dropped from 48.6% in 1933 to 47.8% in 1938 (Hong Sŏngch'an 1985, p. 20). Landlord power vis-à-vis tenants seems to have peaked during the depression.

25. This interpretation is consistent with resource mobilization theory of collection action discussed in previous chapters (see Gamson 1975; Tilly 1978).

CH. 8. JAPANESE MILITARISM AND EVERYDAY
FORMS OF RESISTANCE

1. Through 13 interviews with former peasants (tenants, semi-tenants, and owner-cultivators) in the summer of 1993, I collected oral accounts of wartime experiences. While my sample was by no means representative, such interviews greatly illuminated Japanese war efforts and Korean peasant response to them.

2. For similar developments in Japan, see Dore (1959, pp. 112-14) and Waswo (1977, pp. 135-39).

3. For a discussion of *Naisen ittai*, see Eckert (1991, pp. 235-39).

4. For a discussion of the importance of rural mass organization in Japan for war preparation, see Smethurst (1974).

5. *The Japan Economic Institute Report* (24 January 1992) states: "Until recently Tokyo had not admitted the government's involvement in this inhumane

206 *Notes*

act; however, evidence proving official Japanese involvement was discovered in the Defense Academy's library six days before the prime minister's trip to South Korea [on January 16]. Mr. Miyazawa publicly apologized for what had happened and promised an investigation" (p. 5). The Associated Press also reports: "After issuing denials for decades, the [Japanese] government officially acknowledged today that the army systematically recruited Asian women to provide sex for Japanese troops in World War II. . . . [It] uncovered 127 documents that confirmed army involvement, some of which claimed the women were recruited to prevent troops from raping civilians." The Japanese government offered no estimate of the total, but "historians believe the number of sex slaves totaled between 70,000 and 200,000" (*Iowa City Press-Citizen*, 6 July 1992, p. A1).

6. In addition, there were allegedly 183 secret circles in Korea and arms struggles in Manchuria (see Yi Chaehwa 1988).

7. For empirical works using Scott's model, see articles in the *Journal of Peasant Studies* 13(2) and Colburn (1989).

8. June 1993 interview.

9. June 1993 interviews.

10. See the report by Harold B. Quarton, American consul general in Seoul, in *Records of the Department of State Relating to Internal Affairs of Korea (1940-44)*, reel 1.

11. This finding was initially published in *Minju Chosŏn* (January 1948) by an anonymous reporter investigating the American military government's rice collection policy, and reprinted in Kim Namsik, Lee Chongsik, and Han Honggu (1986, vol. 6, pp. 628-30).

12. June 1993 interview. He added, "I heard many Koreans were killed by Manchurians after Japanese surrender for their mistreatment of Manchurians; Koreans looked down on Manchurians."

13. See the report by Quarton in *Records of the Department of State*, reel 1.

CH. 9. HISTORICAL ORIGINS OF PEASANT RADICALISM IN LIBERATED KOREA

1. Unlike some scholars (e.g., Dahl 1967) who acknowledge only institutionalized political participation, as in elections, I include protest and resistance. As Gamson argues: "[I]n the place of the old duality of extremist politics and pluralist politics, there is simply politics. . . . Rebellion, in this view, is simply politics by other means. It is not some kind of irrational expression but is as instrumental in its nature as a lobbyist trying to get special favors for his group or a major political party conducting a presidential campaign" (1975, pp. 138-39). See also McAdam (1982, pp. 1-59).

2. Figure 5 in Cumings (1981b) lists the counties in which PCs assumed governmental functions. Cumings also details the fate of PCs in the South (see chap. 9). Regarding such committees in the North, see Kim Yongbok (1989).

3. For a comparative study of land reform in South and North Korea, see Kang (1988).

4. For more detailed descriptions of the uprisings, see Cumings (1981b, chap. 10) and "The Quasi-Revolt of 1946" in U.S. Army (1948/1988, vol. 3). Chŏng Haegu (1988) details the uprisings in North Kyŏngsang province.

5. Although uprisings involved many workers and students, thus appearing to be rebellions of the general population against procolonial forces thriving in postcolonial Korea, most protesters were peasants.

6. The other causes listed were police corruption, agitators' use of police corruption to incite the people to violence, careful planning and execution of disturbances by agents from North Korea, infiltration of communists in the schools, the rumor that summer grain collections were not distributed, police failure to plan defense, people's antagonism toward the police, unpopularity of the military government with the masses, failure to inform people of governmental policy, the poor quality of American-installed Korean officials, dishonesty of military government interpreters, attempts to Americanize Koreans too rapidly, and general unemployment because of the number of refugees (U.S. Army 1948/1988, 3:365).

7. For his critique of Henderson's (1968) depiction, see Cumings (1973).

8. Son Hoch'ŏl (1989) presents a good critique of Cumings's (1981b) interpretation of modern Korean history, but focuses on its metatheoretical aspects.

9. Miriam Golden (1988) similarly claims that Italian workers have been able to mobilize continuously due to a long-standing radical socialist tradition: "historical memory" of protest keeps radical aims alive. Drawing on an analysis of various forms of protest in Owens Valley, California, Walton agrees that "historical experience, particularly when it is about previous struggles, . . . is elaborated in legend and historical memory . . . and can become an important resource in its own right for mobilizing participation" (1992, p. 326). For more detailed discussion of this historical experience thesis, see Shin (1994).

10. This historical experience thesis of peasant radicalism is well captured in a very popular historical novel, Cho Chŏngnae's *T'aebaeksanmaek* (10 vols.). A tenant activist, Ha Taech'i, proud of being a grandson of a Tonghak fighter, participates in colonial-period tenancy disputes and postwar political movements, and finally becomes a guerrilla. In a 7 June 1993 telephone interview, the author explained that his stories "are largely based on actual history even though each character was created to stress certain aspects. . . . [Accordingly,] historical continuity of protest movement is not simply fiction, but primarily based on my collection of oral history and other historical facts."

11. Tenancy disputes occurred from 1920 to 1939, but data on the number prior to 1933 exist only at the provincial level. Since a similar geographic distribution of tenancy disputes appeared throughout the 1920s and 1930s (see Chapters 4 and 7), however, this measure should not distort the overall pattern. Also, other dispute aspects such as scale or intensity are not available for the

county level, and there is little written material indicating the degree of wartime "everyday forms of resistance," which must therefore be omitted from analysis. This omission appears not to distort the findings presented below.

12. This nonlinearity suggests that beyond a certain level of experience, further experience had little impact on the chance for uprising, though this point needs to be refined both theoretically and empirically.

13. Outcome data for other tenant demands, such as secure tenancy right, are not available.

14. To include the strength of peasant unions, another major protest organization in the uprisings, would be interesting. Unfortunately, detailed information on county-level peasant unions is lacking, though we can safely assume, as discussed above, that PC strength in general reflected peasant union power in a given county.

15. If there were sufficient counties with no PC, it would be useful to compare them with counties with an NGPC and/or a GPC. The small number of cases ($N = 7$) here makes such a comparison of little meaning.

16. This inference stems primarily from the change in the coefficients' significance level. Another approach considers the amount that coefficients change before and after introducing an intervening variable. In addition to the difficulties in directly comparing the changes because of the logged nature of the dispute measure and dependent variable, such comparison is further problematic since estimates in both models are based on the same sample: a given variable's estimate in Model 1 correlates with its estimate in Model 2. For detailed statistical discussion on this problem, see Clogg et al. (1992).

17. The rationale for including population change*GPC is discussed below.

18. This also illuminates Cumings's insufficiently explained finding that population change is responsible for rebellions only in 41 counties. See Cumings 1981b, table 12.

Bibliography

OFFICIAL DOCUMENTS AND UNPUBLISHED SOURCES

Chōsen sōtokufu [Government-General of Korea]. 1929. *Chōsen no kosaku kanshū* [Tenancy customs in Korea]. Keijō.
———. 1930. *Chōsen no kosaku kankō* [Tenancy customs in Korea]. 2 vols. Keijō.
———, Keimukyoku. 1931. "Chŏngp'yŏng nōmin kumiai kenkyo gaikyō" [A briefing on the case of the Chŏngp'yŏng Red Peasant Union]. Reprinted in Pak Kyŏngsik, *Chōsen mondai shiryō gyōsho*, vol. 6: *1920-30 nendai minzoku undō* [Materials on Korean issues: Nationalist movements in the 1920s and 1930s], pp. 484-539. Tokyo: Asea mondai kenkyujo.
———, Keimukyoku. 1933 and 1938. *Saikin ni okeru Chōsen chian jōkyō* [Recent conditions of public security in Korea]. Keijō.
———, Nōrinkyoku. 1934. *Chōsen ni okeru kosaku ni kansuru sankō jikō tekiyō* [A briefing on tenancy-related issues in Korea]. Keijō.
———. 1935. *Chōsen no shūraku* [The villages of Korea]. 3 vols. Keijō.
———, Keimukyoku. (1933-1936). *Kōtō keisatsu hō* [High police report]. Nos. 1-6. Keijō.
———, Nōrinkyoku. 1937. *Chōsen kosaku nenpō* [Annual report on Korean tenancy]. Vol. 1. Keijō.
———, Nōrinkyoku. 1940a. *Chōsen nōchi nenpō* [Annual report of Korean agricultural lands]. Vol. 1. Keijō.
———, Nōrinkyoku. 1940b. *Nōka keizai gaikyō chōsa-kosaku nōka, 1933-1938* [Survey of the peasant economy—Tenant households]. Keijō.
———, Nōrinkyoku. 1940c. *Nōka keizai gaikyō chōsa-jisaku ken kosaku, 1933-1938* [Survey of the peasant economy—Semi-tenant households]. Keijō.
———, Kōtōhōuin, Kenjikyoku. *Shisō ihō* [Thought report series]. Keijō.
———, Kōtōhōuin, Kenjikyoku. *Shisō geppō* [Monthly thought report]. Keijō.
———. 1907-22. *Annual Report on Reforms and Progress in Chosen*. Keijō.
———. 1923-38. *Annual Report on Administration of Chōsen*. Keijō.

Ch'ungch'ŏng Pukdo. 1930. *Kosaku kankō chōsa sho* [A survey of tenancy customs]. Vol. 1.
Hamhŭng chihō hōin. 1933. "Tanch'ŏn nōmin kumiai kyōgikai jiken" [The incident of the Tanch'ŏn Peasant Union]. Reprinted in Pak Kyŏngsik, *Chōsen mondai shiryō gyōsho*, vol. 6: *1920-30 nendai minzoku undō* [Materials on Korean issues: Nationalist movements in the 1920s and 1930s], pp. 550-73. Tokyo: Asea mondai kenkyujo.
Keijo fukushin hoin. 1933. "Chŏngp'yŏng nōmin kumiai jiken hanketsu" [Court documents on the Chŏngp'yŏng Peasant Union case]. Reprinted in Pak Kyŏngsik, *Chōsen mondai shiryō gyōsho*, vol. 6: *1920-30 nendai minzoku undō* [Materials on Korean issues: Nationalist movements in the 1920s and 1930s], pp. 540-49. Tokyo: Azia mondai kenkyujo.
———. 1934. "Sekishoku Yŏnghŭng nōmin kumiaiin bōdō jiken" [The case of violence of the Yŏnghŭng Red Peasant Union]. Reprinted in Pak Kyŏngsik, *Chōsen mondai shiryō gyōsho*, vol. 6: *1920-30 nendai minzoku undō* [Materials on Korean issues: Nationalist movements in the 1920s and 1930s], pp. 575-606. Tokyo: Azia mondai kenkyujo.
Records of the Department of State Relating to Internal Affairs of Korea (1930-39), 2 rolls; *(1940-44)*, 3 rolls. National Archives of the United States. Reprinted by Scholarly Resources, Inc.
Republic of Korea. 1949. *Chosŏn kyŏngje t'onggye yoram* [Brief statistics on Korean economy]. Seoul.
United States Army. 1948/1988. *History of the United States Armed Forces in Korea*. 4 vols. Reprinted by Tolbege in Seoul.

WORKS IN KOREAN

An Chongch'ŏl. 1990. "Haebang chikhu kŏn'guk chunbi wiwŏnhoe chibang chojik kwa chibang inmin wiwŏnhoe e kwanhan yŏn'gu—Chŏnnam chibang ŭl chungsim ŭro" [A study of local organizations of the Committee for the Preparation of Korean Independence and people's committees in South Chŏlla]. Ph.D. diss., Chŏnam National University.
An Pyŏngjik. 1975. "Singminjiha Chosŏnin taejiju ŭi yŏn'gu" [A study of large Korean landlords during the colonial period]. *Kyŏngje nonjip* 14: 1-18.
Chang Hyŏnch'il. 1935. "Chosŏn suri chohap kwa chungnong kyegŭp" [The irrigation union and the middle class in Korea]. *Sindonga* 5(2): 25-28.
Chang Sanghwan. 1985. "Nongji kaehyŏk kwajŏng e taehan silchŭngjŏk yŏn'gu" [An empirical study of land reform]. Pp. 292-358 in *Haebang chŏnhusa ŭi insik 2* [Perspectives on Korean history in the pre- and postwar era]. Seoul: Han'gilsa.
———. 1988. "Hyŏnhaeng t'oji munje wa haegyŏl panghyang" [The current land problems and solutions]. Pp. 109-91 in *Han'guk nongŏp nongmin munje I* [Problems of agriculture and farmers in Korea], edited by Han'guk nongch'on sahoe yŏn'guso. Seoul: Yŏn'gusa.

Chang Siwŏn. 1980. "Singminjiha Chosŏn ŭi pan ponggŏnjŏk t'oji soyu e kwanhan yŏn'gu" [A study of semifeudal landownership in colonial Korea]. *Kyŏngje sahak* 4: 38-139.
Chi Sugŏl. 1984. "1932-35 nyŏngan ŭi Chosŏn nongch'on chinhŭng undong" [The rural revitalization campaign in colonial Korea, 1932-35]. *Han'guksa yŏn'gu* 46.
———. 1985. "Chosŏn nongminsa ŭi tanch'e sŏnggyŏk e kwanhan yŏn'gu" [A study of the characteristics of the Institute of Korean peasant]. *Yŏksa hakpo* 106: 169-207.
———. 1993. *Ilcheha nongmin chohap undong yŏn'gu: 1930s nyŏndae hyŏngmyŏngjŏk nongmin chohap undong* [A study of the peasant union movement in colonial Korea: The revolutionary peasant union movement in the 1930s]. Seoul: Yŏksa pip'yŏngsa.
Cho Chŏngnae. 1986-89. *T'aebaeksanmaek* [The T'aebaek Mountains]. 10 vols. Seoul: Han'gilsa.
Cho Kijun. 1973. *Han'guk chabonjuŭi sŏngnipsaron* [A history of Korean capitalism]. Seoul: Taewangsa.
Cho Sŏggon. 1988. "Chosŏn t'oji chosa saŏp e issŏsŏ ŭi soyugwŏn kwajŏng e kwanhan han yŏn'gu" [A case study of the investigation process of landownership in the cadastral survey in Korea]. Pp. 9-55 in *Han'guk kŭndae nongch'on sahoe wa nongmin undong* [Rural society and peasant movements in modern Korea], edited by Chang Siwŏn et al. Seoul: Yŏlŭmsa.
Cho Tonggŏl. 1979. *Ilcheha han'guk nongmin undongsa* [History of peasant movements under Japanese colonialism]. Seoul: Han'gilsa.
Ch'oi Wŏngyu. 1985. "Hanmal-Ilcheha ŭi nongŏp kyŏngyŏng e kwanhan yŏn'gu: Haenam Yunssiga ŭi sarye" [A case study of farm management in the late Chosŏn and early colonial Korea: The Haenam Yun family]. *Han'guksa yŏn'gu* 50/51: 275-318.
Chŏng Haegu. 1988. *10 wŏl inmin hangjaeng yŏn'gu* [A study of the October people's uprisings]. Seoul: Yŏlŭmsa.
Chŏng Sŏkchong. 1972. "Honggyŏngnaenan ŭi sŏnggyŏk" [Characteristics of the Honggyŏngnae Rebellion]. *Han'guksa yŏn'gu* 7: 151-206.
Chŏng T'aehŏn. 1987. "Singminji sidae (1910-18) Chosŏn ŭi chabonjejŏk chose chedo sŏngnip e kwanhan yŏn'gu" [A study of the establishment of the capitalist tax system in colonial Korea, 1910-18]. *Kyŏngje sahak* 11: 1-79.
———. 1991. "1930 nyŏndae singminji nongŏp chŏngch'aek ŭi sŏnggyŏk chŏnhwan e kwanhan yŏn'gu" [A study of rural policy change in 1930s Korea]. Pp. 56-107 in *Ilchemal Chosŏn sahoe wa minjok haebang undong* [Colonial Korea and national liberation movements during the last years of Japanese rule]. Seoul: Ilsongjŏng.
Chosŏn Ilbosa. 1986. *Chosŏn ilbo hang'il kisa saegin, 1920-40* [Index of reports on anti-Japanese activities in the *Korean Daily*]. Seoul.
Chu Ponggyu. 1981. "Ilcheha sojak chaengŭi ŭi sŏnggyŏk e kwanhan yŏn'gu" [A study of the characteristics of tenancy disputes under Japanese colonial-

ism]. Pp. 122-46 in *Ilcheha singminji sidae ŭi minjok undong* [Nationalist movements during the Japanese colonial period], edited by Pulbitsa. Seoul.

Han Tohyŏn. 1986. "1930 nyŏndae nongch'on chinhŭng undong ŭi sŏnggyŏk" [The nature of the rural revitalization campaign in 1930s Korea]. Pp. 233-77 in *Han'guk kŭndae nongch'on sahoe wa ilbon chegukchuŭi* [Modern rural society and Japanese imperialism in Korea], edited by Han'guk sahoesa yŏn'guhoe. Seoul: Munhak kwa chisŏngsa.

Han Wugŭn. 1971. *Tonghangnan kiin e kwanhan yŏn'gu* [A study of the causes of the Tonghak Rebellion]. Seoul: Han'guk munhwa yŏn'guso.

Han'guk yŏksa hakhoe. 1991-92. *1894 nongmin chŏnjaeng yŏn'gu I and II* [Studies of the 1894 peasant wars]. Seoul: Yŏksa pip'yŏngsa.

Han'guk yŏksa yŏn'guhoe. 1989. *3.1 minjok haebang undong yŏn'gu* [A study of the March First national liberation movement]. Seoul: Ch'ŏngnyŏnsa.

Hŏ Changman. 1963. *1920 nyŏndae nongmin undong ŭi palchŏn* [The development of peasant movements in the 1920s]. P'yŏngyang: Chosŏn nodongdang Press.

Hŏ Chongho. 1965. *Chosŏn ponggŏn malgi ŭi sojakche yŏn'gu* [A study of the tenancy system in the late Yi dynasty]. P'yŏngyang: Sahoe kwahagwŏn Press.

Hong Sŏngch'an. 1981. "Hanmal-Ilcheha ŭi chijuje yŏn'gu: Kanghwa Hongssiga ŭi ch'usugi wa changch'aek punsŏk ŭl chungsim ŭro" [A case study of landlordism in the late Chosŏn dynasty and early colonial Korea: The case of the Kanghwa Hong family]." *Han'guksa yŏn'gu* 33: 67-115.

―――. 1985. "Hanmal-Ilcheha ŭi chijuje yŏn'gu: Koksŏng Chossiga ŭi chiju roŭi sŏngjang kwa kŭ pyŏndong" [A case study of landlordism in the Late Chosŏn dynasty and early colonial Korea: The case of the Koksŏng Cho family]. *Tongbang hakchi* 49: 113-64.

―――. 1986. "Hanmal-Ilcheha ŭi chijuje yŏn'gu: 50 chŏngbo chiju Posŏng Yissiga ŭi chiju kyŏngyŏng sarye" [A case study of landlordism in the Late Chosŏn dynasty and early colonial Korea: The case of the Posŏng Yi family]. *Tongbang hakchi* 53: 155-214.

―――. 1992. *Han'guk kŭndae nongch'on sahoe pyŏndong kwa chijuch'ŭng* [Social change and landlord class in modern rural Korea]. Seoul: Chisik sanŏpsa.

Hong Sŏnghŭp. 1985. "T'oji soyu wa chiju sojak kwangye ŭi sŏnggyŏk pyŏnhwa e kwanhan yŏn'gu" [A case study of the agrarian landownership and sharecropping system]. M.A. thesis, Seoul National University.

Hwang Namjun. 1987. "Chŏnnam chibang chŏngch'i wa yŏ-sun sagŏn" [Local politics in South Chŏlla province and the Yo-Sun incident]. Pp. 413-96 in *Haebang chŏnhusa ŭi insik 3* [Perspectives on Korean history in the pre- and postwar era]. Seoul: Han'gilsa.

In Chŏngsik. 1949. *Chosŏn nongŏp kyŏngjeron* [On the Korean agricultural economy]. Seoul: Pangmun ch'ulp'ansa.

Kajimura Hideki. 1989. "Pigyojŏk kwanjŏm esŏ pon Chosŏn t'oji chosa saŏp" [The Korean cadastral land survey in comparative perspective]. Pp. 79-112

in *Kŭndae Chosŏn ŭi kyŏngje kujo* [The economic structure of modern Korea], edited by An Pyŏngjik. Seoul: Pibongsa.
Kang Chŏngsuk. 1983. "Ilcheha Andong chibang nongmin undong e kwanhan yŏn'gu" [A study of peasant movements of Andong county during Japanese colonialism]. M.A. thesis, Ewha Womans University.
Kang Hundŏk. 1981. "Ilcheha sojak chaengŭi ŭi sŏnggyŏk e taehan il koch'al" [An analysis of the characteristics of tenancy disputes during Japanese colonialism]. *Han'guksa nonch'ong* 4: 83–156.
Kang T'aehun. 1988. "Ilcheha Chosŏn esŏ ŭi nongminch'ŭng punhae e kwanhan yŏn'gu" [A study of rural class differentiation in colonial Korea]. Pp. 153–306 in *Han'guk kŭndae nongch'on sahoe wa nongmin undong* [Rural society and peasant movements in modern Korea], edited by Chang Siwŏn et al. Seoul: Yŏlŭmsa.
Kim Chinbong. 1970. "Chinju minnan e taehayŏ" [On the Chinju Rebellion]. *Paeksan hakpo* 8: 427–58.
Kim Ch'ŏl. [1965]1988. "Singminjigi ŭi ingu wa kyŏngje" [The population and economy during the colonial period]. Pp. 109–54 *Ilche malgi p'acism kwa han'guk sahoe* [Fascism and Korean society in the later years of Japanese colonialism], edited by Ch'oi Wŏngyu. Seoul: Ch'ŏng'a.
Kim Chŏngsil. 1934. "Chosŏn nongjiryŏng kŏmt'o" [An examination of the Agricultural Lands Ordinance]. *Sindonga* 4(6): 28–35.
Kim Chŏngsuk. 1958. "1934–37 Myŏngch'ŏn nongmintŭl ŭi hyŏngmyŏngjŏk chinch'ul" [The revolutionary advance of the Myŏngch'ŏn Peasant Union, 1934–37]. *Yŏksa kwahak* 4(3): 6–30.
Kim Chunbo. 1970. *Han'guk chabon chuŭisa yŏn'gu* [A study of the history of Korean capitalism]. Seoul: Ilchogak.
Kim Chunyŏp and Kim Ch'angsun. 1963–76. *Han'guk kongsan chuŭi undongsa* [The history of Korean communist movements]. 5 vols. Seoul: Kodae asea munje yŏn'guso.
Kim Kyŏngil. 1987. "Ilcheha ŭi nongŏp kwa kongdong nodong chojik" [Agriculture and communal labor organizations in colonial Korea]. Pp. 502–37 in *Hyŏndae chabon chuŭi wa kongdongch'e iron* [Modern capitalism and theories of community], edited by Seoul taehakkyo sahoehak yŏn'guhoe. Seoul: Han'gilsa.
Kim Namsik. 1974. *Namnodang yŏn'gu charyojip* [Materials on the South Korean Workers' Party]. 2 vols. Seoul: Kodae asea munje yŏn'guso.
Kim Namsik, Lee Chŏngsik, and Han Honggu. 1986. *Han'guk hyŏndaesa charyo ch'ongsŏ* [A collection of materials on contemporary Korean history]. 15 vols. Seoul: Tolbege.
Kim P'ildong. 1990. "Kye ŭi yŏksajŏk punhwa palchŏn kwajŏng e kwanhan siron" [A preliminary study of the historical development of *kye*]. Pp. 54–87 in *Han'guk ŭi sahoe chojik kwa sahoe sasang* [Social organization and social thought in Korea]. Seoul: Han'guk sahoesa yŏn'guhoe.

Kim San. 1934. "Chosŏn nongch'on pŏmnyul munje" [Legal issues in rural Korea]. *Sindonga* 4(10): 99-104.

Kim Sangjo. 1981. "Nongmin i ssaun ilchemal" [Peasant resistance in later years of colonialism]. *Sindonga* 201 (May): 334-58.

Kim Sŏggŭn. 1983. "Singminjiha (1919-32) han'guk nongch'on ŭi sahoe kujo pyŏnhyŏk undong e kwanhan yŏn'gu" [A study of social transformation movements in colonial rural Korea]. M.A. thesis, Chŏngsin munhwa yŏn'guwŏn.

Kim T'aeil. 1990. "Kun tanwi chiyŏk sahoe wa nongmin t'ongje" [County-level local society and peasant control]. Pp. 63-82 in *Chiyŏk sahoe chibae kujo wa nongmin* [Power structure of local society and peasants], edited by Han'guk nongch'on sahoe yŏn'guso. Seoul: Yŏn'gusa.

Kim Yongbok. 1989. "Haebang chikhu pukhan inmin wiwŏnhoe ŭi chojik kwa hwaldong" [The organization and activities of people's committees in North Korea after liberation]. Pp. 180-246 in *Haebang chŏnhusa ŭi insik 5* [Perspectives on Korean history in the pre- and postwar era]. Seoul: Han'gilsa.

Kim Yonggi. 1980. *Naŭi han'gil yuksimnyŏn* [My sixty years of anticolonialism]. Seoul: Kyujang munhwasa.

Kim Yŏngdu. [1928]1987. "'Chosŏn undong' palgan sŏnŏn ŭi pip'an" [A critique of the declaration of the "Korean Movement"]. *Hyŏn'gyedan* 1. Reprinted in *Singminji sidae sahoe undongnon yŏn'gu* [Studies of theories of social movements during the colonial period], edited by Pae Sŏngch'an, pp. 209-17.

Kim Yŏngmo. 1971. "Ilche sidae chiju ŭi sahoejok paegyŏng kwa idong" [The social background and mobility of landlords during the Japanese colonial period]." *Asea yŏn'gu* 14: 107-25.

Kim Yongsŏp. 1960. "Yang'an ŭi yŏn'gu: Chosŏn hugi ŭi nongga kyŏngje" [A study of the land registers: The economy of peasant households in the late Yi dynasty]." Part 1, *Sahak yŏn'gu* 7: 1-95; Part 2, *Sahak yŏn'gu* 8: 59-119.

———. 1970. *Chosŏn hugi nongŏpsa yŏn'gu* [Studies of the agrarian history of the late Yi dynasty]. Seoul: Ilchogak.

———. 1972. "Hanmal-Ilcheha ŭi chijuje: Kanghwa Kimssiga ŭi ch'usugi rŭl t'onghaeso pon chiju kyŏngyŏng" [A case study of landlordism in the late Chosŏn dynasty and early colonial Korea: The case of the Kanghwa Kim family]. *Tonga munhwa* 11: 3-86.

———. 1975. *Han'guk kŭndae nongŏpsa yŏn'gu* [Studies of the agrarian history of modern Korea]. Seoul: Ilchogak.

———. 1978. "Hanmal-Ilcheha ŭi chijuje: Kobu Kimssiga ŭi chiju kyŏngyŏng kwa chabon chŏnhwan" [A case study of landlordism in the late Chosŏn dynasty and early colonial Korea: The case of the Kobu Kim family]. *Han'guksa yŏn'gu* 19:65-135.

———. 1992. *Han'guk kŭn hyŏndae nongŏpsa yŏn'gu* [Studies of the agrarian history of twentieth-century Korea]. Seoul: Ilchogak.

Kim Yŏngsuk and Kim Hŭiil. 1959. "Ronmun <1934-1937 nyŏn Myŏngch'ŏn nongmin tŭl ŭi hyŏngmyŏngjŏk chinch'ul> e taehan myŏtt kaji pip'anjŏk ŭigyŏn" [Critiques of the article "Revolutionary advance of the Myŏngch'ŏn Peasant Union, 1934-1937"]. *Yŏksa kwahak* 3: 69-73.

Ko Chŏngsu. 1958a. "1920 nyŏndae mal 1930 nyŏndae ch'o panil nongmin undong ŭi saeroun ang'yang (1929-1932)" [New anti-Japanese peasant movements in the late 1920s and early 1930s]. *Yŏksa kwahak* 4(2): 40-56.

———. 1958b. "Widaehan sahoe chuŭi 10 wŏl hyŏngmyŏng kwa Chosŏn e sŏŭi nongmin undong ŭi saeroun ang'yang" [The Great Socialist October Revolution and the new peasant movement in Korea]. *Yŏksa kwahak* 4(6): 21-33.

Kwŏn T'aehwan and Sin Yongha. 1977. "Chosŏn wangjo sidae ingu ch'ujŏng e kwanhan il siron" [A preliminary estimate of population in the Chosŏn dynasty]. *Tonga munhwa* 14.

Kwŏn Tuyŏng. 1979. "Ilcheha ŭi han'guk nongmin undong" [Korean peasant movements during Japanese colonialism]. Pp. 143-81 in *Han'guk kŭndaesa ron* [Korean modern history], vol. 3, edited by Yun Pyŏngsŏk, Sin Yongha, and An Pyŏngjik. Seoul: Chisik sanŏpsa.

Miyata Setsuko. 1988. "Chosŏn minjung ŭi chung'il chŏnjaenggwan" [Korean people's view of the Sino-Japanese War]. Pp. 408-35 in *Ilche malgi p'acism kwa han'guk sahoe* [Fascism and Korean society in the later years of Japanese colonialism], edited by Ch'oi Wŏngyu. Seoul: Ch'ŏng'a.

Pae Sŏngch'an, ed. 1987. *Singminji sidae sahoe undongnon yŏn'gu* [Studies of theories of social movements during the colonial period]. Seoul: Tolbege.

Pae Yŏngsun. 1988. "Hanmal ilche ch'ogi ŭi t'oji chosa wa chise kaejŏng e kwanhan yŏn'gu" [A study of the cadastral land survey and land tax reform in late Chosŏn and early colonial years]. Ph.D. diss., Seoul National University.

Pak Ch'ŏnu. 1983. "Hanmal-Ilcheha ŭi chijuje yŏn'gu: Amt'aedo Munssiga ŭi chijuro ŭi sŏngjang kwa kŭ pyŏndong [A study of landlordism in the late Chosŏn dynasty and early colonial Korea: The case of the Amt'aedo Mun family]. M.A. thesis, Yonsei University.

Pak Hyesuk. 1987. "Mi kunjŏnggi nongmin undong kwa chŏnnong ŭi undong nosŏn" [Peasant movements and the policy line of the National League of Peasant Unions during the American military occupation]. Pp. 353-412 in *Haebang chŏnhusa ŭi insik 3* [Perspectives on Korean history in the pre- and postwar era]. Seoul: Han'gilsa.

Pak Kwangsu. 1969. "Chinju minnan ŭi yŏn'gu" [A study of the Chinju Rebellion]. *Inch'ŏn kyŏyuk taehak nonmunjip*.

Pak Kyŏngsik. 1986. *Ilbon chegukjuŭi ŭi Chosŏn chibae* [Japanese imperialist rule in Korea]. Seoul: Ch'ŏng'a.

———. 1988. "T'aep'yŏngyang chŏnjaenggi ŭi han'guggin kangje yŏnhaeng" [Draft of Koreans for forced labor during the Pacific War]. Pp. 49-85 in *Ilche malgi p'acism kwa han'guk sahoe* [Fascism and Korean society in the later years of Japanese colonialism], edited by Ch'oi Wŏngyu. Seoul: Ch'ŏng'a.

Pak Myŏnggyu. 1987. "Ilche sidae nongmin undong ŭi kyech'ŭngjŏk sŏnggyŏk" [The class character of peasant movements in colonial Korea]. Pp. 538-69 in *Hyŏndae chabon chuŭi wa kongdongch'e iron* [Modern capitalism and theories of community], edited by Seoul taehakkyo sahoehak yŏn'guhoe. Seoul: Han'gilsa.

Pak Sangt'ae. 1987. "Chosŏn hugi ŭi ingu-t'oji appak e taehayŏ" [Population/land pressure in the late Chosŏn dynasty]. *Han'guk sahoehak* 21: 101-21.

Pak Sŏp. 1988. "Singminji Chosŏn e issŏsŏ 1930 nyŏndae ŭi nongŏp chŏngch'aek e kwanhan yŏn'gu" [A study of agricultural policy in 1930s Korea]. Pp. 111-50 in *Han'guk kŭndae nongch'on sahoewa nongmin undong* [Rural society and peasant movements in modern Korea], edited by Chang Siwŏn et al. Seoul: Yŏlŭmsa.

Pak Sundong. 1986. *Amt'aedo sojak chaengŭi* [Amt'ae Island tenancy disputes]. Seoul: Ch'ongnyŏnsa.

Sagong P'yo. [1929]1987. "Chosŏn ŭi chŏngse wa Chosŏn kongsan chuŭija ŭi tangmyŏn immu" [The current situation in Korea and the main task for Korean communists]. *Leninjuŭi* 1. Reprinted in *Singminji sidae sahoe undongnon yŏn'gu* [Studies on theories of social movements in colonial Korea], edited by Pae Sŏngch'an, pp. 65-129.

Sin Yongha. 1979. *Chosŏn t'oji chosa saŏp yŏn'gu* [A study of the land survey program of Korea under Japanese colonial rule]. Seoul: Han'guk yŏn'guwŏn.

———. 1985. "Kabo nongmin chŏnjaeng ŭi chuch'e seryŏk kwa sahoe sinbun" [The main social forces of Kabo peasant wars and their social status]. *Han'guksa yŏn'gu* 50/51: 225-73.

———. 1987. *Han'guk kŭndae sahoesa yŏn'gu* [A study of the social history of modern Korea]. Seoul: Ilchisa.

See also Shin, Yongha.

Son Hoch'ŏl. 1989. "Pŭrusŭ k'ŏmingsŭ ŭi han'guk hyŏndaesa pip'an" [A critique of Bruce Cumings's research on modern Korea]. *Silch'ŏn munhak* Fall: 295-330.

Song Ch'ansŏp et al. 1988. *1862 nyŏn nongmin hangjaeng* [The 1862 peasant uprisings]. Seoul: Mangwŏn han'guksa yŏn'gusil.

Suzuki Ikuo. 1989. *Pŏbŭl t'onghan Chosŏn singminji chibae e kwanhan yŏn'gu* [A study of the colonial rule of Korea through law]. Seoul: Kodae minjok munje yŏn'guso.

Yang Kyŏnja. 1933. "Chosŏn sojangnyŏng chejŏng e taehayŏ" [Regarding the promulgation of the Tenant Arbitration Ordinance in Korea]. *Sindonga* 3: 38-41.

Yi Chaehwa. 1988. *Han'guk kŭn hyŏndae minjok haebang undongsa* [A history of national liberation movements in modern and contemporary Korea]. Seoul: Paeksan sŏdang.

Yi Chongmin. 1989. "1930 nyŏndae nongmin chohap ŭi sŏnggyŏk yŏn'gu" [A study of the characteristics of peasant unions in the early 1930s]. M.A. thesis, Yonsei University.

Yi Chunsik. 1984. "Ilcheha Tanch'ŏn chibang ŭi nongmin undong e taehan yŏn'gu" [A study of peasant movements in the Tanch'ŏn area under Japanese imperialism]. M.A. thesis, Yonsei University.

———. 1989. "1930 nyŏndae ch'o hamgyŏngdo chibang ŭi mujang nongmin t'ujaeng" [Arms struggles in Hamgyŏng provinces in the early 1930s]. *Yŏksa pip'yŏng* 4: 157-72.

———. 1993. *Nongch'on sahoe pyŏndong kwa nongmin undong* [Rural change and peasant movements]. Seoul: Minyŏngsa.

Yi Hyesuk. 1988. "Mi kunjŏnggi nongmin undong ŭi songgyŏk kwa chŏn'gae kwajŏng" [The characteristics and process of peasant movements during American military rule]. Pp. 229-78 in *Haebang chikhuŭi minjok munje wa sahoe undong* [National issues and social movements in liberated Korea], edited by Han'guk sahoesa yŏn'guhoe. Seoul: Munhak kwa chisŏngsa.

Yi Hyŏngch'an. 1988. "1920-1930 nyŏndae han'gugin ŭi manju imin yŏn'gu" [A study of Korean immigration to Manchuria in the 1920s and 1930s]. Pp. 209-83 in *Ilcheha han'guk ŭi sahoe kyegŭp kwa sahoe pyŏndong* [Social class and social change in colonial Korea], edited by Han'guk sahoesa yŏn'guhoe.

Yi Kwanggyu. 1990. *Han'guk ŭi kajok kwa chongjok* [Family and kinship in Korea]. Seoul: Minŭmsa.

Yi Sŏngmu. 1980. *Chosŏn ch'ogi yangban yŏn'gu* [A study of the early Chosŏn yangban]. Seoul: Ilchogak.

Yi Yŏnghun. 1988. *Chosŏn hugi sahoe kyŏngjesa* [A socioeconomic history of the late Chosŏn dynasty]. Seoul: Han'gilsa.

Yun Sujong. 1990. "Ilcheha ŭi kojidae e kwanhan il koch'al" [An examination of wage labor in colonial Korea]. Pp. 89-141 in *Han'guk ŭi sahoe chojik kwa sahoe sasang* [Social organization and social thought in Korea], edited by Han'guk sahoesa yŏn'guhoe.

WORKS IN JAPANESE

Asada Kyoji. 1973. *Nihon teikokushugika no minzoku kakumei undō* [National revolutionary movements under Japanese imperialism]. Tokyo: Miraisha.

Hida Okazu. 1982a. "Chŏngp'yŏng nōmin kumiai no tenkai-1930 nendai no akairo nōmin kumiai no jirei" [The development of red peasant unions in Chŏngp'yŏng]. Pp. 317-50 in *Shokuminjiki Chōsen no shakai to teikō* [Korean society and protest in the colonial period], edited by Jirō Iinuma and Chae-ŏn Kang. Tokyo: Miraisha.

———. 1982b. "Yŏnghŭng nōmin kumiai no tenkai-1930 nendai no akairo nōmin kumiai no jirei" [The development of red peasant unions in Yŏnghŭng]. Pp. 53-78 in *Chōsen 1930 nendai kenkyū* [Studies of 1930s Korea], edited by Mukuge no Kai. Tokyo: Sanichi shobo.

———. 1984. "Kimhae nōmin kumiai no tenkai-1930 nendai no akairo nōmin kumiai no jirei" [The development of red peasant unions in Kimhae]. In *Chōsen minzoku undōshi kenkyū* [The history of Korean nationalist movements], vol. 1, edited by Chōsen minzoku undōshi kenkyūjo. Tokyo: Aohisa Bunko.

———. 1988. "Myŏngch'ŏn nōmin kumiai no tenkai" [The development of peasant unions in Myŏngch'ŏn]. Pp. 35-57 in *Chōsen minzoku undōshi kenkyū*

[The history of Korean nationalist movements], vol. 5, edited by Chōsen minzoku undōshi kenkyūjo. Tokyo: Aohisa Bunko.
Hori Kazuo. 1976. "Nitteika Chōsen ni okeru shokuminchi nōgyōseisaku" [The agricultural policy of Japanese imperialism in Korea]. *Nihonshi kenkyū* [Japanese history].
Im Pyŏngyun. 1971. *Shokuminchi ni okeru shōgyōteki nōgyō no tenkai* [Agricultural commercialization in colonial Korea]. Tokyo: Tokyo University Press.
In Chŏngsik. 1939. *Chōsen no nōgyō kikō* [The agricultural system of Korea]. Tokyo: Hakuyosha.
Ishi Yoshikuni. 1972. *Kankoku no jinkō zōka no bunseki* [An analysis of population growth in Korea]. Tokyo.
Kang Chaeŏn and Kim Tonghun. 1989. *Zainichi kankoku Chōsenjin rekishi to tenbou* [History and future prospects of Koreans in Japan]. Tokyo: Rōdō keizaisha.
Miyajima Hiroshi. 1974. "Chōsen Kabo kaikaku igo no shōgyōteki nōgyō" [Commercial agriculture since Kabo reform in Korea]. *Shirin* 57(6): 812–51.
———. 1975. "Chōsen tochi chōsa jigyō kenkyū josetsu" [An introduction to the Korean land survey]. *Azia keizai*.
Namiki Makoto. 1983. "Shokumin chika Chōsen ni okeru chihōminshū undō no tenkai: Hamgyŏng namdo hongwŏnkun no jirei o chūshin ni" [Regional popular movements in colonial Korea: The case of Hongwŏn county in South Hamgyŏng province]. *Chōsenshi kenkyūkai ronbunshū*.
Ōwa Kazuaki. 1982. "1920 nendai zenhanki no Chōsen nōmin undō: Chŏnnam Sunch'ŏnkun no jirei o chūshin ni" [Korean peasant movements in the early 1920s: A case in Sunch'ŏn county]. *Rekishiteki kenkyū* 502.
Pak Munkyu. 1933. "Nōson shakai bunka no kiten toshite tochi chōsa jigyō ni tsuite" [The land survey as a turning point in rural differentiation]. *Chōsen shakai keizaishi kenkyū*. Keijō University.
Shikata Hiroshi. 1937. "Richo jinkō ni kansuru ichi kenkyū" [A study of population in the Yi dynasty]. *Chōsen shakai hōseishi kenkyū* [Studies in the social and legal history of Korea]. Tokyo.
Sudō Yoshiyuki. 1937. "Chōsen kōki no dendō bunki ni kansuru kenkyū" [A study of land deeds in the later Yi dynasty]. *Rekishigaku kenkyū* 7: 2–48.
Suzuki Eitarō. 1943. *Chōsen nōson shakai tōsagi* [Survey reports of Korean rural society]. Seoul.
Wada Ichiro. 1920. *Chōsen tochi chizei seido chōsa hōkokusho* [A study of land tax in Korea]. Chōsen sōtokufu, Keijō.
Yi Chaemu. 1955. "Chōsen ni okeru tochi chōsa jigyō jittai" [Realities of the land survey]. *Shakai kagaku kenkyū* 7: 5.

WORKS IN ENGLISH

Alavi, Hamza. 1965. "Peasants and Revolution." Pp. 241–77 in *The Socialist Register*. New York: Monthly Review Press.

Alexander, Jeffrey, et al. 1987. *The Micro-Macro Link*. Berkeley: University of California Press.
Amsden, Alice. 1989. *Asia's Next Giant: South Korea and Late Industrialization*. Oxford: Oxford University Press.
Arendt, Hannah. 1951. *The Origins of Totalitarianism*. New York: Harcourt, Brace.
Balbus, Isaac. 1971. "The Concept of Interest in Pluralist and Marxian Analysis." *Politics and Society* 1: 151–77.
Baldwin, Frank. 1969. "The March First Movement: Korean Challenge and Japanese Response." Ph.D. diss., Columbia University.
Ban, Sung Hwan, P. Moon, and D. Perkins. 1980. *Rural Development*. Cambridge: Harvard University Press.
Ban, Sungwhan. 1979. "Agricultural Growth in Korea, 1918–1971." Pp. 90–116 in *Agricultural Growth in Japan, Taiwan, Korea, and the Philippines*, edited by Y. Hayami et al. Honolulu: University Press of Hawaii.
Barnhart, Michael. 1987. *Japan Prepares for Total War*. Ithaca: Cornell University Press.
Bornschier, Volker, C. Chase-Dunn, and R. Rubinson. 1978. "Cross-National Evidence of the Effects of Foreign Investment and Aid on Economic Growth and Inequality: A Study of Findings and a Reanalysis." *American Journal of Sociology* 84(3): 651–83.
Boserup, Ester. 1965. *The Conditions of Agricultural Growth: The Economics of Agrarian Change under Population Pressure*. Chicago: Aldine.
Boswell, Terry, and William Dixon. 1990. "Dependency and Rebellion: A Cross-National Analysis." *American Sociological Review* 55: 540–59.
Bowen, Roger. 1988. "Japanese Peasants: Moral? Rational? Revolutionary? or Duped? A Review Article." *Journal of Asian Studies* 47(4): 821–33.
Brandt, Vincent. 1971. *A Korean Village*. Cambridge: Harvard University Press.
Brenner, Robert. 1976. "Agrarian Class Structure and Economic Development in Pre-industrial Europe." *Past and Present* 70: 30–75.
———. 1977. "The Origins of Capitalist Development: A Critique of Neo-Smithian Marxism." *New Left Review* 104: 25–92.
Brocheux, Pierre. 1983. "Moral Economy or Political Economy?: The Peasants Are Always Rational." *Journal of Asian Studies* 42(4): 791–803.
Brunner, Edmund. 1928. "Rural Korea." *Report of the International Missionary Council Jerusalem Meetings*.
Burmeister, Larry. 1990. "South Korea's Rural Development Dilemma." *Asian Survey* 30(7): 711–23.
Calhoun, Craig. 1988. "The Radicalism of Tradition and the Question of Class Struggle." Pp. 129–75 in *Rationality and Revolution*, edited by Michael Taylor. Cambridge: Cambridge University Press.
Chang, Yun-Shik. 1991. "The Personalist Ethic and the Market in Korea." *Comparative Studies in Society and History* 33(1): 106–29.

Chase-Dunn, Christopher. 1989. *Global Formation: Structure of the World-economy.* Cambridge, Mass.: Basil Blackwell.
Chirot, Daniel, and Charles Ragin. 1975. "The Market, Tradition and Peasant Rebellion: The Case of Romania in 1907." *American Sociological Review* 40: 428–44.
Cho, Jaehong. 1964. "Post-1945 Land Reforms and Their Consequences in South Korea." Ph.D. diss., Indiana University.
Ch'oe, Yŏng-ho. 1981. "Reinterpreting Traditional History in North Korea." *Journal of Asian Studies* 40(3): 503–23.
Choi, Chungmoo. 1993. "The Discourse of Decolonization and Popular Memory: South Korea." *Positions* 1: 77–102.
Choi, Ho-Chin. 1970. "The Strengthening of the Economic Domination by Japanese Colonialism (1932–1945)." *Yonsei nonch'ong* 7: 349–78.
Clogg, Clifford, Eva Petkova, and Edward Shihadeh. 1992. "Statistical Methods for Analyzing Collapsibility in Regression Models." *Journal of Educational Statistics* 17: 51–74.
Cohen, Stephen F. 1980. *Bukharin and the Bolshevik Revolution.* Oxford: Oxford University Press.
Colburn, Forrest D., ed. 1989. *Everyday Forms of Peasant Resistance.* Armonk, N.Y.: M. E. Sharpe.
Cole, David C., and Princeton N. Lyman. 1971. *Korean Development: The Interplay of Politics and Economics.* Cambridge: Harvard University Press.
Conde, David. 1947. "The Korean Minority in Japan." *Far Eastern Survey* (February 26): 41–45.
Cumings, Bruce. 1973. "Is Korea a Mass Society?" *Occasional Papers on Korea* 1: 65–81.
———. 1981a. "Interest and Ideology in the Study of Agrarian Politics." *Politics and Society* 10: 467–95.
———. 1981b. *The Origins of the Korean War.* Vol. 1. Princeton: Princeton University Press.
———. 1984a. "The Legacy of Japanese Colonialism in Korea." Pp. 479–96 in *The Japanese Colonial Empire, 1895–1945,* edited by Ramon Myers and Mark Peattie. Princeton: Princeton University Press.
———. 1984b. "The Origins and Development of the Northeast Asian Political Economy." *International Organization* Winter: 1–40.
Dahl, Robert. 1967. *Pluralist Democracy in the United States.* Chicago: Rand McNally.
Davies, James. 1962. "Toward a Theory of Revolution." *American Sociological Review* 27: 5–18.
Deutsch, Karl. 1961. "Social Mobilization and Political Development." *American Political Science Review* 55(3): 493–514.
Deyo, Frederic, ed. 1987. *The Political Economy of the New Asian Industrialism.* Ithaca: Cornell University Press.

Doe, Jin-soon. 1991. "The Periodization of Modern and Contemporary History in North Korean Academic Circles." *Korea Journal* 31(2): 41-55.
Dore, R. P. 1959. *Land Reform in Japan.* London: Oxford University Press.
Duncan, John. 1988. "The Koryo Origins of the Chosŏn Dynasty: Kings, Aristocrats, and Confucianism." Ph.D. diss., University of Washington.
Eckert, Carter. 1991. *Offspring of Empire: The Koch'ang Kims and the Colonial Origins of Korean Capitalism, 1876-1945.* Seattle: University of Washington Press.
―――. 1996. "Total War, Industrialization, and Social Change in Late Colonial Korea." In *The Japanese Wartime Empire,* edited by Peter Duus, Ramon Myers, and Mark Peattie, pp. 3-39. Princeton: Princeton University Press.
Elster, Jon. 1985. *Making Sense of Marx.* Cambridge: Cambridge University Press.
Evans, Peter. 1979. *The Dependent Development: The Alliance of Multinationals, State, and Local Capital in Brazil.* Princeton: Princeton University Press.
Evans, Peter, Dietrich Rueschemeyer, and Theda Skocpol. 1985. *Bringing the State Back In.* Cambridge: Cambridge University Press.
Fanon, Frantz. 1963. *The Damned.* Paris: Presence Africaine.
Federal Council of the Churches of Christian America. 1920. *The Korean Situation.* No. 2. New York.
Foster, George. 1965. "The Peasant and the Image of Limited Good." *American Anthropologist* 62(2): 293-315.
Gamson, William. 1975. *The Strategy of Protest.* Homewood, Ill.: Dorsey Press.
Gardner, Arthur. 1979. "The Korean Nationalist Movement and An Ch'angho, Advocate of Gradualism." Ph.D. diss., University of Hawaii.
Geertz, Clifford. 1963. *Agricultural Involution: The Process of Ecological Change in Indonesia.* Berkeley: University of California Press.
Gella, Aleksander, ed. 1976. *The Intelligentsia and Intellectuals.* Beverly Hills: Sage Publications.
Gleason, Ralph. 1956. *Taiwan Food Balances, 1935-1954.* Taipei: JCRR.
Gold, Thomas. 1986. *State and Society in the Taiwan Miracle.* Armonk, N.Y.: M. E. Sharpe.
Golden, Miriam. 1988. "Historical Memory and Ideological Orientations in the Italian Workers' Movement." *Politics and Society* 16: 1-34.
Goldstone, Jack. 1991. *Revolution and Rebellion in the Early Modern World.* Berkeley: University of California Press.
Gragert, Edwin. 1982. "Landownership Change in Korea under Japanese Colonial Rule, 1900-1935." Ph.D. diss., Columbia University.
Gramsci, Antonio. 1971. *Selections from The Prison Notebooks.* Edited and translated by Quinten Hoare and Geoffrey Nowell Smith. London: Lawrence and Wishart.
Gurr, Ted. 1970. *Why Men Rebel.* Princeton: Princeton University Press.
Ha, Joseph M. 1971. "Politics of Korean Peasantry: A Study of Land Reforms

and Collectivization with Reference to Sino-Soviet Experiences." Ph.D. diss., Columbia University.

Hane, Mikiso. 1982. *Peasants, Rebels, and Outcasts: The Underside of Modern Japan.* New York: Pantheon Books.

Hanushek, Eric, and John Jackson. 1977. *Statistical Methods for Social Scientists.* New York: Academic Press.

Hayami, Yujiro, and Vernon Ruttan. 1979. "Agricultural Growth in Four Countries." Pp. 3–26 in *Agricultural Growth in Japan, Taiwan, Korea, and the Philippines,* edited by Y. Hayami et al. Honolulu: University Press of Hawaii.

Hayami, Yujiro, Vernon Ruttan, and Herman Southworth. 1979. *Agricultural Growth in Japan, Taiwan, Korea, and the Philippines.* Honolulu: University Press of Hawaii.

Henderson, Gregory. 1968. *Korea: The Politics of the Vortex.* Cambridge: Harvard University Press.

Hirsch, Eric. 1990. "Sacrifice for the Cause: Group Processes, Recruitment, and Committment in a Student Social Movement." *American Sociological Review* 55: 243–54.

Ho, Samuel Pao-San. 1984. "Colonialism and Development: Korea, Taiwan, and Kwantung." Pp. 347–98 in *The Japanese Colonial Empire, 1895–1945,* edited by Ramon Myers and Mark Peattie. Princeton: Princeton University Press.

Hobsbawm, Eric. 1959. *Primitive Rebels.* New York: Norton.

Hofheinz, Roy, Jr. 1977. *The Broken Wave: The Chinese Communist Peasant Movement, 1922–1928.* Cambridge: Harvard University Press.

Hoston, Germaine. 1986. *Marxism and the Crisis of Development in Prewar Japan.* Princeton: Princeton University Press.

Huang, Philip. 1985. *The Peasant Economy and Social Change in North China.* Stanford: Stanford University Press.

———. 1990. *The Peasant Family and Rural Development in the Yangzi Delta, 1350–1988.* Stanford: Stanford University Press.

———. 1991. "A Reply to Ramon Myers." *Journal of Asian Studies* 50: 629–33.

Huntington, Samuel. 1968. *Political Order in Changing Societies.* New Haven: Yale University Press.

Jacobs, Norman. 1985. *The Korean Road to Modernization and Development.* Urbana: University of Illinois Press.

Janelli, Roger, and Dawnhee Yim. 1988–89. "Interest Rates and Rationality: Rotating Credit Associations among Seoul Women." *Journal of Korean Studies* 6: 165–92.

Jenkins, J. Craig. 1982. "Why Do Peasants Rebel? Structural and Historical Theories of Modern Peasant Rebellions." *American Journal of Sociology* 88: 487–514.

Johnson, Chalmers. 1962. *Peasant Nationalism and Communist Power.* Stanford: Stanford University Press.

Ka, Chih-Ming. 1987. "Land Tenure, Development and Dependency in Colonial

Taiwan (1895–1945)." Ph.D. diss., State University of New York at Binghamton.
Kang, Jeong-Koo. 1988. "Rethinking South Korean Land Reform: Focusing on U.S. Occupation as a Struggle against History." Ph.D. diss., University of Wisconsin, Madison.
Keidel, Albert, III. 1981. *Korean Regional Farm Product and Income: 1910–1975*. Seoul: Korean Development Institute.
Kimura, Mitsuhiko. 1990. "Money and Prices in Korea after the Opening of Ports." Paper presented at the annual meeting of the Association for Asian Studies, April, Chicago.
Kingstone-Mann, Esther. 1985. *Lenin and the Problem of Marxist Peasant Revolution*. Oxford: Oxford University Press.
Klandermans, Bert. 1984. "Mobilization and Participation: Social-Psychological Explanations of Resource Mobilization Theory." *American Sociological Review* 49: 583–600.
Klein, Ethel. 1984. *Gender Politics*. Cambridge: Harvard University Press.
———. 1987. "The Diffusion of Consciousness in the United States and Western Europe." Pp. 23–43 in *The Women's Movements of the United States and Western Europe*, edited by Mary Katzenstein and Carol Mueller. Philadelphia: Temple University Press.
Koo, Hagan. 1990. "From Farm to Factory: Proletarianization in Korea." *American Sociological Review* 55(5): 669–81.
———, ed. 1993. *State and Society in Contemporary Korea*. Ithaca: Cornell University Press.
Kornhauser, W. 1959. *The Politics of Mass Society*. New York: Free Press.
Krantz, Frederick, ed. 1985. *History from Below: Studies in Popular Protest and Popular Ideology in Honor of George Rude*. Montreal: Concordia University Press.
Ku, Dae-yeol. 1985. *Korea under Colonialism: The March First Movement and Anglo-Japanese Relations*. Seoul: Royal Asiatic Society, Korea Branch.
Lachmann, Richard. 1989. "Origins of Capitalism in Western Europe: Economic and Political Aspects." *Annual Review of Sociology* 15: 47–72.
Lai, Tse-han, Ramon Myers, and Wei Wou. 1991. *A Tragic Beginning: The Taiwan Uprisings of February 28, 1947*. Stanford: Stanford University Press.
Lee, Chong-Sik. 1963. "Land Reform, Collectivisation and the Peasants in North Korea." Pp. 65–81 in *North Korea Today*, edited by Robert Scalapino. New York: Praeger Publishers.
———. 1964. *The Politics of Korean Nationalism*. Berkeley: University of California Press.
———. 1978. *The Korean Workers' Party*. Stanford: Hoover Institution Press.
Lee, Eddy. 1979. "Egalitarian Peasant Farming and Rural Development: The Case of South Korea." Pp. 24–71 in *Agrarian Systems and Rural Development*, edited by Dharam Ghai, Azizur Khan, Eddy Lee, and Samir Radwan. New York: Holmes and Meier Publishers, Inc.

Lee, Hoon K. 1936. *Land Utilization and Rural Economy in Korea.* New York: Greenwood Press.
Lee, Mun Woong. 1976. *Rural North Korea under Communism.* Houston: Rice University Press.
Lee, Peter. 1965. *Korean Literature: Topics and Themes.* Tucson: University of Arizona Press.
Levy, Marion. 1966. *Modernization and the Structure of Societies.* Princeton: Princeton University Press.
Lew, Young-Ick. 1990. "The Conservative Character of the 1894 Tonghak Peasant Uprising." *Journal of Korean Studies* 7: 149-80.
Lie, John. 1992. "The State as Pimp: Prostitution and the Patriarchal State in 1940s Japan." Paper presented at the annual meeting of the American Sociological Association, August, Pittsburgh.
Lim, Hyun-Chin. 1985. *Dependent Development in Korea, 1963-1979.* Seoul: Seoul National University Press.
Mao Tse-tung [Zedong]. 1967. *Analysis of the Classes in Chinese Society.* Peking: Foreign Language Press.
Marks, Robert. 1984. *Rural Revolution in South China.* Madison: University of Wisconsin Press.
Marx, Karl. [1852] 1981. *The 18th Brumaire of Louis Bonaparte.* New York: International Publishers.
———. [1853] 1978. "The British Rule in India." Pp. 653-58 in *The Marx-Engels Reader,* edited by Robert Tucker (2d ed.). New York: W. W. Norton and Co.
———. [1864] 1978. "Inaugural Address of the Working Men's International Association." Pp. 512-19 in *The Marx-Engels Reader,* edited by Robert Tucker (2d ed.). New York: W. W. Norton and Co.
———. [1888] 1987. *The Communist Manifesto.* New York: International Publishers.
Mason, Edward, et al. 1980. *The Economic and Social Modernization of the Republic of Korea.* Cambridge: Harvard University Press.
McAdam, Doug. 1982. *Political Process and the Development of Black Insurgency.* Chicago: University of Chicago Press.
McAlister, John T., Jr. 1971. *Vietnam: The Origins of Revolution.* Garden City: Doubleday Anchor.
McCarthy, John, and Mayer Zald. 1977. "Resource Mobilization and Social Movements." *American Journal of Sociology* 82: 1212-41.
McNamara, Dennis. 1990. *The Colonial Origins of Korean Enterprise, 1910-1945.* Cambridge: Cambridge University Press.
Meade, E. Grant. 1951. *American Military Government in Korea.* New York: King's Crown Press at Columbia University.
Menzel, Ulrich. 1986. "The Newly Industrializing Countries of East Asia: Imperialist Continuity or a Case of Catching Up?" Pp. 247-63 in *Imperialism*

and After, edited by W. Mommsen and J. Osterhammel. London: German Historical Institute.
Michell, Tony. 1981. "Fact and Hypothesis in Yi Dynasty Economic History: The Demographic Dimension." *Korean Studies Forum* 7: 65-93.
Migdal, Joel S. 1974. *Peasants, Politics, and Revolution.* Princeton: Princeton University Press.
Mitchell, Edward. 1968. "Inequality and Insurgency: A Statistical Study of South Vietnam." *World Politics* 20: 421-38.
Mitchell, Richard. 1967. *The Korean Minority in Japan.* Berkeley: University of California Press.
Mohan, Raj P., ed. 1987. *The Mythmakers: Intellectuals and the Intelligentsia in Perspective.* New York: Greenwood Press.
Moore, Barrington, Jr. 1966. *Social Origins of Dictatorship and Democracy.* Boston: Beacon Press.
Moskowitz, Karl. 1974. "The Creation of the Oriental Development Company: Japanese Illusions Meet Korean Reality." *Occasional Papers on Korea* 2: 73-121.
Mueller, Carol. 1987. "Collective Consciousness, Identity Transformation, and the Rise of Women in Public Office in the United States." Pp. 89-108 in *The Women's Movements of the United States and Western Europe,* edited by Mary Katzenstein and Carol Mueller. Philadelphia: Temple University Press.
Myers, Ramon. 1991. "How Did the Modern Chinese Economy Develop? A Review Article." *Journal of Asian Studies* 50: 604-28.
Myers, Ramon, and Mark Peattie. 1984. *The Japanese Colonial Empire, 1895-1945.* Princeton: Princeton University Press.
Myers, Ramon, and Yamada Saburō. 1984. "Agricultural Development in the Empire." Pp. 420-51 in *The Japanese Colonial Empire, 1895-1945,* edited by Ramon Myers and Mark Peattie. Princeton: Princeton University Press.
Nahm, Andrew C. 1975. "Themes of Popular Songs and Poems of the Koreans as Oppressed People." Pp. 188-230 in *Korea's Response to Japan: The Colonial Period 1910-1915,* edited by C. I. Eugene Kim and Doretha E. Mortimore. Kalamazoo: Western Michigan University.
Oberschall, Anthony. 1973. *Social Conflict and Social Movements.* Englewood Cliffs, N.J.: Prentice Hall.
O'Donnell, Guillermo. 1973. *Modernization and Bureaucratic-Authoritarianism.* Berkeley: University of California Press.
Ohkawa, Kazushi, and Henry Rosovsky. 1965. "A Century of Economic Growth." Pp. 47-92 in *The State and Economic Enterprise in Japan,* edited by W. Lockwood. Princeton: Princeton University Press.
Olson, Mancur. 1965. *The Logic of Collective Action.* Cambridge: Harvard University Press.
Paige, Jeffery. 1970. "Inequality and Insurgency in Vietnam: A Re-Analysis." *World Politics* 23: 24-37.

———. 1975. *Agrarian Revolution*. New York: Free Press.
Palais, James. 1975. *Politics and Policy in Traditional Korea*. Cambridge: Harvard University Press.
———. 1982-83. "Land Tenure in Korea: Tenth to Twelfth Centuries." *Journal of Korean Studies* 4: 73-205.
———. 1984. "Slavery and Slave Society in Koryo." *Journal of Korean Studies* 5: 173-90.
Perkins, Dwight. 1969. *Agricultural Development in China, 1368-1968*. Chicago: Aldine.
Perry, Elizabeth. 1980. *Rebels and Revolutionaries in North China, 1845-1945*. Stanford: Stanford University Press.
Pinard, Maurice, and Richard Hamilton. 1989. "Intellectuals and the Leadership of Social Movements: Some Comparative Perspectives." *Research in Social Movements, Conflict and Change* 11: 73-107.
Piven, Frances, and Richard Cloward. 1977. *Poor People's Movements*. New York: Vintage Books.
Polanyi, Karl. 1944. *The Great Transformation*. Boston: Beacon Press.
Popkin, Samuel. 1979. *The Rational Peasant*. Berkeley: University of California Press.
Postan, Michael. 1972. *The Medieval Economy and Society*. Berkeley: University of California Press.
Powelson, John, and Richard Stock. 1987. *The Peasant Betrayed*. Boston: Oelgeschlager, Gunn and Hain.
Redfield, Robert. 1960. *Peasant Society and Culture*. Chicago: University of Chicago Press.
Rhee, Sang-Woo. 1980. "Land Reform in South Korea: A Macro-Level Policy Review." Pp. 319-49 in *Land Reform: Some Asian Experiences*, edited by Inayatullah. Kuala Lumpur, Malaysia: Asian and Pacific Development Administration Centre.
Robinson, Michael. 1988. *Cultural Nationalism in Colonial Korea, 1920-1925*. Seattle: University of Washington Press.
———. 1990. "Forced Assimilation, Mobilization, and War." Pp. 305-26 in *Korea: Old and New*, edited by Carter Eckert et al. Seoul: Ilchogak.
Roeder, Philip. 1984. "Legitimacy and Peasant Revolution: An Alternative to Moral Economy." *Peasant Studies* 11(3): 149-68.
Rubinson, Richard. 1977. "Dependence, Government Revenue, and Economic Growth: 1955-1970." *Studies in Comparative International Development* 12: 3-25.
Rude, George. 1980. *Ideology and Popular Protest*. New York: Pantheon Books.
Rueschemeyer, Dietrich, and Peter Evans. 1985. "The State and Economic Transformation: Toward an Analysis of the Conditions Underlying Effective Intervention." Pp. 44-77 in *Bringing the State Back In*, edited by P. Evans, D. Rueschemeyer, and T. Skocpol. Cambridge: Cambridge University Press.

Russet, Bruce. 1964. "Inequality and Instability: The Relation of Land Tenure to Politics." *World Politics* 16: 442-54.
Scalapino, Robert, and Chong-Sik Lee. 1972. *Communism in Korea*. 2 vols. Berkeley: University of California Press.
Schumpeter, Joseph A. [1942] 1950. *Capitalism, Socialism and Democracy*. 3d ed. New York: Harper and Row, Publishers.
Scott, James. 1976. *The Moral Economy of the Peasant*. New Haven: Yale University Press.
———. 1977. "Hegemony and the Peasantry." *Politics and Society* 7: 267-96.
———. 1985. *Weapons of the Weak*. New Haven: Yale University Press.
Shin, Gi-Wook. 1990. "Resource Mobilization and Peasant Collective Action in Authoritarian Polity: The Case of Colonial Korea." Paper presented at the 85th annual meeting of the American Sociological Association, August, Washington, D.C.
———. 1992. "Rethinking the Micro-Macro Link: Toward an Explanatory Pluralism of Peasant Collective Action." Paper presented at the Workshop on Culture and Social Movements, June, San Diego.
———. 1994. "The Historical Making of Collective Action: The Korean Peasant Uprisings of 1946." *American Journal of Sociology* 99: 1596-1624.
———. 1995. "Marxism, Anti-Americanism, and Democracy in South Korea: An Examination of Nationalist Intellectual Discourse." *positions: east asia cultures critique* 3(2): 508-34
Shin, Susan. 1973. "Land Tenure and the Agrarian Economy in Yi Dynasty Korea: 1600-1800." Ph.D. diss., Harvard University.
———. 1975. "Some Aspects of Landlord-Tenant Relations in Yi Dynasty Korea." *Occasional Papers on Korea* 1: 49-88.
Shin, Yongha [Sin Yongha]. 1978. "Landlordism in the Late Yi Dynasty I and II." *Korea Journal* June: 25-32 and July: 22-29.
Skocpol, Theda. 1979. *States and Social Revolutions*. Cambridge: Cambridge University Press.
———. 1982. "What Makes Peasants Revolutionary?" Pp. 157-79 in *Power and Protest in the Countryside*, edited by R. Weller and S. Guggenheim. Durham, N.C.: Duke University Press.
Smelser, Neil. 1963. *The Theory of Collective Behavior*. New York: Free Press.
Smethurst, Richard. 1974. *A Social Basis for Prewar Japanese Militarism*. Berkeley: University of California Press.
———. 1986. *Agricultural Development and Tenancy Disputes in Japan, 1870-1940*. Princeton: Princeton University Press.
Smith, Thomas. 1959. *The Agrarian Origins of Modern Japan*. Stanford: Stanford University Press.
Snow, David, and Robert Benford. 1988. "Ideology, Frame Resonance, and Participant Mobilization." *International Social Movement Research* 1: 197-217.
Sommerville, John. 1974. "Success and Failure in Eighteenth Century Ulsan: A Study in Social Mobility." Ph.D. diss., Harvard University.

Song, Byung-Nak. 1990. *The Rise of the Korean Economy*. Oxford: Oxford University Press.
Song, Kwang Sung. 1989. "The Impact of U.S. Military Occupation on the Social Development of Decolonized South Korea, 1945-1949." Ph.D. diss., University of California at Los Angeles.
Sorensen, Clark. 1990. "Land Tenure and Class Relations in Colonial Korea." *Journal of Korean Studies* 7: 35-54.
———. 1992. "Korean Peasants: Objects of Myth-making, Myth-making Subjects." Paper presented to Comparative Studies in Ethnicity and Nationality, "Myth, Identity, and Ethnic Conflict," at the Jackson School of International Studies, University of Washington, April 30.
Stinchcombe, Arthur L. 1961. "Agricultural Enterprise and Rural Class Relations." *American Journal of Sociology* 67: 165-76.
Suh, Dae-Sook. 1970. *The Korean Communist Movement, 1918-1948*. Princeton: Princeton University Press.
Suh, Sang-Chul. 1978. *Growth and Structural Changes in the Korean Economy, 1910-1940*. Cambridge: Harvard University Press.
Tawney, R. H. 1966. *Land and Labor in China*. Boston: Beacon Press.
Taylor, Charles, and David Jodice. 1983. *World Handbook of Political and Social Indicators*. Vols. 1 and 2 (3d ed.). New Haven: Yale University Press.
Taylor, Michael. 1988. "Rationality and Revolutionary Collective Action." Pp. 63-97 in *Rationality and Revolution*, edited by M. Taylor. Cambridge: Cambridge University Press.
Taylor, Verta. 1989. "Social Movement Continuity: The Women's Movement in Abeyance." *American Sociological Review* 54: 761-75.
Thompson, E. P. 1966. *The Making of the English Working Class*. New York: Vintage Books.
———. 1971. "The Moral Economy of the English Crowd in the Eighteenth Century." *Past and Present* 50: 71-133.
———. 1978. "Eighteenth-Century English Society: Class Struggle Without Class?" *Social History* 3(2): 133-65.
Thorner, Daniel, Basile Kerblay, and R. E. F. Smith, eds. 1986. *A. V. Chayanov on the Theory of Peasant Economy*. Madison: University of Wisconsin Press.
Tilly, Charles, ed. 1975. *The Formation of National States in Western Europe*. Princeton: Princeton University Press.
———. 1978. *From Mobilization to Revolution*. New York: Random House. Reading, Mass.: Addison-Wesley.
Tilly, Charles, L. Tilly, and R. Tilly. 1975. *The Rebellious Century*. Cambridge: Harvard University Press.
Tong, James. 1988. "Rational Outlaws: Rebels and Bandits in the Ming Dynasty, 1368-1644." Pp. 98-128 in *Rationality and Revolution*, edited by Michael Taylor. Cambridge: Cambridge University Press.
Trewartha, Glenn, and Wilbur Zelinsky. 1955. "Population Distribution and Change in Korea, 1925-49." *Geographical Review* 45(1): 1-26.

Tsurumi, E. Patricia. 1984. "Colonial Education in Korea and Taiwan." Pp. 275-311 in *The Japanese Colonial Empire, 1895-1945*, edited by Ramon Myers and Mark Peattie. Princeton: Princeton University Press.
Um, Ky-Sub. 1984. "On Tenancy and Labor Disputes in the 1920s-1930s." *Journal of Social Sciences and Humanities* 60: 59-75.
Vlastos, Stephen. 1986. *Peasant Protests and Uprisings in Tokugawa Japan*. Berkeley: University of California Press.
Vogel, Ezra. 1991. *The Four Little Dragons: The Spread of Industrialization in East Asia*. Cambridge: Harvard University Press.
Wagner, Edward. 1977. "The Civil Examination Process as Social Leaven: The Case of the Northern Provinces in the Yi Dynasty." *Korea Journal* January: 22-27.
Wallerstein, Immanuel. 1979. *The Capitalist World-Economy*. Cambridge: Cambridge University Press.
Walthall, Anne. 1986. *Social Protest and Popular Culture in Eighteenth-Century Japan*. Tucson: University of Arizona Press.
Walton, John. 1992. *Western Times and Water Wars*. Berkeley: University of California Press.
Walton, John, and Charles Ragin. 1990. "Global and National Sources of Political Protest: Third World Responses to the Debt Crisis." *American Sociological Review* 55: 876-90.
Washburn, John. 1947. "Russia Looks at Northern Korea." *Pacific Affairs* 20(2): 152-60.
Waswo, Ann. 1974. "The Origins of Tenant Unrest." Pp. 374-94 in *Japan in Crisis: Essays on Taishō Democracy*, edited by B. Silberman and H. Harootunian. Princeton: Princeton University Press.
———. 1977. *Japanese Landlords*. Berkeley: University of California Press.
Weber, Max. 1968. *Economy and Society*. Edited by Guenther Roth and Claus Wittich. New York: Bedminster Press.
Wells, Kenneth. 1990. *New God, New Nation: Protestants and Self-Reconstruction Nationalism in Korea, 1896-1937*. Honolulu: University of Hawaii Press.
White, James. 1988. "Rational Rioters: Leaders, Followers, and Popular Protest in Early Modern Japan." *Politics and Society* 16: 35-69.
Wiens, Mi Chu. 1980. "Lord and Peasant: The Sixteenth to the Eighteenth Century." *Modern China* 6: 3-39.
Winckler, Edwin, and Susan Greenhalgh, eds. 1988. *Contending Approaches to the Political Economy of Taiwan*. Armonk, N.Y.: M. E. Sharpe.
Wolf, Eric R. 1969. *Peasant Wars of the Twentieth Century*. New York: Harper and Row, Publishers.
———. 1982. *Europe and People without History*. Berkeley: University of California Press.
Woo, Jung-en. 1991. *Race to the Swift: State and Finance in Korean Industrialization*. New York: Columbia University Press.

World Bank. 1990. *The World Development Report.* Oxford: Oxford University Press.
Yoo, See Hee. 1974a. "The Communist Movement and the Peasants: The Case of Korea." Pp. 61–76 in *Peasant Rebellion and Communist Revolution in Asia,* edited by John W. Lewis. Stanford: Stanford University Press.
———. 1974b. "The Korean Communist Movement and the Peasantry under Japanese Rule." Ph.D. diss., Columbia University.
Zagoria, Donald. 1974. "Asian Tenancy Systems and Communist Mobilization of the Peasantry." Pp. 29–60 in *Peasant Rebellion and Communist Revolution in Asia,* edited by John W. Lewis. Stanford: Stanford University Press.
Zald, Mayer, and John McCarthy. 1987. "Organizational Intellectuals and the Criticism of Society." Pp. 97–115 in *Social Movements in an Organizational Society,* edited by Mayer Zald and John McCarthy. New Brunswick: Transaction Books.

NEWSPAPERS

Chosŏn ilbo [Korean Daily]
Chosŏn inminbo [Korean People's News]
Haebang ilbo [Liberation Daily]
Hansŏng ilbo [Seoul News]
Kyŏngsong ilbo [Seoul Daily]
Tonga ilbo [Far Eastern Daily]
Tongnip sinbo [Independence News]

MAGAZINES

Chosŏn nongmin [Korean Peasants]
Far Eastern Survey
Kaebyŏk [Creation]
Nongmin [Peasants]
Sindonga [New East Asia]

Index

Agricultural Association of Korea (Chosŏn nonghoe), 69, 97–98, 101, 102, 104, 107, 202 *n12*
Agricultural Lands Ordinance (1934; Nōchirei), 74, 123, 126, 178
Agricultural Trust Company (Sint'ak hoesa), 124
Agriculture, commercialization of: colonial period, 18, 44–46, 93, 94; nineteenth-century, 27–28; and rural class, 58, 60, 177; and protest, 162–63, 165, 170–71, 173
Agriculture, depression of: and economy, 60, 68–70, 75, 93–95; and disputes, 70–71, 178; and red peasant union movements, 86, 99; and class structure, 95–96, 99; recovery from, 118
Agriculture, involution of. *See* Involution
All Korea Writers Association, 136
An Ch'angho, x, 87. *See also* Nationalism, cultural
An Kwangch'ŏn (Sagong P'yo), 90
Assimilation policy, 136
Association for Systematic Agriculture (Kyet'ong nonghoe), 198 *n10*

Bukharin, Nikolay, 9

Capitalism, incipient. *See* Capitalism, "sprouts" of
Capitalism, "sprouts" of, 27, 31–32
Chinese Communist Party, 102, 136
Cho Pyŏngok, 154
Ch'ŏndogyo. *See* Tonghak

Chŏnnong. *See* National League of Peasant Unions
Chŏnp'yŏng. *See* National Council of Korean Labor Unions
Chosŏn inmin konghwaguk. *See* Korean People's Republic
Chosŏn kŏn'guk chunbi wiwŏnhoe. *See* Committee for the Preparation of Korean Independence.
Chosŏn nodong kongjehoe. *See* Korean Workers Mutual Aid Association
Chosŏn nonghoe. *See* Agricultural Association of Korea.
Chosŏn nongmin ch'ong tongmaeng. *See* General League of Korean Peasants
Chosŏn nongminsa. *See* Institute of the Korean Peasant
Chosŏn nonong ch'ong tongmaeng. *See* Korean Worker-Peasant League
Clan village (*tongjok purak*), 80, 110
Colonialism-pauperization-revolution thesis. *See* Pauperization-revolution thesis
Comfort ladies (*chŏngsindae*), 136, 205–6 *n5*
Comintern, 82, 85, 88, 89, 102. *See also* December Theses
Committee for the Preparation of Korean Independence (Chosŏn kŏn'guk chunbi wiwŏnhoe), 145
Communist thought, front line of, 111
Co-ops, rural credit (*kŭmyung chohap*), 95

December Theses, 85, 88–91, 100, 106, 113, 200 *n14*. *See also* Comintern

231

Index

Deprivation, relative, 63, 100
Development, definition of, 45
Differential spread effect, 169

Education: night schools, 105-6

Fanon, Franz, 10, 11, 198 *n*7
Farms (*nongjang*), 124, 125
Folk songs (*minyo*), 133, 138, 140, 141, 179
Food riots, 151-52
Forestry Association, 97, 99

General League of Korean Peasants (Chosŏn nongmin ch'ong tongmaeng), 100
Government, U.S. military, 5, 146-49
Grain collection. *See* Rice collection

Historical experience thesis, 157-59, 161, 165, 171-72, 207 *n*9-10
Historical memory, 207 *n*9
"History according to losers," 203 *n*24
Hodge, General, 154

"Image of the limited good," 10
Industrialization, colonial: state policy of, 119-21; barriers to, 125; "pulling" and "pushing" factors for, 125-26, 178. *See also* Modernization, Korean
Inmin wiwŏnhoe. *See* People's Committee
Institute of the Korean Peasant (Chosŏn nongminsa), 73, 200 *n*13
Intensification, agricultural: Chosŏn dynasty, 25-26; definition of, 45; colonial period, 45
Involution: Chosŏn dynasty, 32-34; definition of 45; colonial period, 50
Irrigation Association (Suri chohap), 97-99

Joint Korean-American Conference, 154

Kabo reform (1894), 202 *n*18
Kaebyŏk (creation), 201 *n*1
Kanghwa Treaty (1876), 27
Korean Democratic Party, 158
Kim Il Sung, 78, 82, 113, 203 *n*22
KMT. *See* Kuomintang
Ko Kyŏnghŭm (Kim Yŏngdu), 89-90
Koji, 50
Korea Trust Company (Chosŏn sint'ak), 124
Korean Communist Party, 88, 90, 111, 113

Korean Federation of Youth Organizations, 136
Korean Food Distributing Company (Chosŏn singnyang yŏngdan), 134-35, 147
Korean Language Research Society (Chosŏnŏ yŏn'guhoe), 87
Korean People's Republic (Chosŏn inmin konghwaguk), 146
Korean Restoration Army, 136
Korean War (1950-53), 174
Korean Worker-Peasant League (Chosŏn nonong ch'ong tongmaeng), 66
Korean Workers Mutual Aid Association (Chosŏn nodong kongjehoe): publication of *kongje* by, 65; branches of, 66
Korean Workers' Party (Nodongdang), 78, 175
Kuomintang (KMT), 136

Labor, intensification of. *See* Intensification, agricultural
Labor draft (*chingyong*), 136; resistance to, 139-40
Land reform:
  North Korea: basis of, 5, 175; impact on South Korea, 149, 155, 175; outcomes of, 174-75, 197 *n*1, 207 *n*3; Soviet role in, 174; as revolutionary, 175
  South Korea: basis of, 5-6, 153, 176, 179; outcomes of, 5, 51, 176, 197 *n*1, 207 *n*3; U.S. view of, 148, 151; as liberal, 175; as failed, 193 *n*2
Land survey, cadastral (1910-18): nationalist view of, 40-41, 60; nationalist fallacy of, 40, 42; outcomes of, 42
Land Tax Law (1914), 67
Landlord Association (Chijuhoe), 52
Landlords: stagnant (*chŏngt'aejŏk chiju*), 46-47; dynamic (*tongtaejŏk chiju*), 46-47; parasitic, 47, 64
Lenin, V. I.: view of peasant, 9; on colonialism, 39
Limited good, image of, 10
"Little tradition," 10
Local Youth Leadership Seminars, 136

Managerial farmers (*kyŏngyŏnghyŏng punong*), 30-34
Mao Zedong: view of peasants, 9, 11, 198 *n*7; on colonialism, 39; on revolution 82

Index   233

March First Movement (1919), 53, 65, 86, 146, 177, 200 n9
Marŭm. See Saŭm
Marx, Karl: view of peasants, 9, 16, 198 n7; on British rule in India, 39; on British rule in Ireland, 39; on revolution, 65, 82, 112
Mass society, 154
Migration: from Japan and Manchuria, 5, 85, 150-51, 157, 162, 168, 171, 176, 200 n7; to Japan and Manchuria, 75, 118, 162
Military conscription (chingbyŏng), 136; resistance to, 140
Mobilization: defensive, 19; model, 20
Modernization, Korean: state role in, viii, 3-4, 6; world system's role in, viii, 3-4, 6; economic growth in, 3-4; colonial legacy for, 4, 39; social equality in, 4. See also Industrialization, colonial
Modernization theory, 10, 163
Modernization without development, 46
Mutual aid associations (tonggye), 80, 110

Naisen ittai (Japan and Korea as one body), 135, 142, 205 n3
National Council of Korean Labor Unions (Chŏnp'yŏng), 152, 154
National General Mobilization Law (Kukka ch'ong tongwŏn pŏb), 134
National League of Peasant Unions (Chŏn'guk nongmin chohap ch'ong yŏn'maeng or chŏnnong): U.S. suppression of, 144, 147, 151; organization of, 146; land reform proposal, 148, 149; on rice collection, 150
National University (Minnip taehakkyo), 87
Nationalism, cultural, 87, 88, 200 n10
Neighborhood Patriotic Associations, 136
New Korea Company (Sinhan kongsa), 147, 148, 152
Night schools, 105-6
Nissen yūwa (harmony between Japan and Korea), 135
Nodongdang. See Korean Workers' Party
Nongmin. See Peasants
Nongmin chohap. See Peasant unions
Northeast Asian political economy, 120

ODC. See Oriental Development Company
Office-land system (1466; chikjŏnbŏp), 22

Oriental Development Company (ODC), 40, 123, 147

Pacific War (1941-45), 134, 139, 203 n22
Pak Hŏnyŏng, 154
Pauperization-revolution thesis, 6, 11, 58, 63, 64, 67, 82, 177
Pauperization thesis. See Pauperization-revolution thesis
Peace Preservation Law (Ch'ian yujibŏp), 75, 78, 101, 198 n10
Peasant movement, elitist view of, 113
Peasant unions (post-1945; nongmin chohap): organization of, 144-46; role in uprisings, 152, 155, 161, 208 n14. See also National League of Peasant Unions
Peasant uprisings of 1862, 197 n3
Peasants (nongmin), 71-73, 199 n22, 201 n1; as "sack of potatoes," 9, 74, 198 n7; moral economy of, 10, 13-17, 19-20, 63, 82, 178; political economy of, 10, 17; rational, 12-15, 18-20, 63, 74, 178, 193 n1
"People without history," 203 n24
People's Committee (PC; Inmin wiwŏnhoe):
  North Korea: Provisional, 174; organization of, 206 n2
  South Korea: U.S. suppression of, 144, 147, 151, 153; organizational strength of, 146, 156-58, 160-62, 170; Central Committee of, 148; role in uprisings, 152, 155-56, 159, 160, 162, 165-68, 172, 208 n14
Perspective, colonial (singmin sakwan), 31
Policy, cultural, 65, 75
Polity model, 20
Profintern, 82, 89, 102
Program to Increase Rice Production (Sanmai zoshoki keikaku), 43
Prostitution, 136, 205-6 n5

Rank-land system (1391; kwajŏnbŏp), 22
Reading circles (toksŏhoe), 105
Regulations for the Establishment of Owner-Farmers (Zisaku nōchi settei izi zigyō), 122
Rent: fixed (tojo), 36; variable (t'ajo), 51; share-cropping (pyŏngjak), 36; payment in cash (taegŭmnap), 37
Rent Control Order (1939; Sojangnyo t'ongje ryŏng), 134

234   Index

Resource mobilization theory, 64, 99, 159, 205 n25
Revolution, incomplete, 5, 156, 175
Revolutionary peasant union movements (*hyŏngmyŏngjŏk nongmin chohap undong*), 79
Rice, "famine export" of, 46
Rice collection (*kongch'ul*):
 Colonial period: program, 133, 134; resistance to, 138–39, 143, 179
 Post-1945: program, 149; resistance to, 150–51, 153, 154, 207 n6
Riots, food, 151–52
Rising expectations, 63
Rumors (*yuŏn piŏ*), 133, 138, 141–42, 179
Rural (class) differentiation. See Social differentiation
Rural credit co-ops (*kŭmyung chohap*), 95
Rural Revitalization Campaign (Nosŏn sinkō undō), 135, 204 n19
Rural Revitalization Council, 104
Russo-Japanese War (1904–5), 38

Safety-first strategy, 14, 19. See also Peasants, moral economy of
Saŭm (landlord's agent), 46, 124
Semi-feudal colonial society, 31
Semi-proletarianization, late-nineteenth-century, 32, 34, 40; colonial period, 49–50
Sin'ganhoe, 100, 102, 146, 203 n19
Sino-Japanese War: of 1894–95, 38; of 1937–45, 120, 134
Social differentiation: impact on rural protest, 7, 20, 73–74, 177; 19th-century, 27, 32–35; involuted, 34; colonial period, 46, 50, 60
Social mobilization, 5, 151, 157, 162, 167, 171
Society, semi-feudal colonial, 31
Society for the Promotion of Native Production (Chosŏn mulsan changnyŏhoe), 87
Solidarity: conservative, 13, 110; radical, 13

Spring poverty (*ch'un'gunggi*), 75, 80, 83, 94
Stagnation theory (*chŏngch'eron*), 31
Staple Food Management Law (1943; Singnyang kwanniryŏng), 134
State autonomy, 4
Structural determinism, viii, 7, 15–16, 20, 173, 177
Subsistence ethic, 14, 73, 178. See also Peasants, moral economy of

Taegu riot, 152–54
Taewŏn'gun, 4, 33
Temporary Committee on Tenancy Custom Survey (Imsi sojak chosa wiwŏnhoe), 122
Tenancy Law (Sojakbŏp), 123
Tenancy officers (*kosakukan*), 122
Tenant Arbitration Ordinance (1932; Kosaku chōteirei), 74, 116–17, 122, 126–27, 178, 197 n2
Tojigwŏn (permanent tenancy rights), 14, 41, 42
T'oji taejang, 42, 60
T'oji tŭnggibu, 42, 60
Tokugawa Japan (1603–1867), 14
Tonghak: peasant uprisings of 1894, 38, 153, 197 n3, 199 n5, 200 n13; as thought, 82, 199 n5; impact on later protest, 207 n10
Total war, 114, 135, 179
Trust Business Ordinance (1931; Chosŏn sint' agŏpnyŏng), 124

Village, clan (*tongjak purak*), 80, 110

World War I, 43
World War II, 15–16, 112, 144, 171, 176

Yangban, 22, 52, 80, 110, 193, 195, 202 n18
Yang'an (land register), 31, 35, 42, 60
Yi Kwangsu, 87. See also Nationalism, cultural

www.ingramcontent.com/pod-product-compliance
Lightning Source LLC
Chambersburg PA
CBHW030619230426
43661CB00053B/2063